For Allen,
With love

[signature]

3/9/05
[signature]

Hi, How are you?

[signature]

THE MIDDLE OF EVERYTHING

Michelle Herman

MEMOIRS OF MOTHERHOOD

University of Nebraska Press : Lincoln and London

Library of Congress Cataloging-in-Publication Data
Herman, Michelle.
The middle of everything : Memoirs of motherhood / Michelle Herman.
p. cm.   ISBN 0-8032-2426-5 (cloth: alkaline paper)
1. Herman, Michelle. 2. Authors, American – 20th century – Family relationships. 3. Authors, American – 20th century – Biography. 4. Herman, Michelle – Childhood and youth. 5. Mothers and daughters – United States. 6. Grandparent and child – United States. 7. Maternal deprivation – United States. 8. Motherhood – United States. 9. Herman, Michelle – Family. 1. Title.
PS3558.E6825Z467 2005 813'.54–dc22 2004014200

For Grace

CONTENTS

Acknowledgments

Deep and wide and probably forever unpayable debts of gratitude are owed to Lee Martin and Erin McGraw – heavensent readers, colleagues, and friends without whose encouragement I would never have written this book – and for help, faith, and support well beyond the call of duty, I owe many thanks, too, to Jim Phelan, M. V. Clayton, my guardian angel/penpal Ladette Randolph, and the unsinkable, secretly hopeful Marian B. S. Young.

Thanks are also due to Floyd Skloot and Alison Lurie, to Carolyn Harpster and Robert Firestone (who couldn't possibly know how much help they've been), to Renae Carlson, to the Ohio Arts Council and the Ohio State University College of Humanities, and to my beloved students, past and present, at Ohio State.

To my parents and my brother, Mort and Sheila and Scott Herman; to my husband, Glen Holland; and most of all to my daughter, Grace Jane Herman Holland – for her permission despite ambivalence, for this book's title, and for everything else on earth – I am thankful every day.

Finally, to the healers – Michael Hernandez, Marlene Kocan, Sarah Knox, and Janet Meltzer – I am grateful, for once in my life, entirely beyond words.

Superstar

Long ago and oh so far away

My daughter has no idea what she's talking about.

Her hand is fisted, two inches from her mouth, and she is singing into it, a song of her own invention:

Oh baby, oh baby
Why don't you call me no more?
I'm always callin' you-oo
But you're busy callin' someone else
I wanna know who that other girl can be
And why you don't love me no more

Every night for the last two weeks, as part of our bedtime routine, she has performed for me this way, the lyrics and what passes for a melody improvised on the spot. Most of the other parts of the nightly ritual have been in place for years (the bath, the snack, the chapter her father or I read to her); the last time something new was added was a year and a half ago, when she began to want to read by herself for an hour at bedtime, the last thing she'd do before closing her eyes. The performance – that's what she calls it – occurs after the bath and before snack, before I read the evening's chapter of *Little Women*.

The stage is just beyond the foot of my bed. I am supposed to sit on the bed, my back against the wall – as far as possible from her in the small bedroom. From the hallway, she announces that the performance is about to begin. She enters at a run, sliding into place, and starts to sing as soon as she clears the doorway.

You ain't never gonna find someone
Who loves you half as much as I do
Babe – oh, babe

"Where does she get this stuff?" my husband says. She sings for him too, the nights he's on bedtime duty. On his nights, they're reading The Five Little Peppers and How They Grew. Genteel poverty is very big around our house lately. Genteel poverty, and romance. And horses. Horses she discovered through Black Beauty and a series of "children's chapter books" called Pony Pals, but unlike poverty and romantic love – neither of which I am in any hurry to have her encounter outside of books – horses have become a part of her life: she and her father are taking riding lessons together. This is the first thing they've had in common since she was five and they spent hours painting or making collages or building skyscrapers – or, on Sundays, Noah's ark – out of Legos or the criminally expensive quarter-inch-thick wood-plank blocks I bought them for Valentine's Day the year she was two.

"She listens to music," I say. "She lives in the U.S. at the start of the twenty-first century."

"She doesn't even watch TV."

He sounds so bewildered I actually feel sorry for him, although my usual response to his anxiety about the future (or, more specifically, about our daughter's semi-immediate future, her adolescence) is to get irritated. She'll make mistakes, she'll have her heart broken, she'll suffer – so what? It happens to all of us. The only way not to feel pain is to teach yourself not to feel anything at all. "Is that what you want for her?" I've asked him, daring him to say yes.

Well, he wouldn't dare. But I'm almost sure he thinks it.

"She doesn't even like Britney Spears," is what he says now.

I'm a little surprised he even knows who that is. He doesn't read magazines or listen to the radio, and the last album he bought was by the Ramones. But we have cable – I had it put in for his fortieth birthday so he could watch basketball and football on ESPN – and late at night, when he comes in from working in his studio, he flips channels for an hour, sometimes two, trying to wind down enough to go to sleep. Bits of pop culture flash at him this way, too fragmented for him to make sense of them.

The fact is, there's a lot he doesn't know. He doesn't know that his eight-year-old daughter has been asking me questions lately about love. That she has told me she has a crush on a boy in her class. "How can you tell?" I wanted to know. I wasn't trying to give her a hard time or to convince her that she was wrong (because, for one thing, I remember *my* first crush; for another, I try never to give her a hard time – I figure she has the rest of the world for that). I really wanted to know. I always want to know.

"I feel funny when I'm around him," she told me.

"Funny how?"

"Embarrassed. Weird. *Very* weird."

This is a child who is normally so precise about language that once, when she was four and overheard me tell a friend that she had begun saying things were "cool," in imitation of the older girls she saw every day that summer at the pool, she took it upon herself to start pronouncing things she admired as "glorious" or "wonderful" or "gorgeous," never using the same word twice in a single day – a child who will stop and think for a full minute, right in the middle of a sentence, if she doesn't have the perfect word at hand – so her resorting to the all-purpose "funny" and "weird" was itself a sign, I understood. *A sign of what?* I could hear her father asking. But that would mean I'd have told him about this conversation, which I had no intention of doing. It would mortify her; it would make him miserable. And I do my best to keep both of them happy – for better or worse, I believe this to be part of my job on earth – and this, I have discovered, sometimes involves keeping secrets. Which happens to be the part of motherhood and marriage that suits me least. I hate keeping secrets, any secrets.

Still, I don't want this – my daughter's first crush – to be mortifying to her or a source of misery to her father. So I keep my own counsel. This way, I'm the only one who suffers. And that's a secret, too.

I fell in love with you before the second show

By the time I was my daughter's age I'd already been in love for three years, and by the time I was seventeen I'd been in love four times. I'd also had four boyfriends, which sounds symmetrical until you fill in the names.

I was in love with a boy named Irwin from the ages of five to thirteen, and never mind that I never told him or that I didn't even lay eyes on him once during the final year of my devotion, since we went to different junior highs. My family moved when I was eleven years old, and though it was only a matter of blocks, from an apartment building in Sheepshead Bay to one in a neighborhood the very name of which was terrifying to me – Gravesend – in Brooklyn such a move was like relocating to a distant city: new school, new library, new subway stop, new life. And I was stubborn (or sensitive, or high-strung, depending on who you asked), so I held on to the old life longer than anyone considered reasonable. Thus I spent seventh grade in a state of shock, and besides the ongoing daydream of Irwin, the smartest boy in the class (which made him my perfect match, since my father insisted I was the smartest girl in the class – in any class, anywhere, any time) and also my costar year after year in the class play (which actually constituted the only time we ever talked directly to each other: his Maestro to my Gigi, the Lost Note; his Nanki-Poo to my Yum-Yum; his Don José to my Carmen), what I chiefly remember about that year was the one friend I had, and that I never told her about Irwin. I was hoping that not talking about him would help me get over him. It was starting to be embarrassing, being in love for so long with someone who had so little interest in me he hadn't even bothered to say goodbye or wish me luck in my new school.

I fell in love with Howie the summer after seventh grade – we met at a bungalow colony where I spent a weekend visiting a girl who lived in my new building on Gravesend Neck Road – and I didn't fall out of love with him until the end of ninth grade. Since I skipped eighth grade, this only amounted to nine months. But they were busy months. My family moved again, right after Howie and I met, and for those busy months in which my life changed once more, he was my boyfriend. I wore his ID bracelet, with four links removed so it would fit on my wrist.

After Howie, who played football and had to ride the subway for two hours to see me, all the way from Bayside (Queens! – practically another country) to the D train stop at Kings Highway, I fell in love with David. We made out every Saturday night, at parties, one whole summer, and then on Monday he would tell everyone he'd only been "goofing around." Then the next Saturday he'd apologize to me and we'd make out again. This was the summer I began to understand what I should have figured out in elementary school: that when it came to love, I was a slow learner.

Next was Steven, and with him I tried something else: I was *not* in love, not one bit. I'd known him all summer but I hadn't paid him much attention; I was too besotted with David. Steven hung out with the rest of us on the paddleball courts at Brighton Beach Baths (the boys in cut-off jeans, fringed at the bottom, the girls in bikinis and sweat socks and sneakers), but he was a little older, a little patronizing toward us. I was caught off guard when he called to ask me out at the end of the summer.

I had only recently stopped being chubby, a word that had been used to describe me since fifth grade – and that I hated for its lack of dignity at least as much as the condition of my body it denoted – and I still looked like a stranger in the mirror. I was spending a lot of time in front of the mirror in those days, too, and not just admiring and being surprised by myself but also because I had started wearing eye makeup and I needed lots of practice putting it on, my nose three inches from the mirror, since I was terribly nearsighted: a black stripe of eyeliner and a white stripe just above it.

Steven, who assured me I was the first girl he'd ever loved, and who tried to use logic to persuade me that I was in love with him "but didn't know it yet," was three years older than I, a senior in high school. This was both flattering and disconcerting (and sometimes both at once). He was forever reminding me that I was only fourteen, that he knew things I wouldn't know for a long time.

He had to take three buses from Bay Ridge, way at the other end of Brooklyn. This he did not only every Saturday night, for our proper dates – which my parents allowed just once weekly – but several times a week besides, so he could meet me at my school and walk me home. The girls I knew couldn't decide whether to be impressed or scornful. They were sympathetic, however, when I worried aloud about whether my "loving him as a friend" was sufficient grounds for the relationship. Sufficient or not, I wore his Fort Hamilton High class ring on a gold chain around my neck all through my sophomore year.

I met John during a Vietnam War moratorium at my school. We were all lined up outside wearing black armbands over our coat sleeves, when a boy who knew a girl I knew told a girl *she* knew that a friend of his wanted to meet me. My attraction to him was so swift and uncomplicated, I broke up with Steven immediately. By then I was fifteen and had given up eye makeup, passed through a brief "collegiate" stage featuring Weejuns and knee socks, and moved on to feathers and beads and Frye boots and Indian skirts that swept the ground.

I didn't fall in love with John the way I had with David (or with Howie, for that matter, the first time I saw him standing by the jukebox in the rec center at the Sunshine Bungalow Colony, bobbing his head to the Young Rascals' "Sueño" – or even with Irwin, back in kindergarten), but not only did that not disturb me, it was actually a relief. I wasn't in the kind of danger I'd been in with David – the danger of being crushed by my own hopes and humiliated by my expectations – and yet I wasn't without feeling, as I'd been for too long, going out with Steven. Steven had in fact been trying to convince me, over the final few months of our relationship, that I was unfeeling – that I was cold (which wounded me, as he must have known it would, even though I knew it wasn't true) – and when I broke up with him, he accused me of heartlessness. "How can you say that?" I remember asking him, in tears. "You know that's a lie." And he did know. All he meant was what anyone means when he calls someone heartless: he meant I had no heart for him.

A week or two into my relationship with John, he told me, "You gotta hear my friend Russell's band," and then I did, and it was all over for John. I'd been only a little bit in love with him, anyway – and no one could have stood a chance with me against Russell, who seemed to me the boy I'd been waiting to meet all my life. He was perfect. Even now I can remember *how* perfect I felt he was, even if I can't remember why.

Russell at fifteen was wildly self-confident – delusionally self-confident for a kid whose grades were barely passing (later I would do his homework for him) and who was – although it would be many months before I found this out – disliked by nearly everyone in school but John and me. And it's not fair, really, to say I can't remember why I so adored him. What I remember is that he seemed to have no fears, no doubts – and in particular no self-doubt – no anxiety, no troubles.

I suspect now that I wanted to *be* him at least as much as I wanted to be with him.

He was a cute guy, too, and carefully unkempt in the style of the times. He sold pot to the other boys out of his basement, which had its own entrance with sliding glass doors. His parents lavished him with absurdly expensive and inappropriate gifts: a lightly used powder blue Jaguar V12 the minute he had his driver's license; a motorboat; a trip to Europe for both of us when he turned sixteen (which caused a crisis in my house that my father is still talking about – usually in the context of "Just wait till *your* daughter's sixteen and tells you she's going to Europe for the summer with her boyfriend").

He was the drummer in his band, which practiced in his basement. (Later on, there would be two drummers, "like in the Grateful Dead," the boys told me. Later still, the new lead guitarist – another David with whom I would eventually fall in love – explained that two white drummers equaled one black drummer. He had a mordant streak, which I admired very much.)

Russell was the only one with a place to practice, which was doubtless why he was in the band. His parents didn't mind the noise or care if we got high. They didn't even seem to notice when a nitrous tank was hauled in one day. It's possible that his father, a dentist, was the one who supplied the nitrous tank. We named the band after him – the dentist-father – and for a little while I was its lead singer. I wrote songs, too. I wrote the lyrics, and the rhythm guitarist, a sweet, earnest boy named Robby, wrote the music. I didn't know it then – he never told me – but he was in love with me. I should have known: he treated me so gently, with such kindness. But it never crossed my mind that this had anything to do with love.

Your guitar, it sounds so sweet and clear

There are other things I don't tell my husband. For example, that our daughter has lately taken an interest in my love life before he came on the scene, asking questions about my old boyfriends. And that three weeks ago she wanted to know if "French kissing" was for real or if her friend Anna had made it up. Anna is five months younger but she has an older sister and watches a lot of TV. She lives across the street, and in the manner of "street friends" (as opposed to "school friends," which at least in principle a child chooses among), she and my daughter are close. They often play together after they get home from their respective schools – Anna's is Christian evangelical – and on weekends sometimes it's as if Anna lives with us: she'll knock on the door before breakfast, and if my daughter has nothing scheduled that day, chances are she'll still be at our house at dinnertime.

After I ascertained that the basic facts were in place (when sex education comes from Anna, I always have to double-check), I said that while French kissing was real all right, it wasn't something she needed to worry about yet (and also that by the time she was old enough to do it, it wouldn't seem disgusting). But my daughter, an only child in a half-Jewish, half-Southern Baptist, leftist household, wasn't ready to let it go. She asked if it would be all right if she tried it with me before she did it with a boy, so that she'd know what to expect. I declined, and this exchange became another secret for me to keep.

Till now, that is.

But you're not really here

By seventeen I'd established the pattern of my love life: love some too much, love some not at all, love some just enough but not enough to matter – and let there be no correlation between those coordinates and the ones representing "actual" relationships. Roughly fifty percent correlation, actually – the same odds as random throws of the dice.

The pattern of my love life, I should say, until I stopped rolling the dice. I got married, had a child. I was already edging toward forty when I did this, and while "middle age" hasn't brought me peace of mind – it's just given me a set of entirely different things to worry about – my relief at setting down the dice and walking away from the table was considerable. The odds as I've described them may not sound that bad, but I always felt as if I'd lost even when it looked like I was winning.

Perhaps this was because I had the vague idea that there was a fourth variation, some other kind of romantic outcome, one I never saw in action. The big win – that was how I thought of it. You can lose your shirt – lose the ranch – hoping for the big win, and it seemed to me that no matter how many times I rolled, there were only those three outcomes, that same imperfect correlation.

It's just the radio

My daughter is in her leopard-pattern pajamas. She leaps, she spins, she flings her long hair around in a manner disarmingly and alarmingly like my own in the days when I was still dancing. Not that I've given up dancing, exactly. I still think of myself as someone who dances, and sometimes I miss doing it. I just don't go anywhere anymore where dancing takes place. Most nights I'm in bed with a book by ten, and I can hear my daughter down the hall turning the pages of *All-of-a-Kind Family Downtown*. Sometimes I fall asleep before she does.

I am never awake when my husband comes to bed, except on the nights when he quits working an hour or two later than usual and I'm getting up an hour or two earlier than usual in order to get some writing done before it's time to wake our daughter at seven. Then we say hi – *good morning, good night, have a good day, sleep well* – and I head into my study, closing the bedroom door behind me. Chances are good I won't see him again till dinnertime. And then there are days we don't see each other awake at all, when he comes to bed at four and I wake up at six, when I'm on after-school pickup duty and he's in his studio all afternoon, working straight through dinner and not coming in for leftovers until we're upstairs – our daughter is in the shower and I'm across the hall, in my study, reading student stories or checking my e-mail, listening with one ear for her to call me in to check her hair for traces of shampoo before she turns the water off – and I'm asleep, of course, when he comes up at four a.m. again.

Some days, we see each other for ten or fifteen hurried minutes in the early evening – when he's on pickup duty and I don't get home from campus till it's time to start making dinner, and he hasn't been out to his studio yet and is jumpy but trying not to rush me as I tell him what needs to be told about my day, and as soon as he can reasonably excuse himself he goes out the back door to get his workday started at five p.m.

It's not the "family life" I envisioned for myself, but then whose is? Besides, for years and years I didn't envision any sort of "family life" at all. It was all I could do to get from love affair to love affair, and it's no small thing to note that my husband was the first – the only – boyfriend I ever invited to move in with me. He is in fact the only *person* I have ever lived with, other than my parents and now our daughter. I lived alone for seventeen years, from the summer day I moved out of my parents' house in Brooklyn till the summer day the man who would become my husband moved in with me to this house I'd bought myself in the middle of America. We joked that we'd have to hang a moose head in the living room (which I'd painted pale, pale pink and furnished with a flowery chintz couch and rose-colored curtains and a Victorian lady's desk with a kneehole so small I had to search for months to find a chair that would fit into it). We never hung a moose head. The living room is still pink and Victorian, though the couch is stained (mud, chocolate, Juicy Juice) and the delicate chair broke years ago.

It was a surprise to my daughter when she found out about other people's lives, just as it surprised me when I visited my junior high school best friend's house for the first time and met a mother who insisted her whole family sit down for dinner together every night at five-thirty, who *made* dinner every night (even if it was spaghetti sauce from a jar or Rice-A-Roni) no matter how tired she might have been – must have been – after a full day at her job "in the city." I think of her sometimes when I make my own speedy dinners at the end of an exhausting day: pasta and a sauce that doesn't take long if you start it with canned crushed tomatoes instead of smashing them yourself or starting with fresh ones the way I used to when I lived alone and had all the time in the world; vegetables stirred up with olive oil and garlic and lots of salt, the way my daughter likes them. I'm still in my "teaching clothes" when I get dinner started on those nights, but as soon as things are sizzling in their pans I go upstairs and change back into the "writing clothes" I'd left on a hook in the bathroom when I changed out of them before leaving for campus. My daughter always nods approvingly when she sees me in my sweatshirt and leggings again: "That's better." But when she was three and four years old she used to dress up her Barbies and Kens in purple sequined gowns and sparkly silver-flecked tuxedos and send them off to work that way – Barbie to her study to write, Ken to his studio to paint. When I remarked that they were awfully well dressed for what they were about to do, she explained patiently that this was the difference between Barbie life and ours. "It's not *supposed* to be real."

Honestly, I have no idea what other people's lives are like. My daughter probably has a much better idea than I do, since she so often visits other children, has dinner with their families, even spends the night sometimes and sits down to a Sunday morning pancake breakfast with other people's mothers and fathers.

I do know, because she told me, that the first time she saw a father in a business suit come home from work and set down his briefcase in a hallway, she giggled and her friend looked at her curiously. But it was an image she knew only from certain books I'd read aloud to her – Betty MacDonald's *Mrs. Piggle Wiggle*, say, with all those 1940s fathers and their jobs and pipes and evening newspapers. "I didn't know it was *real*," she told me that night. "I thought it was just a book-thing." I could tell she was put out, that she felt I should have told her.

There are lots of things I should tell her, but I haven't sorted them all out yet. Still, there's plenty she's figuring out on her own. Just this past Thanksgiving, when her father was watching the Dallas Cowboys play and she and I were trying to decide if we had the strength for a board game after all that food, I mentioned that when her father and I were first living together I had sometimes watched football on TV with him, just to keep him company. She smiled knowingly. She said, "Well, yes, people do a lot of funny things when they're in love, don't they."

Don't you remember you told me you loved me, baby?

I finished high school six months early. I doubled up on gym and added Spanish, wrote an extra paper for English and one for French, and I was out by winter break. Two weeks later – just after New Year's, 1972 – I started college. I was not quite seventeen, living at home and riding my bike down Bedford Avenue to the Brooklyn College campus every day. I was still doing Russell's homework, but by the following fall he would be away at college and have a new girlfriend to write his papers for him.

My first college paper, that first semester, was for Freshman Comp. The teacher, a graduate student in English named Loren Loverde, to whom I owe a great debt – I can only hope he reads this book and knows at last how great a debt – had us choose a subject we were "irretrievably fascinated with" and write an essay about it. We got our papers back full of marginal notes and questions – the first writing I had ever done that was returned to me with anything but *Excellent!* scrawled at the top (actually, that's not exactly true; in the lower grades there was usually a second comment – something along the lines of *Handwriting?* or *Neatness!* – below the praise).

We rewrote our papers. Once more they were collected and returned to us, the margins dense with comments.

We spent the entire fifteen weeks of the semester on one essay, rewriting single paragraphs again and again and turning them in, then collecting our marked-up papers and rewriting them some more. We experimented with concentrating on different aspects of our subjects. We learned to be ruthless about what Mr. Loverde called "universals" – generalizations and assumptions – as we tried to get at what we really thought, what we truly knew, and what we still wondered about the thing that mattered most to us. We rewrote our essays in their entirety at least four times, and finally we read them aloud to the class.

There were essays on religion and on rock music and on being a vegetarian. There was one on what it meant to be a first-generation American, and one on why the writer hoped to practice medicine someday. There was one on U.S. foreign policy, which surprised and impressed me. One on apartheid – ditto. I was humbled by the thought that when allowed to choose freely, when no teacher had supplied a list of topics and told us to pick one, someone my age – some seventeen- or eighteen-year-old who'd grown up in Brooklyn, like me; who was still in Brooklyn, like me, still living with his or her parents, still sleeping in the same old room – would consider these global matters, these high-minded political matters, the most compelling possible subject.

Me, I wrote about love.

What astonished me was that I was the only one who did. It still astonishes me.

Said you'd be coming back this way again, maybe

Once, about fifteen years ago, I received a letter from an old boyfriend, someone I'd dated in college and for the better part of a year afterward. Another drummer – Norbert. I don't even know how he found my address. I was about a thousand miles from New York by then, even farther from home than I am now, and I hadn't heard from him since his first wife had left him (the wife he'd broken up with me to marry; we had kept on seeing each other right up through the week before the wedding). He was reexamining his life. He wanted to tell me he was sorry he had treated me so badly during the years we'd been involved, wanted to say that he couldn't believe how stupid he had been. He'd been lucky, he said, lucky to have me. He just hadn't known it then.

This is the only such letter I have ever received, and it shocked me into a puzzled silence that was so unlike my normal state, the boyfriend I had then became worried. That was José, for whom I had moved to Omaha, from Iowa City, where we'd met while we were both in school. I didn't tell him about the letter because he hated hearing about my old boyfriends, but I walked around startled and silent for days, and couldn't stop thinking about it.

What Norbert had said was true: he had treated me badly. But what occurred to me then was that I'd invited it – I'd practically begged for it. And I'd had no idea I was begging for it, either. I thought my willingness to be ignored or dismissed or taken for granted or spoken to rudely, even cruelly – or set aside periodically for another, more alluring girl – was charming. Was *lovable*. With Russell, with Norbert – with a lot of other boys, and later men – I was, I imagined, the world's greatest girlfriend. What could be more appealing than not asking for anything, ever? Than accepting what was given and not complaining, not saying, "Please, sir, I'd like some more"? It made me perfectly self-sufficient, and wasn't that what they all wanted? Except I knew I wasn't self-sufficient. I thought it would be enough to look, to sound, to seem as if I were.

I was in my thirties before I was able to see that my willingness to stand there and be ignored must have looked (sounded, seemed) like the antithesis of self-sufficiency. That I must have seemed desperate, and desperately hopeful.

I *was* desperately hopeful.

Baby, baby, baby, baby, oh, baby

My daughter asked me recently why "all songs are about love." She knows a lot of songs. She knows all the standards because I used to sing them to her (and sometimes even now she'll catch herself singing "The Very Thought of You" or "It Might As Well Be Spring" and she'll stop, embarrassed) and lately she's begun listening to pop music on her own, listening to the radio, digging through my records. She has discovered the Beatles, Bonnie Raitt, Aretha, Gladys Knight and the Pips.

"Practically every song is all about 'I love you and you don't love me' or 'I used to love you and now I don't and so I'm sad' or 'Don't you know I love you more than that other girl does?' Why *is* that?"

I tell her that there are some songs that aren't about love. I remind her of some songs she herself knows very well. "Yellow Submarine," for example. "Big Yellow Taxi." She doesn't laugh, though – she just shakes her head – so I don't mention "Mellow Yellow" and "Follow the Yellow Brick Road" as I was going to. " 'This Land Is Your Land,' " I say. " 'Climb Every Mountain.' " She rolls her eyes. " 'The Star Spangled Banner.' "

She isn't persuaded. They're the exception, not the rule. *Love* rules.

I love you – I really do

I'm so ashamed of myself. I used to sing that song, "Superstar," to her, as part of the bedtime routine – the last part, right after I'd read to her and she'd had her snack. But not just "Superstar." I also sang "Close to You" (birds suddenly appearing and stars falling out of the sky every time my beloved was near) and "Someone to Watch Over Me" (I knew I'd meet him someday) and "It Had to Be You" and "Bewitched, Bothered, and Bewildered" and "If I Fell" and "And I

Love Her" and "Taking a Chance on Love" and "They Can't Take That Away from Me," and when I started to get desperate, when it was getting on toward eleven and she still wasn't asleep, I'd pull out "Al Di La" (where he walked, flowers bloomed) and "More" (than – what else? – the greatest love the world has known) and what I wonder now is: what did all those songs *do* to that receptive little brain?

Loneliness is such a sad affair

She doesn't want me to sing anymore – in fact she says, "Mama, *don't* sing, please" or "Sing to *yourself*, silently" – but she is, as I've said, seriously interested, all of a sudden, in my romantic history. She knows the names of all my old boyfriends. She is particularly interested in the last few, the ones she calls my "grown-up boyfriends," the men I was involved with in the years right before I met her father. She asks sly questions about them. She'll remark, of something I own – my cheval glass, for example – "Oh, I love this, you know?" and I'll say, "Yes, I love it too. It's the sort of mirror I always wanted," and she'll say, "Ah, did one of your old boyfriends give it to you? Because he knew that?" And I'll say, "Yes, in fact, one did," and she'll want to know which one. I tell her Clifford. She nods sagely: she knows all about Clifford. She knows that when she was born, he came around and sang to her. He'd written a song for her (which was just like him – which was part of why I'd loved him) and he got down on one knee with his guitar and sang it for her on the front porch.

She likes to reel off a list of my old boyfriends – the boys and men she sees as failed candidates for the position of her father – and mention one or two things she knows about each one, and then sigh and tell me again how glad she is that I didn't love any of them enough to make them her father. That's how she sees it, which I suppose is as good a way as any.

You'd think it would trouble her that I was involved with so many men before I met her daddy, the man in *her* life. It doesn't seem to, though. She treats my life story – my love-life story – as if it were a book, a good book that absorbs her but that doesn't necessarily have any bearing on her day-to-day own life.

Once in a while, though, she will ask me *why* I didn't love any of my other boyfriends enough to marry them. She's trying to make sense of love, I know. Thus far, she has been satisfied by my telling her how wonderful I thought her father was, what a good father I knew he'd make.

"And you were right," she says with satisfaction.

But soon she's pawing in my jewelry box again, looking for the ring from José, whom I loved dearly but not quite enough; the brooch from Clifford, whom I loved too much – recklessly, and foolishly; the minuscule diamond studs from Nick, whom I didn't love at all.

And I can hardly wait to be with you again

The days pass, and the weeks, the months, one after another, each one pretty much like the one before but for the small surprises, the ups and downs of what I can only assume is not that great a variation on "ordinary" family life, whatever that may be. It is the family life I have made for us, improvising as I go. My daughter is growing up, little by little, watchful and curious and so beautiful and bright it makes my heart ache in a way that reminds me of what it felt like to fall in love. She, I often find myself thinking, is "the big win" – the one person I have ever adored who adores me right back, just as fiercely, just as deeply; the one person in whose company I am always glad to be, no matter what my mood has been (indeed, the very sight of whom can instantly dispel my gloom). That her father and I can see both of ourselves in her – her gentleness and reserve, her ability to concentrate fully on whatever she is doing for however long it takes, her interest in taking things apart to see how they work and her ability to put them back together, all his; her passion, her sense of drama, her effusiveness in language, her desire to put everything into words, to talk things over endlessly, all mine; her sensitivity so acute she can't bear the noise and visual overstimulation of most movies, or the trumped-up anxiety of cartoons, a legacy from both of us (as is perhaps her bossiness) – well, this is part of it, part of my feeling that she is what I bet the ranch for, without even knowing I was placing a bet.

The days pass. The dinners are made, the dishes washed, the lunches packed, the classes taught, the bills paid, the homework and the piano books zipped into the backpack that hangs on a hook by the door. The pages – some worth keeping, most not – pile up in my study, and in my husband's studio, out back behind the house I used to live in by myself, another small, glowing still life of a Rose of Sharon from our yard, or my grandmother's Shabbat candlesticks, or his grandmother's velvet pincushion stuck through with silver pins, is hung up on a nail until tomorrow.

When my husband comes upstairs to bed, he tries not to disturb me, but I sleep lightly and I always wake up, momentarily, just long enough to say hello. And that is all I say, he tells me: *hello*, in a cheerful, wide-awake voice, right before I turn over and go back to sleep. I seem happy to see him, most nights, he says. And this is true, I am.

What to say to make you come again?

Here's what I believe about romantic love.

I believe it makes you a better person.

I believe that *every time* you fall in love, you become a little better than you were before.

I know how naïve this sounds. I know I should be embarrassed to admit to such beliefs. But it so happens that I am not embarrassed easily.

A writer I admire – a woman twenty-five years my elder, a brilliant and wise writer, and not just someone worthy of respect but someone I do respect and to whom I usually defer – once took me to task for saying something along these lines, for insisting, as we talked over dinner one night, that romantic love had "redemptive powers." We had been talking about a story by Chekhov. The conversation had turned into an argument, which had swiftly turned personal. I hung my head when she scolded me. But I didn't take it back – not even with her.

Love improves you.

I don't care how foolish it looks, written down in black and white. Because I believe it with all my heart. I believe it even though I spent years making a fool of myself for love, making mistakes in the name of love, losing weeks or months of my life mourning the death of love. I believe that being in love makes one better, and I believe that being in love makes *life* better. And I don't mean just that it makes life *seem* better.

This is what I mean to tell my daughter, when the time comes.

And this: that I don't think it matters if it's an irrational, imprudent, pointless, helpless, wrong, or stupid sort of love, as so many of my own loves and half-loves have been. Because even when love comes to nothing, it makes you more than you were. Even when you know it's going to come to nothing. Even when it's just a little bit of love, a sideline-to-your-life sort of love, a temporary insanity love, a crush. Even when it's only yearning unfulfilled or half-fulfilled. Even when it comes to sorrow in the end.

Love exercises you. Your heart expands to make room for someone else – even if it's just for a while, even if there are already plenty of people in it. Your soul stretches and bends to accommodate the complexities of another person's soul; your mind works furiously to make sense of someone else's life and history and numerous peculiarities – and you have to be alert, you have to really wake up and listen and pay attention: you can't sit alone in your room, you've gotta come hear the music play, which you can't *do* sitting alone in your room with a notebook and pen thinking about your own lonely place in the universe, or rolling another piece of paper into the typewriter as you try to make sense of something somewhat related to something that happened to you or almost happened to you five or ten or fifteen years ago, or tap not quite silently on a laptop you lug along with you everywhere you go, in case you have half an hour between all the other things in your life now, trying to make progress on a novel that is, in fact, about love.

Love helps. Love hurts (and *scars*, and *burns* and *mars* – I know that song too; I am beginning to think I know too many songs) but it also helps. It helps keep life's basic, unchangeable facts, our isolation inside our own selves and our own histories, our separateness – and our dread and terror and the despair that comes and goes, the sadness, the failures – from overpowering life itself. It sweetens all the rest. It makes you feel, however fleetingly, at the center of things. The lead actor. The star. The one who matters most, doing the thing that matters most. You *are* the star. And the thing that matters most takes over your life: it makes everything else less important, less relevant. It feels like the reason we were all put on earth. It's ridiculous, but it feels wonderful. It feels essential. It is essential. Ridiculous and essential.

It makes your life sing.

And afterward, and forever, you have that song. It's yours.

Come back to me again and play your sad guitar

I saw Norbert – the one who wrote me the letter of apology – not too many years ago. He lives in Israel now, with his Israeli second wife. He's earns his living as a musician, as far as I know the only one who does among all the boys who played music when we were young. He was in Columbus for a percussion convention, and he called me. We had lunch; he showed me pictures of his children – he had two then – riding camels on vacation. We exchange e-mails now from time to time, and just the other day he wrote to tell me that his third child had arrived – "Life never stops with the surprises," he said – and that he and his family were planning to leave Israel soon, to return to the U.S. to live.

Russell, my high school boyfriend, turned up at a reading I gave in New York when my first book came out, and he looked almost exactly like his father had looked, all those years ago. And now he is a dentist, like his father. He has taken over his father's practice on Ocean Avenue, in Brooklyn. He's married too, of course – or he was then – and when I saw him he had two kids, he told me, but that was over a decade ago, so who knows what's happened since.

Robby, the rhythm guitarist in the band we named after Russell's father – Russell's own name, now – e-mails me every couple of years, just to say hello, to send his love. I never loved him, not even a little bit – not that way, as we used to say – and I was surprised to find out recently that he had loved me "that way" for a while, the year we were fifteen. My best friend from high school, who lives in Petaluma, is forever running into people from our high school in Brooklyn (most of whom seem also to have moved to California) and sometimes they'll remember that she and I were close back then and they'll ask about me. But this time, the woman hadn't known me. She had known Robby, though, and what she asked my old friend was, "So, whatever happened to that girl Robby used to sing with, the one who treated him so cruelly and broke his heart?"

"Who else did Robby sing with?" my friend asked me when she called to tell the story. "Who would that have been?" But it had to have been me. There hadn't been anyone else.

Steven, the boy who called me heartless, used to phone me once every few years, always to reminisce about the same handful of shared experiences: the time we went to the Rolling Stones concert at the Garden and had to leave early because of my curfew; the shopping trip to a store called Id, where I supervised the purchase of his first pair of bell-bottoms in honor of his acceptance to Clark University; how we saw *Easy Rider* together on our first date. Every time we talked, he'd congratulate himself on being the one to get me started reading the Sunday *Times*, when my father read the *News* in those days. What I remember about this is that Steven called the "Arts and Leisure" section "Section Two," in a knowing, insider's way, which impressed me (even though it didn't help his cause – his campaign to make me "admit" that I loved him). I had no idea then that no one referred to the sections of the paper by their number. But I've never had any desire to hurt his feelings, and so I never once mentioned this when he called. I never mentioned, either, that all I remember about the *Easy Rider* date is what I was wearing – the matching purse and shoes, the knee socks, the kilt (I wouldn't make that up: I wore a kilt to *Easy Rider*). And black eyeliner, and white eyeliner, two perfect stripes.

Robby is still single; Steven is married and has a daughter.

The mordant lead guitarist lives in a small town in Maine with his wife, their children grown and gone. He runs a bagel shop.

I like knowing where they are, what they're doing, whether they have someone who loves them.

For years I had no idea what had become of John, the boy for whom I broke up with Steven, but just a few months ago my brother told me he'd run into him in the town where he lives in New Jersey. John was working there, in the post office. My brother was mailing a package. Scott – my brother – hadn't even known John. He's four years younger than I am and missed everything that went on in my life except when I went out of my way to include him, which wasn't very often. Still, there in the post office, when the guy behind the counter glanced at

Scott's return address and said, "Herman. I once went out with a girl whose last name was Herman, years ago, in Brooklyn," my brother swears he was sure right away that it was me, even before they got to neighborhood, high school, dates of attendance, my first name. "How is that possible?" I asked him, and Scott shrugged. "You went out with everybody."

I hadn't even known he was paying attention.

John seemed no more surprised, according to Scott, than he was. Once they established that yes, it was that Herman, they shook hands over the counter and John told Scott to give me his regards.

I don't know what happened to Howie. Or to David, who kissed me with such apparent meaningfulness and then convinced me each week to come back for more despite everything he'd said during the seven days preceding – but oh how I wish he would show up again, just long enough for me to find out how he turned out. I'd get in touch with him myself if I could, but there are too many Davids in the world, and too many of them share his last name.

I'm glad to say I know how Irwin's life unfolded. I tracked him down years ago. I called his mother – she was still at the same address, the same phone number, in Sheepshead Bay; all I had to do was call Information (after almost thirty years, still at the same address!). She told me that he lived in Ohio – two hours from here, in Cincinnati – and gave me his phone number and address, and I wrote to him. He called me when he got the letter. He remembered the little girl I'd been – remembered some things about me that I'd forgotten. The "I love Paul" button I wore the year we were ten, the spider plant Miss Schiff let me take home, to the dismay and bitterness of everyone else in the first grade, my refusal to play certain games I claimed were "too childish" (what I remembered was that there had been games I was afraid to play, fearful I'd get hit with a misaimed ball, or possibly that someone would intentionally aim a ball at me). I reminded him of the comedy routine he and Stewart Grodman had performed on the last day of sixth grade as part of the goodbye party Mrs. Rosenbloom threw for us, the one at which he had declined to sit near me, though I got up my nerve to ask him. He didn't remember that at all.

He didn't remember that Robin Schultz and I performed "Red Rubber Ball."

Then there were things he remembered differently from the way I did. He was sure it had been the Captain and Little Buttercup in H.M.S. *Pinafore*, not Nanki-Poo and Yum-Yum in *The Mikado*. And he hadn't played the Maestro in *The Lost Note*, he said. That was Stewart Grodman.

We talked for hours. We time-traveled together. We caught up, too. He had married in his early twenties; he was still married. He had two nearly grown children and one still young. He'd spent years as a steelworker, he told me, before he finally decided to go to college and then on to grad school in biochemistry.

And a few years after that phone conversation – two or three years ago – he drove up to Columbus and had dinner with me and my family. My husband, who is not normally or naturally social, was polite and as friendly as I have ever seen him be to anyone. My daughter studied Irwin carefully. I studied him carefully, looking for the boy I'd first met close to forty years before. He looked only vaguely familiar. In the pictures he showed me of his sons when they were young I could see more of him, the boy I had known and loved.

My husband and daughter mostly listened to the two of us, and after dinner they gave us some time alone. We talked as easily as if we'd known each other all our lives, instead of three and four decades ago. We looked at pictures – the class pictures, every year from kindergarten through sixth grade, which I had saved and kept in photo albums. We had been in the same class every year, "tracked" in a group coded the "IGC class," which we weren't supposed to know meant "intellectually gifted children."

We talked about my minute-long scream in the last act of our fifth-grade operetta version of *Carmen*, and about Mrs. Greenfield in fourth grade, who hated both of us for unknown reasons, and how we didn't tell our parents that. We talked about the girls who didn't like me (he insisted they had been jealous because I was smarter and more talented, which was kind, if dishonest, of him; they didn't like me, I knew even then, because I was peculiar – bookish and bossy, theatrical, too hungry for attention). We talked about the old neighborhood, and all the children in our class – looking at the photos, between the two of us we were able to name every single child – and how we imagined they might have turned out. We talked about what had been on our minds and in our hearts back in those days.

He was a sweet, smart, lovely man, and it was a pleasure to spend time with him. I realized I was pleased with myself – my old self, my long-ago self – for having chosen well. It struck me as we sat talking that I had loved him most of all, despite how young I'd been. I'd loved him acutely – unreservedly, and steadfastly – without having to tell him, without the need for him to know. That had made it very pure, I thought. And even though he'd ignored me – even though he hadn't known what to do with me; even though he hadn't known a thing about what I felt – I was glad I'd felt what I had, back then. My own inclination to give love, long before I knew anything about love – long before he knew anything about how to receive it – struck me as a great gift. And all at once it seemed to me selfish not to share this gift with him. Never too late, I told myself, and took a deep breath, and confessed.

It wasn't easy, not even after thirty years. I blushed as I spoke. I even stammered, which I don't recall ever in my life having done before.

And when I was done, he smiled. He said, "I know."

"You know?"

He shrugged.

"What do you mean, you *know*? Now or then?"

He looked abashed – perhaps because I sounded so agitated. Well, I *felt* agitated – mortified for my five-year-old, my nine-year-old, my eleven-year-old self.

"Both, I guess." He said this cautiously. "You know, I knew then, so . . . of course I know now."

Was he *sure* he'd known then?

"Well . . . yeah. It's not the kind of thing you forget."

No, I said, what I meant was: was he sure he hadn't figured it out looking back and was now imagining he had known at the time?

"I'm sure," he said.

And: "I was lucky," he said.

Lucky to have known that he was loved? Lucky to have *been* loved? Lucky to have been loved by me?

But I couldn't ask. It seemed too much to ask.

And then I thought: it doesn't matter. Whatever his answer might have been, it wouldn't matter.

Because he was right – he had been lucky. Lucky on all counts.

And so have I. Not just to have loved, but to have failed to hide it.

This, I realize, is exactly what I mean to tell my daughter – that I have been lucky. That I am lucky, still.

And that I wish the same for her. To love, and to fail to hide it.

Enough Friends

My daughter and her best friend are playing with their stuffed snakes. I can hear them arguing – the snakes, not the girls – in the next room.

The girls are Grace and Kristin, ages eight-and-a-half and ten; the snakes are River, Stormy, Coby, Andrew, Mist, Breeze, Taffy, and Taffy. One of the Taffys belongs to Grace (who belongs to me). The other, its identical twin, is Kristin's.

River and Breeze are identical, too, and so are Stormy and Andrew (apparently the snake-makers didn't have anywhere near as much imagination as these girls do), but Grace and Kristin looked at me as if I were the dumbest person on earth when I asked once why *they* didn't have the same names. Later Grace took pity on me and explained that it had to do with their personalities: Taffy and Taffy not only looked alike, they *were* alike. The other look-alikes (and here she laughed in amazement that I could have thought otherwise) were *completely different* from each other.

By now I know that each of the snakes has a distinct, well-defined persona (stalwart, jocular, fearful, and so on), a gender (half the snakes are male, the other half female), a best friend among the other girl's snakes, and a "crush" – a word the girls use both for the type of emotional attachment (as in *he has a crush on her*) and to denote the object of that attachment (thus, Mist's crush is Andrew, and Andrew's is Mist. In the snakes' world, all crushes are reciprocated).

The snakes aren't shouting anymore, and in spite of myself I lift my hands from the keyboard and listen closely. It's just the girls talking now – "as themselves," as they would say – agreeing that after playing with the snakes all morning they're both finally tired of it. Now they're trying to make up their minds what to do next. Grace is enumerating the possibilities, and she and Kristin are considering each in turn, as seriously as if they were deciding foreign policy. They're talking quietly enough so that if I want to know what's going on I have to make an effort to eavesdrop (and, shamefully enough, I do – although a moment ago I had been telling myself piously that I was doing my best not to listen, that I was trying to concentrate, for godsakes. It's always one way or the other when you're a mother. Or at least that's how it's been for me).

In the end they decide to be the Beatles, another favorite game these days. They both love the Beatles, which is considered a sign of eccentricity in their school. It's not that they don't like 'N Sync, they are constantly having to explain: 'N Sync is their *second* favorite band. To them, the Beatles are brand new and thrilling and entirely cool – so cool, they tend to forget that the music they're in thrall to is decades old. When Grace saw the present-day Paul McCartney for the first time on TV not long ago, she burst into tears. The last time she "knew" him was from *Let It Be*, and although she recognized him right away when I called her into the room and pointed, his appearance shocked her. As soon as he started singing "I'm Down," though, she relaxed. "It's still really him," she said with a sigh, and by the time his set was finished, she wasn't crying anymore.

She and Kristin have memorized the lyrics to dozens of Beatles songs. They have favorites: "Love You To" (with all that sitar, and George Harrison's mournful lyrics about how quickly time passes) is currently Grace's; Kristin's is "Maxwell's Silver Hammer," because it makes her laugh ("the story and the music are both funny," she marvels). Last week it was "You've Got to Hide Your Love Away" (Grace) and "And I Love Her" (Kristin). The week before, "No Reply" and "Help!"

When they play at being Beatles, Grace is always George and Kristin is Ringo. They are best friends. They have paired off the Beatles just as they have paired off their snakes: George and Ringo, John and Paul. And they have given them personalities, too – so specific and precise that I've heard one remind the other, "No, he would never say that." Most of what they know is from the movie *Help!*, which they claim is their all-time favorite live-action film, just as *Yellow Submarine* is their favorite cartoon.

They like to debate the various merits of each Beatle – and to make fun of me because they know that "my Beatle" in 1965 was Paul. "Oh, naturally," says Grace. "You *would* like 'the cute one.'" I don't know why she says this – how she can possibly know this about me – but since she's right, there's nothing I can say in my defense.

At the moment Ringo is both girls' favorite, but when I ask them why, they become uncharacteristically inarticulate – "He just *is*."

In their formulary, Ringo is the funniest and the most accessible – the "most normal," they tell me. John is the smartest and also "the leader." George is the shyest, the most interesting, and the best musician (this last, I'm sure, is received wisdom from my husband). Paul is – as he has been to all girls since time immemorial – the cutest, but Grace and Kristin's lexicon also accords him the title of "the sweetest" ("You can tell this because he sings lead on all the sweetest songs," Grace explains, and she has a point. "John sings lead on most of the sarcastic ones." Ditto. And George, they've noted, tends toward the gloomy).

Grace wept when the real George Harrison died, and the day after, she and Kristin decided to write a condolence letter to Ringo. They could only imagine how hard it would be for either of them to lose her best friend, they told him. *Please write back. You are our favorite Beatle. From your friends, Grace and Kristin.*

They wondered for a long time whether they should say "your friends" or "your fans." I was in my study, eavesdropping again. They were worried that Ringo would consider it presumptuous if they called themselves his friends when they didn't even know him. Finally they came in to ask me what I thought. This is not something they do very often, so I knew how serious they were, and how troubled.

I told them that in my opinion "friends" would be fine – and not just fine but lovely – since it was likely that Ringo had a great many more fans than friends, and everyone, no matter how famous, can use another friend or two.

They considered this for a moment. Finally Kristin nodded thoughtfully. "You know," she told Grace, "I think your mother might be right. Especially now, what with George and all. If your best friend dies, you probably feel like you're all alone in the world."

Grace looked pretty close to tears herself, thinking about this.

I didn't have the heart to tell them that I had no idea if George and Ringo had been "best friends" – and that actually I doubted it, for all sorts of reasons. I don't want to be the one who forces these children to "face facts," who drags them away from the dreamy state of imagining and inventing in which they live.

Besides, when it comes right down to it, there's only so much I *can* explain.

• • •

My mother never eavesdropped on me and my best friend. She couldn't have; she was too depressed – a condition that was described to me when I was very young as "the same kind of sickness that Abraham Lincoln had," which I suppose was meant to reassure me, to make her condition sound more dignified. There was no inherent dignity in the way my mother spent her days – in bed, "resting" with her eyes open (which I knew because despite strict orders to leave her alone, I was always sneaking in, trying to talk to her or hold her hand, or else just sitting on the edge of the bed watching her) – but by invoking Lincoln my father managed only to worry me more. For years I had a picture in my mind of the famous president, Honest Abe himself, in his tall black hat, lying in a too-small bed (a Goldilocks image that somehow crept in to the picture), staring at the ceiling, too sad and listless to move. How did anything get done? I wondered. How on earth did he manage to run the country?

And because my sense of time wasn't very well-developed, I was fearful about what might happen to all of us, with nobody in charge.

I remembered this – the last part of it – when Grace couldn't sleep for several days following the botched presidential election of 2000, afraid that something terrible would happen. She couldn't rest until we had a president, even the wrong one (although she worried then that the world would "go to hell in a handbasket," as her father had darkly predicted).

In my childhood, I wasn't worried about what would happen at home – my mother sad as Lincoln, unable to take charge – so much as I was just plain lonely. My father and my grandmother were capable of taking charge of everything (and they were always tussling over who was really in charge, so that by the time I was Grace's age I sometimes thought it was no wonder my mother had retreated to her bed). I felt safe enough. I just had no one to talk to.

Not at home, I didn't. But when I was three we moved from the building on Brighton Fifth Street, in which we lived just down the hall from my grandparents – from the apartment in which my mother had grown up, sharing a room with her three older brothers – and into a brand-new building one D-train stop away, in Sheepshead Bay. There I found my first best friend (I'll call her A——, the first in a long line of best friends).

I escaped to A——'s family's apartment, one floor below ours, every chance I got. With A——, when we were five or six, I acted out the plots of Broadway shows and Hollywood musicals. We would listen to the cast recording albums on her parents' record player and sing along, using appropriate gestures, stopping the record as necessary for scenes unilluminated by song, taking turns assuming the best roles (Eliza, Maria, Julie Jordan, Laurey). And when we weren't singing "The Rain in Spain" or "People Will Say We're in Love," we were winding up the tiny ballerina in A——'s jewelry box and dancing along with her – not improvising, either, but taking turns choreographing, then teaching it to the other and practicing till we got it right.

At Grace's age, we spent most of our time together drawing and making up stories to go with the drawings, although sometimes we skipped the drawing part altogether and just lay on A——'s bed side by side as we told each other stories we made up on the spot.

If an adult came into the room, we stopped what we were doing. It was embarrassing to be caught holding hands and singing, in what we believed to be harmony, about how when love came so strong, there could be no right or wrong (both of us in tears because Bernardo was dead), or solemnly grande plié-ing at each other as the jewelry box tinkled out "Für Elise," or pointing to a drawing of five girls dressed in high fashion circa 1963 and one dowdy, lonely girl drawn way at the edge of the paper, arms crossed protectively in front of her, and explaining that the popular girls have excluded and mocked our isolated protagonist, but . . . (and here the sheet of paper was lifted, and the next scene revealed). But even if it hadn't been embarrassing, we still wouldn't have wanted anyone to see or hear what we were up to. It was nobody's business but ours, so we went silent – and if we needed to communicate with each other when we weren't alone, we used "G-talk," a language I can't remember how we learned and which I have yet to meet anyone else who spoke in her childhood (and thus I concluded years ago that A—— and I must have made it up – but recently my husband, while rounding the full range of cable channels late one night, stumbled across a movie that featured a brief G-talk exchange, he says, and although he can't remember the name of the movie or anything else about it, he swears it was "that crazy 'gadigadaga language' of yours," and that it was translated with subtitles).

I can still speak G-talk fluently (*idigI cidigan stidigill spidigeak Gidigee-tidigalk flidiguidigentlidigy*) and two years ago I taught it to Grace, who would amuse herself by speaking it rapidly to me in public places. Last year she decided to teach it to Kristin, and now they use it often, and with great pleasure – they call out greetings to each other at the end of the school day, making plans for future play dates and reporting the news since last recess – and I am the only one who can understand them.

In A——'s and my childhood, there was no one who could understand us.

. . .

I remember what it was like, before A——, and how much my life changed when she entered it.

From my vantage point of forty-four years later, I know this: that I am bereft when I am told that we – my mother and her enormous belly, my father, and I – are leaving the only home I know, just down the hall from the one my grandparents live in, and moving into a new apartment in Sheepshead Bay. I have never heard of Sheepshead Bay, but I am assured that it is nice, and not very far away at all, and that the new apartment will be much bigger and better, that my new little brother or sister and I will have a bedroom of our own to share, with linoleum featuring pictures of Mother Goose characters, as if any of this information will help me in any way.

My father has decided that our one-bedroom apartment is too small, and that it's time to leave Brighton Beach, where I was born and where everyone in the building knows me and calls me *mamaleh*;

where when I wake up wide awake at five-thirty, unable to go back to sleep as I'm supposed to, I can quietly let myself out of our apartment and, still in my pajamas, make my way down the hall and knock on Grandma and Papa's door, and gravely observe as Papa wraps himself in his t'fillin and says his morning prayers and then downs a shot glass of homemade schnapps (which I watch him make with mission figs and vodka in giant bottles he keeps under the kitchen table), and eat breakfast with him before he goes to work at the Biltmore Hat Company, far away in The City, Manhattan.

Looking back, I understand that my father must have thought it would be better for my mother, better perhaps for all of us, to put some distance – even just one subway stop – between us and my grandparents, but without them, I think, I will be the loneliest child in the world. I am *already* practically the loneliest child in the world.

Until I met A——, I had no friends. As much as I loved my grandmother, she wasn't my playmate or even my confidante, not then. Later, much later – when I was in my early twenties, living on my own – she did become my confidante, a great surprise and thrill for both of us. We fell into the habit of talking on the phone for hours late at night, after my grandfather was asleep. But in my childhood, she had no time for that sort of leisurely, intimate relationship. When we were together, I would follow her around, watching her work and listening to her talk. She was never idle, not for a second, and all the while she worked (it's amazing to me now that she found so much housework to do in a three-room apartment), she told me stories about coming to this country, including every detail she could wring out of her memory about the journey she had made from Poland as a teenager, alone, and about life at her sister's apartment on the Lower East Side when she first arrived, and about the boys who'd courted her and how my grandfather had edged them all out, and about the button factory where she'd worked before my grandfather insisted that she quit ("I'll give you the three dollars a week to stay home," he said grandly – and this when they were only courting, not even yet engaged! she reported, still proud of it after half a century) and her life as a young wife and mother, and my mother's childhood – there was no end to her stories, and I loved them; I loved listening to her and I felt happiest, safest, when I was alone with her in her apartment. But I didn't feel as if I had a *friend*.

And my grandfather was fun, he was gentle and funny, and he knew how to comfort me without words – he was the only one who did – but when he was around he didn't play with me, either. And my father? My father was awe-inspiring; I idolized him. But he could not be talked *to*, nor did he have any interest in playing. I didn't expect him to – he was above playing, as I saw it – but later, when my brother came along, he was faced with a child who did expect to be played with (not that my father gave in; he seemed baffled by this turn of events). What my father required from *me* was devotion, rapt attention. This I was glad to give him, but it wasn't friendship.

The only other person in my life was my poor mother, and I was *not to disturb her*, my grandmother was forever telling me. I hardly needed to be told. I longed for her company, but I was afraid of making her cry, afraid of the gloom that surrounded her, afraid of how fragile she seemed. Even when I did try to talk to her, I whispered. I told her good news only – that I'd missed just one word on the spelling test (*cigarette*), that I had been chosen for the lead in the class play, that my second grade teacher, Mrs. Pullman, had announced to the whole class that I was going to be a writer because of the poem I'd written about the newly built Verazzano Bridge ("shining like a necklace in the night").

It's possible I thought I might break her, just by speaking to her in an ordinary tone of voice about ordinary things. How could we have been friends? (Later we were – and we are, now, and have been for over three decades – but back then, although she lived among us, I hardly knew her. I have only the vaguest memories that are directly *of* her.)

There was no one at home for me to tell my stories to, to speak with about what was on my mind, to sit down on the floor and play a game with.

But there was A——.

A—— lived with *her* pregnant mother, her father, and her Grandma Belle (lucky A——!) one floor below us. They had just moved in, too. She was five months older than I, and glamorous – not just older but much taller; not just taller but more grown-up, too. She was poised.

She was demanding. She was *formidable*. I adored her. I adored and admired her, both.

I had never admired anyone but my father and my grandmother. Before A——, I hadn't known it was possible; I hadn't known there might be other people in the world who were worthy of admiration. I also hadn't bargained for what would come along with admiring someone who wasn't linked to me by blood: that I would worry, constantly, that I might displease her and fall out of favor with her, that I would lose her for good.

Over time, this became part of the fabric of my life, as basic to it as my longing for my mother, my affection for my grandfather, my worship of my father and my grandmother – my adoring, admiring devotion to A—— and the low rumble of worry that she could easily be lost to me forever. Devotion and dread: my constant companions.

. . .

I am four, five, six, seven. I spend as much time as possible downstairs with A—— and her family. I am perfectly happy there. It is the anti-Herman household.

A——'s mother has a job. She is the first mother I have ever met or even heard of who goes out into the world each morning, like a father. Each evening she returns in time for dinner, which her mother, whom I call Grandma Belle just as A—— does, has prepared. Grandma Belle takes care of all the housework and the children – A——, and then the baby, A——'s little sister, when she arrives. Grandma Belle is a different sort of grandmother from mine. She doesn't have a Yiddish accent, and her hair is dyed red. She seems to have no power or authority, either, unlike my grandmother. She takes care of things as per her daughter's instructions – she "helps"; she doesn't run the household. It's her daughter who makes all the decisions.

A——'s mother is imposing, "stylish." She wears makeup. She is tall, too, like A——. Like the father in the family. They are large and we are small.

A——'s father is soft-spoken and pleasant. Except for his height, he doesn't frighten me. He is handsome and rather charming, in his quiet way. He always seems delighted to see me: he smiles very nicely and asks how I am today. But aside from that, he hardly speaks at all.

A——'s mother makes up for his silence: she never stops talking, and her voice is loud – it's a big, hoarse, booming voice, a commanding voice. It fascinates me, but oddly enough it doesn't frighten me. She yells at me to *eat something, damn it* – for at that age I have to be persuaded to eat; I eat hardly anything at all except white bread and Temptee whipped cream cheese – and I take this as a sign of love.

The apartment itself is the antithesis of ours, and not just because it is laid out differently, in a different "line" than ours, with one more room (a room for Grandma Belle). A—— and her sister share a bedroom just as my brother and I do, but ours is bigger. It is the only way in which our apartment is superior to theirs.

They live in a showplace – this is the word A——'s mother uses for it. She's proud of it, proud of all her things, and she expects her mother to take good care of them – the lamps and little tables and figurines and framed pictures. The living room is decorated in shades of red and pink and there is nowhere one can walk without bumping into some object: a marble-topped round table just big enough to house one porcelain lady dressed in pink and her pink umbrella, or a plush rose-colored velvet loveseat, or a spindly floor lamp, or the grandfather clock. There is a sofa, also velvet, with many little tasseled brocade pillows; drapes; a French provincial-style telephone on another minuscule table; a coffee table with claw-footed legs; shelves on all the walls displaying well-dressed old-fashioned ladies and the occasional gentleman, children holding hands, ballet dancers, dogs and cats, cunning baskets full of flowers. China treasure chests spilling china treasures. Colored glass bottles. Vases. Candlesticks. Little bowls, little plates, little glasses. Little lamps with glass shades, roses painted on the shades. *Things* – this is chiefly what I remember – things everywhere.

As there are in our place, but our things aren't there for show. We have stacks of stuff. It is all stuff no one knows what to do with. The effort that's been made toward "decorating" even I can tell is meager. We have mock Danish modern – a kidney-shaped coffee table – and the kind of couch (black tweed, flecked with bits of white and gold) that curves around the corners. Boxy fifties armchairs (which I love, for this is where I read, my legs flung over one side; I cannot imagine where A—— finds a place to read). A floor-to-ceiling lamp with plastic ivy curling around the cage that holds three tubes of light; another cage-lamp atop a "corner table," a triangle that fits behind the sofa's curve, with three glass globes concealing bulbs – a pink globe, a green globe, a yellow globe. And then there are stacks: of magazines, of books – both my parents are readers, like me – and of household items no one can be bothered to put away, or which no one knows where to put away; there are many things in our place that have no place.

Things are in disorder, but I am very orderly. I'm quiet, too. I am obliged to be, when I'm at home – and no matter how many hours I spend at A——'s, eventually I must go home, back up to our apartment on the third floor.

If the weather is good, I duck out to the fire escape, which overlooks the "play area" (a triangle of concrete sidewalk enclosed by a chain link fence) and beyond that, Avenue Z. But whether I am just outside the living room or in it, sitting sideways in my favorite armchair, I wear a costume dress that Grandma made for me, and I am in my own world, thinking or reading – already I am reading obsessively; I have discovered that reading keeps me from feeling lonely (a few years later I will make the same discovery about writing, which it turns out is even more effective) – or drawing pictures on stationery my father brings home from his new job at the life insurance company, the job I know he hates, but which he has taken so we can afford this move.

The move has not in fact accomplished what he must have hoped. In our new home my mother spends more time than ever lying down behind the closed bedroom door, and my grandmother visits almost every day (which is a relief, though it isn't the same as having her just down the hall, or as comforting as being with her in her apartment). For her part, Grandma is taken aback by my frequent absences, and I have the distinct impression that she doesn't think very highly of A——.

Not that she sees much of her. We never play in my family's apartment. A—— will come upstairs to "call for me" and then the two of us take off, downstairs to her place or outdoors to the play area.

With a brother on the scene, I am no less lonely than I was before, but it's more crowded in the apartment – and it's worse, it seems to me, to be lonely when you're not alone. My brother uses up the little bit of attention and energy my mother has available, and this, naturally, is infuriating. I have been waiting a long time – forever – for her attention, and now that she has roused herself, at least part of the time, she turns not to me but to him.

There is nothing about the baby that seems useful to me. Small as he is, he takes up a lot of space and makes a lot of noise. This I find shocking: I have been told so often to be quiet, my mother is resting. I turn the pages of a book, make scratches on paper. These are my only sounds. Now I must be quiet both for my mother and for my baby brother, who is often sleeping. We live in silence or in whispers unless it is one of the times when my brother is crying – or one of the times when my father is shouting. Or when my mother is sobbing.

After Scott is born, my father and my grandmother shout at each other whenever they are both in the apartment at the same time. For a while she is banished – my father yells at her that she is trying to "take over" – but she is reinstated when it becomes obvious that we cannot manage without her help. I weep with relief then, but I can't bear the way he talks to her when she comes back – or the way he will lose patience with my mother and demand, despairingly, that she pull herself together. I can't bear my mother's hand-wringing and sobbing (my father cannot bear it either, I can see for myself: her sobbing infuriates him; his fury makes her cry harder) or the way she fusses over my brother. I am less and less willing to be quiet for her sake when she is resting.

And so I flee for A——'s apartment. Even though at her place we have to be careful not to disturb anything, it is far more relaxing to me to play there than in our place, where there is not something but some*one* we have to be careful not to disturb, and where there is often someone disturbing us. At A——'s, no one bothers us, and no one cares how much noise we make as long as we don't disarrange or break anything, Grandma Belle reminds us every day. Since our games are not the sort of games that make a mess, we aren't in the least constrained by this. Grandma Belle is satisfied, and we play – content, engrossed, spinning out our stories, acting out our plays, dancing and singing and drawing and speaking in our own secret language – for hours, day after day. Year after year.

• • •

Grace and Kristin rarely make a mess, either, and when they do, it's the kind of mess that is tidied up in a matter of minutes: stuffed animals dropped into baskets and nets, model horses dumped into their bins, costumes swept back into the play clothes trunk.

They have been best friends since the day they met, just over a year ago. Grace was in second grade then, and on that day she came home excited and relieved: at recess, within the sea of children screaming and running in circles, playing capture the flag and foursquare and tag, she and "this third grader I've seen before but never talked to" somehow managed to connect and within minutes were rounding up their teams of imaginary horses, naming them and telling each other what each of them were like.

Looking back, they don't marvel over this as I do. As far as they're concerned, it was "no big deal": all the girls at school were already paired up, and in retrospect they believe it had just been a matter of time for them, too. They don't remember (at least not viscerally; if asked, they'll talk about it with detachment) how lonely they had been before they found each other. Grace had been at the school for a year, ever since we'd transferred her into it in the middle of first grade (when the "arts alternative" public school she'd been attending fell apart suddenly and dramatically, in ways that called for immediate action); Kristin had been there from the first day of kindergarten. Until they met, neither one of them had had a special friend at school. Kristin's mother says her daughter had resigned herself to loneliness, that she used to bring a book out to recess – a practice that was, if not forbidden, strongly discouraged – and find a secluded place to sit on the ground and read, three times a day. Grace spent two out of the three daily recess periods standing near a tree in the corner of the yard, "looking pathetic" on purpose, hoping someone from her class would come and ask her to play. She told me this a few months into second grade. What about the third recess? I asked her. What was different about that one? "That one, I pretend to be having fun. So they won't think I'm completely pathetic."

Now she doesn't have to pretend or be pitiful. She and Kristin are a perfect match – they can play together for eight, nine hours at a stretch and still beg for more time when told they have to part. They talk on the phone after they have left each other, and when Grace is not with Kristin or on the phone with her, she is often planning what they will do the next time they are together.

The nearly two-year age difference between them doesn't seem to matter – not yet, anyway, although I imagine it will, sooner or later, as even the five-month age difference between A—— and me eventually mattered. (Grace, however, has pointed out that since she is more interested in matters of love than Kristin is, it's possible that the "boy crazy stuff" – which Grace knows is coming because she's had experience with it, in the form of two teenage girls to whom she was deeply attached when she was younger – will kick in for both of them at roughly the same time despite the difference in their ages.) That Kristin was in third grade and Grace in second when they met troubled only the other third graders – who, for the first few weeks of the new alliance between the girls, made fun of them both: Kristin, for "playing with a second grade baby," and Grace, for "trying to act big." Neither Grace nor Kristin seemed especially moved by these taunts, not because they are above being hurt by other girls (Grace would come home in tears when the girls in her class told her, as they periodically did and still do from time to time, that she was "weird"), but simply because this was a taunt had no heft or weight for either of them. If the other girls had really wanted to torture them, they would have to have suggested that one had lost interest in the other. Luckily, the girls at school aren't that shrewd: no one thought of this.

By now, everyone at school – it is such a small school that all the children know one another and know who the best friend pairs are – accepts that Grace and Kristin are "bests," an inviolable pair. They are both weird. This seems to be accepted as a fact of grade school life.

2

Thanks to the way our birthdays fall out on the calendar, A—— is a year ahead of me in school. That first year, when she starts half-day kindergarten and I am still at home, is a misery. But the following year I am in school in the afternoon, and she is in the abbreviated-day first grade, which lets out at one. Even though we overlap at P.S. 209 for no more than an hour, we are almost even now, as I see it, and I feel better.

It gets a little rocky after that – when she is in second grade and I am in first, when she is in third and I am in second – for she is popular, tall and beautiful, accomplished, perfectly at ease in the social situation that all children understand is the real point of school, and I am uneasy, anxious, short and "chubby," worried, frightened. She has other friends; I have none.

But I remember this, too: knowing, always, that she loves me best.

I know this because she tells me, and because we still play together after school and on weekends, and we take dancing and "drama and elocution" lessons together once a week and afterwards, at the store under the subway station, we buy comic books together – DC Romance comics we read while walking home, then immediately swap.

I am jealous of the painting lessons she takes on Saturdays at the Brooklyn Museum, but my father says the neighborhood is bad; he won't take me there. Instead, I have piano lessons, and so we each have something the other doesn't. There is always this tension between us, it seems, once we pass the age of eight or nine: who has what, who is better at what, who will succeed.

I am a better writer. She is a better singer. But I sing and she writes, too, so we find we can't leave each other alone with our talents.

I sleep at her place now very often, in a "hideaway bed" – a trundle bed – that is pulled out every night for her and her sister. I sleep in the crack between her mattress and her sister's. I like her sister, though I keep this to myself: it is to be understood that she is a pest, beneath notice.

When she, the little sister, grows old enough to play with us – when she is four or five and we are seven or eight – A—— occasionally, grudgingly, agrees to include her in some subordinate role and I am secretly glad. It is almost like having another friend, and I am eager – desperate – for friendship. But even as A——'s sister joins us in our games, my brother, exactly A——'s sister's age, is left out in the cold – upstairs, where one has to be quiet, and it doesn't really matter if you make a mess. Most of the time, I don't even speak to him.

He says now – with the affability that is one of the hallmarks of his personality – that we didn't get to like each other until I was twenty, and he was seventeen, and I moved out of the house. Almost my first act when I moved out, into an apartment in the Village, was to invite him to dinner – just the two of us, grownups together, without our parents – as if we didn't even have parents.

Now that we are both parents ourselves, we get along very well and are fond of each other, although we see each other only once or twice a year and rarely talk (a function, we have apparently agreed to assume, of the several hundred miles between us and how busy we both are – with our work, with our families). I sometimes think that if we had been close as children, if our childhoods had had more in common – if there had been anything at all between us other than the fact of blood relation and living in the same small space – we'd be more alike now, would have more to talk about. As it is, we treat each other with bemused affection: my work, my interests, my disordered house are all a puzzlement to him, as his life is to me.

And when we do talk, it is about the children. His oldest child, Sean – with whom I've been head over heels in love since I first took him in my arms when he was a few hours old – is nearly seventeen, and now that he's a teenager and in and out of teenage trouble all the time, I am at long last of some use to him (as the one grownup in the family who understands teenage trouble, having been – unlike his parents in their youth – a teenager in frequent trouble myself, something I happen to remember as if it were only yesterday), and for my brother, talking to me *about* Sean is a comfort. I'm very glad to be a comfort. My niece, Jamie, thirteen and a half, will almost certainly be in need of me too before long (and Scott in need of comfort about her). The youngest, Greg – not much older than Grace, and a bookworm to boot (the only one of my brother's children who has never been disappointed by my birthday presents) – should be all right for some time. This is how Scott and I talk, when we do. *So far, so good,* he says.

We almost never speak of the past, of our own childhood. I don't suppose I'll ever know what my absence meant to him. I don't even know if he noticed it. Or, if he did, if he remembers that now. He has told me that he doesn't remember our mother's depression, insisting that it must have been over before he was old enough to have grasped it. But that's as far as the conversation has ever gone. It's not something we talk about – what we remember, what it meant. What it still means.

· · ·

When Grace and Kristin are together, at Kristin's house or ours, they will sometimes sit side by side on the bed, each with her own book, and read for hours in companionable silence. I had a friend – one friend (B——, who inevitably followed A——) – with whom I could do this, too. We were twelve, in seventh grade. Even after thirty-five years I remember how serene I felt, sitting at one end of her bed, my back against the wall, under the poster she had tacked up ("The unexamined life is not worth living") as she sat at the other end. Her big sister in the room next door, playing "Angel of the Morning" on her guitar. The Ramblers on the turntable downstairs, in the living room decorated with African masks and Peter Max posters, the stereo turned up loud enough so that B——'s mother, freshly home from work and cooking dinner, could listen from the kitchen. And B—— and I with our paperbacks (*Marjorie Morningstar* or *Cat's Cradle* or *The Mask of Apollo* or Salinger's *Nine Stories*. We were children with catholic as well as semi-grown-up tastes).

It was my first experience of solitude-in-company, and for me it was the ideal state – one I tried and failed for the next twenty years to recapture in romances, succeeding finally only in my mid-thirties. Before then, the men in my life were always either too much present, or not nearly enough.

That Grace and Kristin are exactly present enough for each other is a blessing. I still marvel over this sometimes as I watch them together – as much amazed as I am pleased – because for years Grace had no use for friends at all. Until she was five she tolerated other children when she was obliged to, at preschool, in her "creative movement" class at the ballet company downtown, in playgrounds or swimming pools, but she would never choose the company of a child over that of one of her parents. There was a little boy in New York, the son of a close friend of mine, whose company was not intolerable, but it never occurred to her that he might be a more attractive playmate than her father or me.

The trouble was, Glen and I were both first-rate playmates. He was good for complicated block towers that took up the whole play-room, skyscrapers Grace could fill with tiny plastic people, or giant multileveled Noah's arks that she'd populate with her vast collection of model animals. And when they weren't building and populating, they were painting or drawing or making sculptures out of clay or papier-mâché.

I wasn't much good with blocks, but I excelled at making dioramas, and I kept a box full of collage materials at hand – sequins, feathers, strips of shiny paper, lace – as well as bins of beads and buttons for jewelry-making. Or else we baked cookies and decorated them with violently colored homemade icing, or sewed fabric scraps into shawls for her dolls or a few of her favorite stuffed animals, or made little pillows and blankets for them. Or we hauled out all the stuffed animals or the bin full of model dinosaurs and "made them talk." Her father wasn't any good at this, so it was always I who accompanied her into the hearts and minds of the characters she had painstakingly differentiated. Ally the bossy alligator; Cowie the maternal, somewhat impatient cow, and her sister, Little Red Cowie, affectionate and needy; and Buffy, a squat, non-cuddly brown buffalo, who was timid and inclined to feeling left out – these were among the animals I was regularly assigned, and woe unto me if I "made them talk" in a way that betrayed the personalities defined for them by Grace.

Often we became characters ourselves, as directed by the *auteur*: orphan girls forced to scrub floors or sew or make a meatloaf or a pot of soup (a lot of dinners got cooked this way, as I coaxed Grace to incorporate real food into the game) or doctor and patient or mother and daughter – with our real-life roles reversed – or sisters who worked on a farm or in an orchard. I spent countless hours picking pretend berries, apples, and peaches, and plucking and digging out vegetables and tossing them into imaginary baskets.

And I remember it being fun, almost all the time. Because Glen and I took turns with Grace, we rarely became restless or impatient, and never desperate – something I've heard other parents who spend a lot of time with their children talk about (and which I remember fearing, when I was pregnant). It was a pleasure to play with Grace. She was never boring. And when *we* began to bore her, she would simply switch games, and we became interesting again.

I wouldn't have thought twice about her lack of interest in children her own age if her preschool teachers hadn't brought it up. They were concerned by the lengths to which she'd go to avoid playing with other children during the three hours she spent at the university's child care center. "Incidents" were reported to me, in a whisper. I would ask Grace about them on our way home, and she would relate, matter-of-factly, that another girl had joined her in the toy kitchen, or at the doll house or the sand table or wherever else she had been playing by herself "perfectly happily" for some time, and that she had excused herself ("nicely," she'd assure me) and moved on to the plastic animals or cars or blocks – whatever toy was not in use by other children at the moment.

"But why couldn't you have included her in your game?" I'd ask obediently (for this was what the teachers had told me to ask her).

"Because it was a one-person game."

"Couldn't you have expanded it to make it a two-person game?"

"Of course I could have, but then I wouldn't have been including her in *my* game. It would have been a different game."

"Right," I'd say, "but what if – "

"*Mama*," she'd say. "You asked, I answered."

I could see why the teachers – underpaid, undertrained, overworked – had turned the matter over to me.

"All right, then. So instead of including her in your game, would you consider playing a different sort of game sometime, maybe something like the games you and I play together? And see how it goes?"

A glance in the rearview mirror: she was incredulous. She didn't even dignify my question with an answer.

And the thing was, I understood. I felt terrible. We'd ruined her for children. The preschool teachers talked to me, as diplomatically as they could, about her "social skills" – which, they pointed out, was what preschool was supposed to help her develop, so that she would be ready for the primary grades (Grace complained about this all the time: "Why do they call it *school* if all we ever do is play, play, play? When does the learning start?"). Naturally I worried, and I felt guilty. Still, I thought – but managed not to say – her social skills with *us* were just fine. She was a joy to take to a restaurant or an art museum. She held up her end of a conversation better than most adults I knew.

It did occur to me during those years that because she got to call all the shots when she played with us (did Glen really care whether they built with Duplo, Lego, wooden blocks, or Lincoln Logs? did it matter to me whether we made Playmobil figures, dinosaurs, or stuffed animals talk?), when the time came for her to play with other children, it would require her to make an adjustment. But I figured we would cross that bridge when we reached the shore. In the meantime, I studied her for signs of incipient interest in children – or at least a little reluctance when she turned away a neighbor child who'd come knocking ("Sorry," she'd say cheerfully, "but I'm busy playing with my mama right now"). I suggested play dates with the girls in her creative movement class, because she seemed to like them better than her preschool classmates – or at least she was content to hang around with them after dance class to eat trashy snacks from the vending machine and make solemn trades (three Skittles for three M&Ms, one twist of licorice for two potato chips) while we mothers continued the conversation (about our marriages, about our parents and their marriages, about sex, about what our children would and wouldn't eat these days, about the schools we meant to send them to next year) we'd been having while the girls were behind the closed dance studio door for the last hour. Grace declined all offers.

Not that this kept her from calling these girls – and the neighbors she rejected, and the children in her preschool class with whom she wouldn't share the toy kitchen – her "friends." Once, in the playground, a little girl approached her where she was pushing Elephanty and Christmas the Frog and Sophie Sofanisba in the baby swings, and asked, "Do you want to be my friend?" and Grace looked startled and then said, politely, "No, thank you, I already have enough friends."

Had she known the word "acquaintance," I'm pretty sure she would have used it. But back then "friend" was a catchall word that had to cover everyone she knew and didn't actively dislike.

Certainly, when an actual friend came her way for the first time – the day before kindergarten, ten weeks past her fifth birthday – it was like an explosion in her heart.

. . .

She met Tenara at kindergarten orientation, at the school she used to go to, and even now, close to half her lifetime later, she remembers every detail of their first encounter. She likes to reminisce about how, at first, when "this strange girl I never saw before in my whole life" wandered over to the corner of the classroom where Grace and her father were building with blocks, and asked to join them, she was horrified. "At first I thought" – and here her voice fills with the outrage she remembers – " 'who does she think she is? I don't even know her!' But then something happened, and I just looked at her – and she looked at me – and we started playing together, and that was that. We were best friends."

She says it was like the moment in *West Side Story* – her favorite movie after she "outgrew" (she says) *The Music Man* and before she discovered *Help!* – when Tony and Maria lay eyes on each other for the first time at the dance in the gym. Everything else went out of focus. "I forgot all about Daddy," she says. "It was like that song they sing later, about 'only you, you're the only one I can see.' "

Tenara was – is – a bright, lively, confident, remarkably self-possessed little girl who had arrived in Columbus, in the U.S. itself, just weeks before. Her mother whispered, as we stood watching the girls begin to play together, that she still hadn't grown accustomed to the ease with which her daughter made her way in the world. She told me a condensed version of her life story – how she'd left the States for Israel at sixteen, sure she'd never return, how she'd met her husband, what sort of work they'd both been doing all these years, what had gone into their decision to come "home," and how they'd ended up in Columbus because that was where Doug, her husband, had found a job – and we liked each other (though nothing in the room went out of focus for us). I told her that Tenara seemed to have "taken Grace on" and she laughed: yes, that was Tenara all over.

Tenara was the first person outside our family who interested Grace. She was a dramatic, dynamic little girl, telling elaborate stories that made her own eyes grow big, and dressed in layers of clothes – long skirts, one on top of another; peasant blouses that left her naval showing – that reminded me of my own style during the years I faithfully attended Grateful Dead concerts up and down the East Coast, and both Laura Nyro shows at the Fillmore East, early and late, on Christmas Eve.

Tenara's English was spattered with Hebrew, and sometimes, when the girls were first getting to know each other, she would lapse entirely into the language she had always before spoken with other children. English was the language of her parents, of home. Grace was fascinated by this, and from my post in the room next door when the girls played at our house after school, I heard her asking questions about it. Tenara was the first child of Grace's own age with whom she had ever had a real conversation – the kind of conversation she was accustomed to having with us.

But this was a crash course in friendship.

On day three of kindergarten, Grace told Tenara at recess that she loved her, and Tenara said, "You can't love me. You only think you do. You don't know me well enough."

When I picked Grace up at school that day she greeted me in tears, which it seemed she had been holding back all afternoon. As soon as we were in the car she told me what had happened and asked if Tenara was right. I remember thinking that she had met her match, but what I said was, "Nobody can tell you how you feel. You're the only one who knows that."

"But Tenara seemed so mad about it. How could she be mad about someone loving her?"

By the time she got this question out she was sobbing. I remember gripping the steering wheel and willing *myself* not to cry, because I couldn't bear that she had been rejected, because I wanted so much to protect her from hurt of any kind, and because I was awash in guilt: I *had* protected her, for too long, and it was hitting her so hard now because she had no defenses against it.

I had always known I'd have to have this conversation with her, but I hadn't expected to have it until she was twelve or thirteen. I had imagined that it would have to do with romance, with some unworthy teenage boy whom she had scared away with her intensity, her passion, her willingness to speak her mind and announce exactly how she felt – her utter inability to play it cool. (The apple, I knew from the start, hadn't fallen far from the mother tree. Even as a newborn she'd made every passing feeling clear. She was madly expressive, full of desires. "You'll never have to guess what this one's feeling," a friend pointed out when she was three months old.)

"I'm not saying it makes *sense* for her to be mad about this," I said carefully. "Nor do I think she actually *is* mad. I think she's just . . . alarmed. Because the thing is, people sometimes are alarmed by that kind of declaration."

Sobbing. Coughing. Sniffling in the back seat. "*What* kind?"

Sighing in the front seat. "Look, I am not about to suggest that you aren't feeling what you obviously *are* feeling, or that you shouldn't feel it. But" – and here I hesitated – "sometimes it might be wise to keep those feelings to yourself."

There it was: the opposite of what I had been telling her *and* showing her – not to mention what I'd granted her by blood – for the last five years.

"Why?" she said. Not a wail. Simple curiosity. She had stopped crying.

"That's a good question, isn't it? Why wouldn't people want to know what other people are feeling? It's mysterious to me, I have to admit, but the fact is that sometimes people don't feel worthy of being loved, so they hate to hear that someone loves them. It makes them think there's something wrong with that person."

"Like . . . 'how can you be so stupid that you love me?' "

"It could be something like that. But sometimes it isn't that at all. Sometimes it's just that strong feelings, like love, can make people nervous."

"They don't make *me* nervous. They make me happy."

"Yes, well" – I laughed – "I think that's probably true. They make me happy, too. But not everyone feels that way. Everybody's different. You already know that, right? And for some people, maybe instead of feeling happy when they find out they *are* loved, they get scared. 'Whoa!' they think, 'that's too much feeling!' "

By now she was laughing too, but there was a little sob behind it, and she was still sniffling.

"They're not really mad, you know," I told her. "They seem mad, and they might even think they're mad, but they're not. They're just . . . misunderstanding. They don't know themselves how lovable they are."

"But that's sad, isn't it?"

"It certainly is."

She thought this over, silently. I thought it over, too. I made myself keep silent the rest of the way home.

In the end, she agreed that whatever Tenara's reasons had been for responding as she had, it would be wiser not to say anything more on the subject, at least for a while. It was her first lesson in the politics of emotion.

A lesson that has served her well, with all the other friends she's had since then, starting soon after that conversation – because once the gates opened, they opened wide. Even though Tenara remained her best friend all that year and for most of the year that followed, she began almost at once to make other friends. There was Cassie and Metzlal and Whitney and Sarah and Marissa . . . and finally Kristin, a new *best* friend. And that early lesson has served her particularly well with Kristin, whose reserve is extreme, and whose alarm at emotions expressed has occasionally been a source of some amusement to Grace, now that she's grown accustomed to it.

Tenara, as it turned out, quickly got over her anxiety about being loved. These days she's the one who comes on stronger. And it's not just that Tenara "warmed up" (although indeed she did, by the beginning of the second week of school); it's also that as Grace has grown older, she's become more like her father – that is, her personality seems to have made more room for his genes and his lessons. She's more reserved than she once was, less insistent on making her feelings known the instant she feels them. She's still my daughter, full of passions easily expressed – and compared to someone who is genuinely reserved, like Glen or Kristin, she's a powerhouse extrovert – but she's tempered what she has been both taught and given by me, with what Glen has bestowed upon her, and the combination (as she is quick to point out lately) works much better than either style does on its own.

When Grace and Tenara are together now, it's Tenara who will throw her arms around Grace and cry, "I love you to death! You're still one of my best friends in the world! I miss you so much, you little honeybunch." Grace giggles at this, and she doesn't draw away or tense up (as Kristin would; Kristin would barely tolerate such a thing, and then she'd run as soon as she was released), but it takes her aback, I can tell. Maybe *because* she's used to Kristin now, or maybe because she'd never go quite that far herself. But she navigates these emotional channels surprisingly well, having made the adjustment – late, I know, and with a fair amount of trauma, but very thoroughly – to the world of Other People: the various worlds of all the other people, one world per person. She has her passport; she travels freely.

3

Grace and I have a game we play sometimes when we're alone together. She calls it "Hard Questions in the Swing." We were in the backyard – she was swinging; I was sitting in a rocking patio chair, drinking a glass of wine – when she thought it up. But we play it now during dinner, on nights when Glen isn't ready to take a break from working in his studio and join us, or if we're driving somewhere, just Grace and me. It's a private sort of game.

And it's not really a *game*. She'll ask me, say, if I had to choose between publishing another book and keeping her as my daughter, which would I choose?

I'd choose her, I tell her.

But you'd be sad?

Yes, very sad.

If the choice doesn't make you sad, it's not a good Hard Question in the Swing.

The questions aren't always about her. She wants to know: If I could bring back only one of the cats I used to have – Cadence and Elizabeth, who lived with me for many years before Grace came along – which one would I choose? If I could return to New York City (for which she knows I pine) to live, but could never again visit a beach (which she knows I love, almost more than anything, and for which I also pine), which would I choose?

I can't help pointing out the existence of Far Rockaway and Brighton Beach – "just to name two," I say – but she sticks to her guns: no beaches, not anywhere. She clarifies the question, makes it harder. "You don't get to leave *Manhattan*. There's no beach *there*, right?"

I'm supposed to ask hard questions too, though I try not to ask any that will make her *too* sad, or upset – or conflicted. I'd never ask which parent she would choose if she could only keep one of us, or which set of grandparents; I'd never ask her to pick just one – or three, or five – of her stuffed animals. But I've asked her, "If you could pick three people in your life now – not counting relatives – you could continue to know for the rest of your life, who would you choose?"

A good "Hard Question in the Swing" takes a long time to answer, and this one did, once she got past Kristin.

In general she doesn't think I'm brutal *enough*. She wants to be asked *hard* questions, she says. And I know, really, that that's why she invented the game: not to ask but to answer hard questions. So from time to time she coaxes me along toward asking something tougher than I would otherwise consider. Once, toward the end of the summer, as we sat together in the bench swing on our front porch, playing the game, she confessed to a "secret wish" that she could have known me when I was her age. "I bet we would have been friends," she told me.

I sighed, and gave her what I knew she was asking for.

"So . . . if you had to make a choice, and we could both be eight years old and be friends but it meant that you'd have a different mother, which would you choose?"

This was a good one, I could tell. This took so long I closed my eyes and rocked us in the swing for ten minutes. I might have dozed off; it was late. In summertime I let her stay up almost as late as she wants to.

"I'll keep you as my mother," she said finally. Regretfully. I was about to say, "All right, then," but she went on, "That is, if you're *absolutely* sure you couldn't split yourself in half and be two people at the same time – girl and mother both?"

I was, alas, absolutely sure.

• • •

Like Grace, Kristin has had one other best friend. Hers was a girl she met at a class at the neighborhood rec center when she was three or four. The girls attended different schools when they were old enough to start, but they remained close, close enough so that when the other girl's family moved out of town, Kristin became severely depressed for several months. Even after she recovered, though, she was still subdued and lonely – until Grace came along.

The girls saved each other. I often think this and I don't believe I'm being melodramatic: I truly don't know what they would have done without each other, how they would have managed to keep on, as lonely as they were. And it's largely because of Kristin that I can't bear to think of moving Grace out of what we still call her "new school," even though it's now been over two years since she made the switch. This school, a throwback to the Eisenhower small-town fifties, was meant to be a temporary remedy: when we transferred her into it, we were just marking time, keeping our daughter safe, while we tried to figure out what to do next. Tenara's parents, Joanie and Doug, decided to try another alternative public school, but I was too angry, too bitter, too cynical about the system – certain that any school that was working well would have the plug pulled on it the way our arts school had – to bring myself to chance it.

The new school was imperfect – so far from perfect, by my reckoning, it wouldn't have made even the first cut when I went on my initial rounds (that is, if I'd included any private schools on my list of schools to visit, which I had not; Glen and I had never considered the possibility that we wouldn't send our daughter to public school). But perfection was the least of our concerns when we made the switch. We'd given up on perfection; we were willing – grateful – to settle for *quiet* (and indeed, the new school was so quiet that on the day I brought Grace to visit, right before she started attending daily, she turned to me as we walked down the hall toward what would be her classroom and said, "Where do they keep the children? In another building?"). We were grateful for the absence of chaos. We still are.

But there is a morning "flag ceremony" each day, complete with patriotic songs Grace had never heard before and was expected to know by heart (and so I gritted my teeth and taught her "God Bless America" and "The Star Spangled Banner." I didn't mind "You're a Grand Old Flag" – the melody more than made up for the lyrics – and I discovered that "America the Beautiful" still had the power to make me teary, as it did when I had to sing it during my school's flag ceremonies). Some mornings, after the pledge (through which Grace remains proudly silent), they sing "The Buckeye Fight Song" – the Ohio State football anthem. This one she never did manage to learn, and I couldn't help her with it. "I don't see what it has to do with anything," she says.

There is a dress code she and I both hate: navy blue, white, light blue, khaki, and a hideous dark green plaid. The mothers are called "Mrs." whether we like it or not (that I am called "Mrs. *Herman*" is a particular source of irritation to me; there is no room in the school's universe for a mother whose name is her own).

A month after Grace started there, they had a "celebration of the fifties" that failed to mention abstract expressionism, beat poetry, or music other than the likes of "Chantilly Lace." The children were given a "dress-down day" and told to wear clothes appropriate for the occasion, and I capitulated and bought Grace a poodle skirt when she declined my suggestion that she dress in black "like a Beatnik." "No one will know what that means," she said.

At the old school, the music teacher, Mrs. Myers, had taught the children to read music and let them try out different instruments; she played Beethoven and Mozart for them, and the children talked about what they had heard (and she never once told them what they were "supposed to hear," the way my early music teachers did). There were dance and theater classes several times a week. I watched Grace's kindergarten class act out the first Thanksgiving, improvising all their lines, and one afternoon Mr. White lowered the art room's acoustical ceiling tiles and had the children paint them, lying on their backs, pretending to be Michelangelo painting the Sistine Chapel.

At the new school, in "music," they sing songs, often from Disney movies, in preparation for two annual performances – and when they're not rehearsing (which means, essentially, for the first week or two of the school year and the last few weeks, late May and early June, after the spring concert), they watch videos of musicals. In "art," that first year, they copied Disney cartoons. (Disney is very big at the new school, which mystifies poor Grace, who knows just two Disney movies: *Bambi* and *Fantasia*.)

Still, we left the old school – which I had chosen so carefully after months of classroom observations and conversations with teachers and principals, in a city with some of the worst public schools in the U.S. – because we had no choice. Grace's last day there was the day her teacher called me to come in – "She's all right, she hasn't been hurt, but . . ." (it was the first time I'd ever known Mr. Trent to be at a loss for words, which frightened me almost as much as the call itself) – and I found her sitting perfectly still and alone at her table for four. Two of the other three chairs had been overturned, and Grace was weeping soundlessly at her empty table, tears slipping down her cheeks, her hands pressed together tightly in her lap, while all around her the classroom was in turmoil: two children were rolling around on the floor fighting, chairs were being thrown – and crayons, and tissue boxes – and everyone was shouting or shrieking. One little boy was in a corner. He had pulled his pants down to his ankles and he was howling.

Tenara was in a different first grade class, since the school made a point of sprinkling its brightest children among the different classes at each grade level, just as it distributed its most troubled children, so that every class had "a good mix" at every level. That was the idea, anyway. In practice, first graders with serious behavior problems were put in Mr. Trent's class. Not only was he the only male teacher in the primary grades, presumed to be able to "handle" the more violently disturbed – and violent – kids, but he was easily the most gifted classroom teacher in the school, with a reputation for being able to teach anyone, anytime (even the girl who ate the soap out of the soap dish in the corner sink, and the kids who couldn't yet write their names, who didn't know their own birthdays or even the name of the city in which they lived; even the kid who was forced to stay up all night by his father – to keep him company, the little boy explained one day when I was helping out in the classroom, as I did every Thursday, and I'd had to wake him, as I often did). Tenara had a less gifted teacher, but was in the less tumultuous classroom – a tradeoff, Joanie and I had agreed miserably a week or two into first grade.

Although Grace and Tenara were in different classes, they saw each other at recess twice a day, and when we left the school in February, while I mourned the loss of Mr. Trent and "arts through the curriculum," for Grace the worst of it was starting all over at a school in which she didn't know anyone, and leaving Tenara, who stayed behind to finish out the school year before transferring.

That the private school Grace now attends is small enough to have allowed her and Kristin to find each other even though they are in different grades – so small there is just one class of twelve to twenty children at each grade level – is the best thing about it. In the end it's probably the most important reason we keep Grace there in spite of everything.

If I said this out loud to Glen, he'd scoff. We keep her at the school because there's nowhere else to send her, not unless we move to the suburbs, which neither of us can bear the thought of doing. And after all, her second grade teacher was excellent, and in the upper grades, we have been told, there are other good teachers in whose classrooms she will land. There's a terrific band teacher now, and a new art teacher on the way; I like the looks, too, of the fifth grade.

I'm taking this friendship-thing way too seriously, Glen would say. Growing up, he changed schools every two years as his family moved from one small town to another in East Texas. Because he was a boy, he didn't have "best friends" the way Grace has – but he had friends, and he was taken from them almost as soon as he felt completely comfortable with them. His life story features a trail of lost people, names that go with anecdotes (about frogs, rabbits, snakes, and swamps) and nothing else, names he isn't quite sure he's got right, faces he can't quite remember. And while I moved only three times – each time just a subway stop or two farther from Brighton Beach, where I was born – I hated it. The first time, I left my grandparents behind, which was bad enough (my mother pregnant, my grandmother abandoned: the two events tied together in my mind); the second time, I left behind everything I knew. Everyone in my grade school went to one junior high, and I to another. And in the move and in the change of schools I left behind A——, to whom I had been so devoted for so many years. It didn't matter that things between us were already changing by then: A—— would soon be starting junior high; she already had her period; she had *breasts* – and I was still a little girl, still chubby, a bookworm, somberly declaring that I was an "author," dressing in A——'s hand-me-downs and wearing pale pink gold-speckled eye-glasses with thick, smudged lenses. I would catch up to her somehow,

I kept telling myself. Or the differences between us wouldn't matter. Our friendship went deeper than that: we were *sisters*.

The day the movers came I hid in the bedroom I had shared with my brother for seven years, and I wept. I didn't care that in the new apartment I would have my own room, that I would be allowed to decorate it any way I liked, that the new building had a swimming pool. I would be all alone again. I couldn't bear it. I would die, I thought. I would die of loneliness.

. . .

I didn't die. I was saved by B——.

We met on the first day of seventh grade, locating each other in the schoolyard by what seems in retrospect like radar. By the end of the day, we were a team. A tense, lonely, desperate team.

My desperation was always just below the surface, not quite hidden, and starting out at a new school where I didn't know a soul made it impossible to keep it submerged – to have any control at all over it (control that would have allowed me to pretend to be okay, as I had so often done in grade school). For her part, B—— was paralyzed by shyness, the result of which was that she had managed to get all the way through grade school without making a single friend. But she appealed to me as soon as I laid eyes on her. She had an air of separateness – cool, remote, superior – that drew me to her and had me trying to amuse her, impress her, anything to get her attention.

It was a drill, I suppose, that I knew well. Not that this crossed my mind, then. I went knocking on a closed door and got her to let me in. She wasn't going to; she surprised herself. But no one had ever knocked so loudly or with such determination. I barreled my way in, as I have barreled my way into people's hearts all my life.

B—— and I became best friends with a level of intensity that suggested we were in a foxhole together. And I suppose that junior high (or "middle school," as it's called now, as if renaming the limbo between grade school and high school has done a thing to address its multitude of failures, miseries, and outright horrors) *is* a sort of war zone. Certainly B—— and I felt there were enemies everywhere. The only good guys I can remember from that period were certain teachers: Mr. Inemer, the English teacher we worshiped, who had us read Sons and Lovers and taught a creative writing class; Mr. Cetron, who taught social studies, and on whom we all – not just B—— and I, but all the girls – had romantic crushes; Mr. Weissman, the science teacher, about whom I can remember nothing except that he told sarcastic jokes that held us in a sort of terrified, awed thrall.

There were two or three children with whom B—— and I had tentative, awkward relationships – other misfits, for one reason or another. One was brilliant and riddled with self-doubt; it's possible she was even more desperate than I, and her neediness kept me at arm's length. Another was a sleepy, striking, sultry girl who seemed to me mysterious and fascinating: she wasn't Jewish, which was exotic enough, and she lived with her mother, grandmother, and older brother above a store on Coney Island Avenue and Avenue U. Her hair fell into a perfect flip; secretly, I tried to copy her likewise perfect handwriting. The other girls in our class ignored her, but the boys all had crushes on her that were made evident to us by the way they stared, slack-jawed. They never talked to her. They didn't talk to B—— and me, either, but that was because *we* were invisible.

Invisible, and inseparable.

After school and on weekends, B—— and I stuck together. *Huddled* might be the better word. Sometimes one or the other of the two girls we considered our subsidiary friends – but never both at once, for they didn't know what to make of each other – joined us; mostly we were alone together.

We spent nearly all our time at B——'s house – another anti-Herman household. B——'s mother had a job, just as A——'s had (in fact, I am almost certain that they were both bookkeepers. Is it possible that all the mothers in Brooklyn who had jobs in the 1960s were bookkeepers?). B——'s mother bustled around taking care of things, went out to work all dressed up and came huffing home carrying two overfull bags of groceries she began at once to empty and out of which she made what I considered to be elaborate dinners for which I was usually invited to stay.

They ate wonderful food – Ronzoni spaghetti with delicious sauce from a jar, instead of Goodman's noodles with ketchup, as we did, and steamed bright green vegetables (my grandmother cooked fresh green beans and carrots and spinach, but she boiled them until they were baby-food soft, their true colors faded; at home we ate canned). Even their convenience foods were of a different and apparently superior kind (their brand of canned ravioli was of a better class than ours, I could tell just by looking at the label's muted, serious-looking color scheme).

There were cookbooks in their house. They had a house – an actual freestanding "private" house, the first I'd ever set foot in. They had an attic, a pantry, a square of backyard, a dog, a hamster, a staircase.

B—— and I, as close as we were, argued frequently. For a shy girl, she had a lot of opinions she wasn't afraid to voice, and for a chubby, nearsighted, sad, and otherwise friendless girl, I held my own pretty well. Still, our arguments broke my heart and worried me. B——, on the other hand, never seemed worried. She seemed certain she couldn't lose me no matter what she said, or how harshly she said it. She was right, but I was never able to figure out how she knew that.

4

My concern about how Grace would fare when she discovered that she couldn't always be in charge, and that she would have to learn to live with other children's wants, turned out to be unfounded. Perhaps because Tenara was as used to calling all the shots as Grace was, or because they were both kids who happily generated lots of language, they seemed to enjoy all the negotiation involved in their decisions about what to play and how to play it. They debated, made lists, drew up plans of who would be in charge when: they had a system.

But really it didn't matter – they didn't need the system, or the lists; they debated for the fun of it – because, as Grace reminded me not long ago when I asked if she remembered this period of adjustment, the two of them "pretty much always wanted to do the same thing anyway."

She said this ruefully, for in the years since then, they have both changed – inevitably, as Grace admits she knows – and when they get together now they have to work sometimes to find something they both want to do.

Still, Tenara was on her list of the three people she would want to know for the rest of her life, right up there with Kristin and her godfather, Michael. And when Tenara came to spend the night one weekend recently, after the girls hadn't seen each other in months, once they got past the first hour it was "almost just like old times," Grace told me the next morning. During dinner, Tenara told a long, convoluted story about an argument she'd had with one of her new friends, and at the end she said, "And this is one of the nicest girls I know at my school!" Then after a moment she added, "And I am *not* being facetious." I laughed out loud with pleasure to hear her using the word, and both girls looked at me as if I were crazy. But Grace knew what had pleased me. "It's just *vocabulary*, Mama," she said. "It's not that big a deal."

They slept in one bed, curled up tight. Surrounded by stuffed animals. They looked like two puppies. Two brainy, talkative puppies. Their legs were tangled together. Grace had one arm flung across Tenara's face.

· · ·

It was in B——'s house that I was introduced to the pleasures of a sit-down family meal. At five-thirty every day, all of them stopped what they were doing and ate together at the same table. This dumbfounded me, and even if I hadn't loved the food, I would have been thrilled and grateful to be part of the ritual. And then one Saturday afternoon B——'s parents took me with them to Greenwich Village, another ritual of theirs, and a trip I remember in its every particular even now, over three decades later.

My first croissant, a visit to Pottery Barn (which in those days was a single big store, and really looked like a barn), a tiny crowded jewelry shop up a narrow flight of stairs, in which B—— and I were each allowed to pick out one gift for each other. We both chose earrings (mine were my first pair that dangled; I have them still). B——'s family, I felt that day, had introduced me to the world I was meant to live in. All I'd seen of Manhattan before this was Rockefeller Center and the Automat – where my grandparents would sometimes take me on a Sunday for the movie, the stage show, and then lunch – and once or twice the offices of the insurance company where my father worked without enthusiasm on weekdays, reserving his passion for the police-and-fire beat he covered for the *Daily Mirror* on weeknights and weekends.

I decided that when I grew up I would live in Greenwich Village, and I did: I moved into an apartment on Christopher Street within days of my graduation from Brooklyn College (and for this I held B——'s parents responsible – as did my parents, but not as gladly).

By the end of the summer after seventh grade, B—— and I were no longer as close as we had been. She spent the first half of summer at a Y camp, where she learned a lot of new protest songs and how to sniff glue in a paper bag, and by the time she got home she felt, she said, as if she hardly knew me anymore. I was going steady by then – with Howie, my first boyfriend – and B—— was disdainful, not least because I'd met Howie at a bungalow colony in the Catskills, where I'd been the guest of a new friend. B—— said that my new friend and her bungalow colony were bourgeois. "Besides," she added bitterly, "you didn't even pick her for a friend. She just happens to live in your building" – which, for good measure, she pronounced bourgeois as well.

And then my family moved again. Not far – six blocks north and seven blocks east – but far enough so that even though B—— and I were still together for ninth grade, once we started high school we were separated. I'd broken up with Howie by then and had started dating Steven; the girl who'd lived in my building vanished into it (and, thanks to the peculiarities of New York City's zoning system, she went to yet a third high school); and before long I had a new best friend.

C—— sat next to me in tenth grade homeroom. Our first conversation, I remember, was about the boy *she* was in love with. His name was Billy. I remember that I gave her some earnest advice about him – by then I considered myself an expert – even before I knew *her* name.

And then all through high school we kept each other alive. That's what I believe, though Glen undoubtedly would say I'm taking this too seriously. But C—— and I talked every day for hours. Her parents were always driving her out of their apartment – they found fault with everything she did – and she slept at our place several nights a week. She was sixteen when she left home for good, and after that it was to our apartment that she went "home" for holidays. I provided her with a place to go, which was what she needed most. In return, she kept me company, which was what I still needed most. Company, and the feeling that I was completely understood. From A—— to Z——, that was what I asked for, and what I received.

. . .

Z—— was my last best friend. We met when I was thirty-four; she was thirty-one. I was single – aggressively single, I suppose, in retrospect. I'd been living alone for fourteen years and had had one boyfriend after another for longer than that, a good twenty years. She – like me, a writer and a teacher – was married to the man who'd been her second boyfriend.

It's possible that we romanticized each other's lives.

Although it didn't seem to either of us at the time that this *was* possible.

We knew too much about each other's lives, we were sure, not to see them clearly. We knew too many of the intimate details of each other's dissatisfactions. And yet it seemed to me that being married – happily or not – meant you'd have someone to count on, night and day, and how bad could that be? Plus she had the option, if she chose to exercise it, of having a child, which I longed to do by then.

What she made of my life, which she entered right in the middle of a bad breakup (I was being dumped that fall by Clifford, with whom I was wildly, if most unwisely, in love, and who up to the day before he broke up with me had been claiming I was the one true love for whom he'd been searching all his life), I still can't imagine.

Ten months after that breakup, ten months after Z—— and I first met, I returned from a month at Yaddo, the artists' colony, to a second, even more devastating breakup, and it was in the wake of this new misery that Z—— and I moved from friendship to best friendship.

I had planned a trip to Mexico with the man Z—— referred to as the Very Bad Boyfriend: we were to celebrate his having completed and defended his dissertation that June, and his move, as soon as I returned from Yaddo, to Columbus – where I'd finagled him a short-term teaching job in his field, since he'd had no luck on the academic job market on his own. I'd traded all my frequent flyer miles – all those trips back to New York! – for the two plane tickets; I'd put down a nonrefundable deposit on the hotel reservation.

After the Very Bad Boyfriend announced that he had fallen in love with someone else, that he'd been seeing her for months and "probably shouldn't" go to Cancun as planned, Z—— went with me instead.

Far from home, while I recovered not just from this latest blow but from the one before (which, I suddenly realized, I hadn't given myself a chance to do: I'd flung myself into a romance with the Very Bad Boyfriend just days after Clifford had cut me loose) – and come to think of it, I hadn't given myself any time to think things through after José and I had split up, either (my God, I told Z——, I was in three-in-a-row relationship recovery!) – the week Z—— and I spent together on the beach compressed several years' worth of the work of our getting to know each other. We sat up talking half the night each night on our hotel room balcony, drinking rum and Diet Coke. In the morning, I went down to the beach and dragged a chair into the water so that waves came splashing up around my waist. I would read nineteenth-century novels for six, seven, eight hours a day. Z——, blond and fair-skinned, sat on the balcony, in the shade, reading too or writing in her journal, in a big straw hat and an ankle-length, long-sleeved white dress, taking no chances. If I turned back and looked up at her, she would wave. At sundown she would join me on the beach and we would walk a little while along the shore as the Mexican boys called out to her, "*Blanca!*" and tried to sell us silver jewelry, and then we would go out to dinner or up to our room, where we would make quesadillas on the electric stove that was always shorting out and shocking us (a bad connection, we guessed, but neither of us had the Spanish to explain this to the desk clerk, so it kept shocking us all week).

We came home not only closer than we'd been, but as close as it was possible, we thought, for friends to be – certainly closer than we were to anyone else, and closer, it seemed to me, than I had ever *been* to anyone else. It still seems that way to me, when I think back on it: Z—— was my last best friend, and my *best* best friend.

Our friendship, in the form it first took in Cancun nearly a year after we met, lasted for four years – through on-again, off-again ventures of mine with both recent ex-boyfriends; through a frantic period of actual dating, for the first and last time in my life (blind dates and why-not-give-it-a-try dates with just about anyone who asked, double dates with colleagues setting me up with their single friends, dozens of dinners and movies and concerts – the dreariest Saturday nights of my life); through my husband's and my courtship and our "wedding" (we eloped; only Z—— and her then-husband knew that we were getting married, and they were our witnesses and dinner partners afterwards); through the birth of my daughter and most of the first year of her life; and through Z——'s breakup with her husband and the start of the relationship for which she'd left him – but just barely through that. By the time I was thirty-nine we weren't best friends anymore. For a while we weren't friends at all.

Four years is a good run, I know. Between A—— and Z——, I've had only two other best friends for that long. And in Iowa and Nebraska, where I lived for two years apiece after I left New York and before I landed in Ohio, I managed to go through *four* best friends, one after another (during a period in which I had just one boyfriend – as if I couldn't have a best friend and a boyfriend I could count on at exactly the same time). Most of my best friendships, like most of my romantic relationships, have lasted for no more than two or three years. Some have lasted only a few months.

I am still on friendly terms with most of my ex–best friends, just as I am with most of my ex-boyfriends – even the Very Bad Boyfriend. I've lost touch with A——, which grieves me. But the last time I saw her, sixteen years ago, I discovered that we couldn't manage even a brief conversation as adults. We had seen each other, or talked over the phone, from time to time over the years – during high school and in college – but when I tracked her down again, just as I was finishing graduate school, it had been ten years since we'd last talked, and our reunion was a failure. Her life seemed frivolous to me: she was a full-time wife, carefully groomed and tanned, with a baby she left in the care of a full-time nanny. I was grimly serious, determined to prove that I'd turned out well. The gulf between us was uncrossable.

Still, I am pretty sure that once enough time has passed – another five years, or maybe ten – I'll get in touch with her again. I'm less earnest than I was as a freshly minted M.F.A., with much less to prove; I like to think I wouldn't be so eager for her approval, or so disappointed in her for not being in a position to offer it. Besides, it's unimaginable that years of motherhood – not to mention menopause

– won't have changed her, too. I haven't written her off. (But then I haven't written anyone off – less because I don't want to than because I can't.)

The woman who was my best friend in my twenties, in New York (I'll call her U——, several best friends before Z——), is someone I will go years without talking to, but then there will be a little flurry of activity between us, and we'll talk for a long time on the phone, two or three times in the same month, or exchange long, chatty e-mails. Even though our lives are very different now (she is a lawyer, in private practice; she lives alone in a studio apartment in Hell's Kitchen), what ties us together is our history – the fact that in the late 1970s we lived next door to each other in the Village; that later, though we lived in different neighborhoods, we saw each other almost every day and wrote songs together and performed them at parties; that for years we ate dinner together several times a week, and talked over every aspect of our lives, exhaustively; that once, when a man with whom I was hopelessly in love treated me badly in a careless way, she went to see him and told him how thoughtlessly cruel he had been, and demanded that he call me and apologize – which he did.

While a series of men paraded through my life during those years, it was U—— I counted on, U—— whose availability, fidelity, and devotion to me really mattered. Now it is as if we are family to each other. We have each other for life, whether we see each other or not, even if years pass between phone calls, even if I go "home" to New York for a weekend and don't get in touch with her.

I felt this way about my junior high school best friend, too. B—— and I had wandered off in separate directions in high school, where we found other best friends for whom we were better suited – but we remained connected, more like cousins than friends, tied to each other by links, however tenuous in the present, forged in the past. All through college, where we came back together for four years (and where she and C——, my high school best friend, regarded each other warily), and afterwards, when she went to medical school and I moved to the Village to write, we were close in this way, family to each other, if not quite friends in the present, until her death, not many years ago. We hadn't seen each other since her med school graduation, when her mother gave a party for her, but we had talked on the phone and written letters to each other, and when she got sick – it was ovarian cancer – we began talking often, at least weekly, for the first time since we were children.

I lost another close friend to ovarian cancer several years later – a friend from high school who hadn't been a "best" or even second-best friend then, just a girl I was friendly with, the girlfriend of one of my boyfriend's friends. We liked each other, and sometimes we spent time alone together, but it was a relationship based on our boyfriends' connection, and when we graduated and went to different colleges, we lost touch for years. We reconnected much later, after she wrote to me care of the publisher of my first book, and later still, when I had the chance to spend a sabbatical – the first of my career – in New York, it was she who found my family a place to live, in the building next door to hers, and her husband who made the arrangements that would allow us to barter for the rent, which was the only way we could possibly have afforded it.

Her son and my daughter were born two days apart, and that year, the year of my sabbatical, that Grace and Silas were both two, the four of us, mothers and children, spent a lot of time together. She had been on an extended leave from her job at Brooklyn Family Court – an unpaid leave she kept extending – and she spent most of that year trying to decide whether to quit altogether to be with Silas full time. Finally she did quit, and only a few months later the cancer was diagnosed.

That year we lived next door to each other, we became as close as sisters. That was how I saw it, though when I said it to her, she laughed. Unlike me, she *had* sisters, and her relationships with them were troubled, painful.

When she was dying, however, her relationships with both her sisters were better. Everything else stopped mattering, then, the way it's supposed to and hardly ever does.

It's been three years that she's been gone – three years and six days, as I write this – and I miss her all the time, still. It's she, more than any other friend I've ever had, whom I wish I could call to talk to about Grace and Kristin, the talking snakes, the way the girls pretend to be the Beatles and listen to the records she and I played for our children when they were two years old – the records she and I listened to together when we were fifteen, though our boyfriends weren't interested (for them, it was nothing but the Who, the Dead, Led Zeppelin). We liked the Dead and the Who too, but when we were alone together, it was the Beatles we listened to. And Joni Mitchell. The Incredible String Band. Dylan. Music the boys had no patience for.

I remember sitting with her in her parents' house one afternoon and listening to George Harrison's *All Things Must Pass* for the first time, how she had pulled me by the hand and said, "You've got to hear this, this album is incredible, it's perfect." George was "her" Beatle the way Paul was mine.

I realize I can't even assign her a letter of the alphabet, since I met her when I was fifteen, right after C——, but we only became close twenty-five years later – after Z—— entered my life, in fact. She doesn't fit in neatly anywhere. So I'll call her by her name, which was Vicki.

5

Grace and Kristin are listening to *Rubber Soul*. They're in the playroom, with the stereo in the living room cranked up – they're listening to the album on vinyl; the only CD player in the house is in Grace's room – and I'm making dinner in the kitchen, which has a doorway into the playroom. As I pass by with a pot full of water, I see that my daughter has held up her right hand to stop everything – no talking now! – because the rare song by George Harrison has come on. They listen in respectful silence to "Think for Yourself," and when it's over, I hear Grace tell Kristin that she's asked me not to play *All Things Must Pass* anymore, although in the days and weeks immediately following Harrison's death we listened to it all the time. Kristin wants to know why. "The song 'My Sweet Lord' makes me too sad," Grace tells her. "Because he sings about how it's going to take so long, and he's talking about getting to see God. But it turns out it *didn't* take so long. . . ."

And Kristin says – and this is why, or part of why, she is my daughter's best friend – "That *is* sad." For a minute the two little girls bow their heads to contemplate the sadness of life itself.

But then they're up and dancing, halfway through "The Word."

Later, the album over, the stereo silenced, Grace tells Kristin what she has already told me – the way she's decided to think about George's death, something that makes her feel better about it. "Think how lonely John was in heaven all by himself. Now the two of them are together. It always helps to have someone with you. Even if it's not your *very* best friend."

She's right – that's what I'm thinking, listening in. Any good friend is a help, a hedge against the loneliness. And for the first time a fleeting thought comes to me: that Vicki is there too, with George.

This is what happens when you are a mother. You start to think, sometimes, like a child. It's not always a bad thing. For a moment, anyway, the thought of Vicki with her Beatle, up in heaven, was a comfort to me.

• • •

By the time I re-met Vicki, Z—— and I were no longer best friends. We'd "split up" by Grace's first birthday, which came right around the time Z—— ended her marriage and began living with someone else. That we have settled into another sort of friendship now – with the occasional flare-up, reminders of the bitterness we both felt when the bond between us first loosened, the righteous gloom of abandonment on both sides – has been a relief to both of us. As I've said, it's not unusual for me to end up "still friends" with my ex-bests. One or two, I admit, have disappeared angrily from my life, the way Z—— almost did, but most have just downshifted, as Z—— and I finally were able to do after months of anger, arguments, periodic furious silences, tears.

These days Z—— and I talk fairly often, though there are weeks when we fall out of contact altogether. Because we don't rely on each other anymore for day-to-day conversation, there are weeks when we're both busy and come close to forgetting about each other. Or, worse, one of us is busy and forgets the other, who feels neglected. Even now, we can hurt each other badly. The year I was in New York, spending so much time with Vicki and her son – Z—— and I were still estranged then, but we had reached the point of trying to pretend we weren't – I remember how angry and hurt I was when she came to New York for a few days and stayed with someone else, a friend of hers from grad school, a woman with a child around Grace's age, with whom I myself had become friendly that year. I could barely bring myself to speak to Z—— when she came out to the playground with her old friend and the friend's daughter, for a prearranged date with Grace and me – and Vicki and Silas. And when she talked to me, she didn't meet my eyes.

It's been over eight years now since Z—— and I last talked for hours on end, on the phone or in person. We get together, for dinner or lunch or shopping, once or twice a year. Still, if something goes wrong – or if something goes especially right – we are among the first people the other will call.

It's a peculiar category, the ex–best friend. Not as well-defined as ex-husband, ex-boyfriend. Ex-sister, ex-cousin – these don't even exist as categories. Once a sister, always a sister, whether you're getting along or not. I suppose that's why I think of these ex–best friends as family: people who belong to me, one way or another, no matter what.

But even though Z—— and I belong to each other, we aren't central to each other's lives anymore. That's what caused the friendship to change. It's always what causes it, I think: that shift from centrality. It's what turns a best friendship into . . . something else. Not "just friends" – a term that has never made much sense to me, anyway, since it implies that the relationships that really matter involve sex, which I have not found to be true at all. What I *have* found is that the process of unbecoming best friends and becoming some other kind of friends is more difficult for me to manage than a romantic breakup. It's not only that there is no word for it. It's also that unlike the end of a romance, which requires a decision to change the nature of the relationship, and which so often leaves at least one of the participants feeling lost, cut off, struggling to move the other person out of the central place in her life, when best friends stop being best friends, there's hardly ever a *decision*. It's hard to know how to think about it, what to do, how to behave. With Z——, as with A—— through Y——, we both found our attention pulled elsewhere. Our relationship simply followed the center of gravity – the two separate centers of gravity. We each turned away, and the tie between us loosened.

But it could never be undone altogether. Even if we wanted it to, which we both don't.

. . .

Grace comes home from Kristin's in tears. Her father, who was on pickup duty, is bewildered – she cried all the way home without explanation – and when the two of them get into the house, he is saying, "But it was time to go home, what did you expect me to do?" and she is saying, between sobs, "But that's not the *point*." It takes me a good fifteen minutes to get the story out of her. Her play date with Kristin, it turns out, had forcibly ended before the snakes, who had been arguing "for a *very* long time," had had a chance to make up.

She doesn't blame her father, she says. It's true that he stood firm, as did Kristin's parents, telling the girls it was time to stop playing and tidy up because Grace had to get home for dinner. But at that point Grace suggested to Kristin that the snakes make up quickly before she left, and Kristin refused. "My snakes are still angry," she said. "They don't feel like making up." Grace can hardly get this sentence out, she's crying so hard.

"Why don't you call her?" I say. "Dinner can wait a few minutes."

Glen gives me a look that says I'm being overly indulgent, that I'm encouraging something I shouldn't be. When *we* argue, this is generally what it's about. But I'm not going to argue; I'm not even going to give him my look that says *trust me on this, it's more important than you think* – because I know from experience that at that point he would become impatient enough to say something.

"Are you sure?" Grace asks, and I see her glance anxiously toward her father.

"I'm sure," I say.

I watch her steel herself as she goes to the phone, but I try not to listen in to the conversation, for I know myself to be perfectly capable (though I would never allow myself to give in to this capability – I don't think) of grabbing the phone from her and telling Kristin that if her snakes don't make up with Grace's, I will smack her silly.

The snakes don't argue often, but when they do, it can get ugly, especially if it goes on for more than a few minutes: Taffy and Taffy shouting at each other, River and Breeze calling each other the most horrendous names, accusations and counter-accusations flying. I have taught my daughter – my poor daughter, writer's child – that there is no such thing as a "bad" word, that words are neutral in and of themselves, like rocks (even the biggest and sharpest of rocks, as long as they're on the ground), and can be used to hurt someone only when used *against* that person. Aimed, and hurled. And that sometimes a rock picked up idly and tossed without purpose – hand to hand, or into the sky, or even just dropped back on the ground – can hurt someone too, so one needs to use care always, to think about what you hold in your hand before releasing it. I have taught her to pay attention to both the beauty and ugliness, whether obvious or subtle or potential, inherent in language, as in stone. Thus, when a word is used in anger by my daughter, it is chosen – aimed and hurled – after serious consideration.

By her snakes, too. And by Kristin's, because even though she hasn't been raised by a writer, she – like Grace's other best friend, Tenara – takes more care with language than most children do. This may have something to do with why Grace has picked them. Or why they've picked her.

Grace has had to explain the rock analogy to Kristin, and I'm not sure she's convinced by it, even though her snakes have been granted her large and complex vocabulary, and when they turn to insults and name-calling every word is chosen, not merely resorted to. It doesn't surprise me that Kristin has declared that she wants to be a writer when she grows up.

The bitter arguments between the snakes – in which it's every snake for himself, and never mind best-friendship – is the closest Grace and Kristin ever come to arguing. They let the snakes take care of that part of their relationship, which seems to me very smart of them. If Z——and I had had spokessnakes to do our fighting for us, it's possible we would have handled those first months of unhappiness between us with less acrimony.

Grace and Kristin's snakes talk for ten or fifteen minutes while I set the table and keep the pasta warm, and when Grace hangs up she is smiling tremulously and is ready to sit down to her spaghetti and "smooth tomato sauce" – the plainest possible sauce, with no lumps – and steamed artichoke and a vinaigrette dipping sauce. This happens to be her favorite meal, and I am pleased with myself for having it ready for her on a night that it is called for.

It isn't even that she needs cheering up. She's fine now. I'm the one who's still upset. *She* doesn't know how precarious these relationships can be. Certainly she has no idea that they can end, that there may come a time when she and Kristin won't even know each other. That even if the friendship doesn't end, it's likely to change over time. She doesn't know any of this and I don't want her to know, despite how frank I've been about everything else. We've never "done" Santa and she knows I'm the Tooth Fairy; she's understood how babies are made since she first asked me – when she was four – and just the other day we had a talk about artificial insemination, because it had dawned on her that it wasn't fair that a woman who lived with another woman couldn't become pregnant (and when I explained how artificial insemination worked, she thought it was brilliant; she slapped the kitchen table and said, "Man! Why doesn't *everybody* do it that way, then?"). I've never flinched from answering any of her questions about death, or God, or masturbation. And if she *asked* me if Kristin would be her best friend forever, I'd tell her the truth – what I think, what I can guess. But she's not going to ask me because she doesn't know there's a question to ask. She hasn't tried to picture what it would be like not to have Kristin in her life. She can't envision what it would be like not to have a best friend at all. I'm the one who can envision that – who doesn't have to. Who knows.

· · ·

Naturally it has occurred to me that at forty-seven I should have long outgrown the need for a best friend. I have a husband, a child, plenty of *good* friends, ex–best friends, a great many colleagues, students, former students. Meaningful work. A job I enjoy. A house and a garden I neglect. Who has time for a best friend?

I don't have time. But still I yearn for it. *Still*, when I am about to meet a woman of roughly my age and inclinations (all it takes is to be told: she's a writer – or an artist or a composer or an actress – and better yet, that she is this and a mother too; and better still, the mother of a girl about Grace's age), I am lost in hope, filled with preparatory joy. And then I meet the woman and she's not right for me at all – there's nothing there for us – and I fall into gloom. I am ashamed of myself, I scold myself, I feel like a fool. *You're too old for this, this is absurd, what are you doing?*

But here's what I'm doing: I'm looking for her. Still. The friend. The one who'll last forever.

. . .

I have embarked on each of my best friendships confident that I had found her (or, once in a blue moon – or, more precisely, once a decade – as I got older, *him*): the perfect friend, the one and only. With boyfriends I was never able to imagine perfection or forever, not even when (and possibly especially when) I was most desperately in love. I could always see the ending blinking in the distance (the far distance, yes; farther by far, every time, than the end would turn out to be, for I was optimistic always, even in my understanding of the finite). When things started to go awry with a boyfriend, I was quick to think: *All right, then. With the next one, I'll. . . .*

But I have been stunned, every time – every time, as if for the first time – by the loss of a best friend.

One expects the course of love to be rocky; one knows the possibility exists that someone – possibly both ones – will fall out of love, or that the match will turn out to be too flawed to last, an error of judgment, a case of mistaken identity.

And the fact is, I have settled for much less, in love – much, *much* less – than the perfection I seek in friendship. I have cut men, and before that, boys, a considerable amount of slack – so much slack it has sometimes been hard to see the line that connects us at all.

I've fallen for men despite numerous entries in the debit column – despite thoughtlessness or self-centeredness or all-out narcissism; or despite politics, bad taste (or none) in literature, drunkenness, even dishonesty. I've fallen for men because of their charm, charisma, wit, intelligence, or talent; because I liked the way they looked or moved or smiled or laughed; because of certain books they'd read and what they had to say about them, or the music they liked, or the jokes they told and how they told them. In a best friend, none of this – not even all of this – has ever been enough. In a best friend, it's had to be all of this *plus*. *Plus* meant someone who would understand me. More:

someone who would never misunderstand me, whether I was able to explain myself or not.

It's not that I wouldn't have liked to be understood by a romantic partner. It's that I never expected it. In a romance, understanding would have been a bonus – gravy. In friendship, it's the meat, the whole point of the undertaking.

That's not all.

In my best friendships, I've expected never to be let down, not even in the smallest way. In my romances, I was always sure I *would* be let down (and I always was, too). In friendship, I've required kindness, generosity, scrupulous honesty at all times. Insight. Sympathy. *Wisdom*. (And in romance? Who expects wisdom in romance?)

And here is something else: in my romances, my greatest pleasure, always, was at the beginning – the flinging myself into each new love affair, the flying-through-the-air of love before the landing – while in friendship, the beginning was the part I couldn't wait to get past. With each new best friend, I rushed as quickly as I could through getting-to-know-you and into the counting-on, all-history-unburdened, I-know-what-you're-feeling, I-know-everything-about-you, call-me-anytime-you-need-me-day-or-night part of the relationship. The stable, comfortable, day-to-day, mundane, how-did-you-sleep-last-night, shorthand-conversation part. The part with the frank and tender familiarity.

I always felt that a little familiarity went a long way with a boyfriend.

But with a friend! I couldn't wait until she felt as familiar to me as I was to myself, until she knew *me* so intimately she could guess what I might do or say before I'd even had a chance to think it through myself, let alone actually do or say anything. It was the part I never expected to get to with a man: the part with the complete and perfect understanding.

Unless the man in question was a friend, and not a lover. Then my expectations along those lines went way up.

• • •

I once knew a woman who didn't have any friends. Actually, I didn't know her at all; I knew her husband. Her husband was *my* friend, and when he first told me this about his wife, because I'd asked (what I'd asked was who his wife was close to, who she counted on for moral support, because the way he had described her – busy every minute with difficult, demanding work and kids and house, devoted to him in ways that sounded too good to be true – she sounded like a woman near the edge), I assumed he wasn't telling me the truth. Not lying to me so much as lying to himself. Or else bragging (*my wife doesn't need any friends! She has me*). Or maybe just not paying enough attention to *notice* who his wife's friends were, since he was busy all day long with difficult, demanding work himself, and at home, he'd told me (sheepishly? or was he bragging?), he would continue working long past the time his family had gone to bed.

Under scrutiny, his claim held up. The wife worked full time at the kind of job that has no down-time, at a breakneck all-day pace, and at day's end she did the cooking, supervised the homework and the music practice, got the kids to bed. It was she who kept track of the children's activities and doctors' appointments and clothing sizes, and the ups and downs of *their* friendships. In her "spare time," she ran on a treadmill while listening to novels on tape. "She has no time for friends," her husband said, and although I raised an eyebrow (neither he nor I had "time for friends," either – and yet here we were, talking on the phone for a few minutes between classes, between committee meetings, between knocks on our office doors), I didn't say a word. It was a matter of priorities, I told myself. Wasn't I forever telling myself I had no time to do the laundry, and making time somehow to go shopping for more clothes instead?

My friend's wife had one sister, with whom she had an uneasy, not at all close relationship, and there were women in her office with whom she chatted while they went about the day's work. She had a colleague or two in town with whom she was on friendly terms. Oh, and college roommates – they kept in touch sporadically. But no, he said, no *friends*. Not the kind you're talking about, anyway. Not even a leftover friend from her former, presumably less busy life? I wondered out loud, marveling. No. It was as if her life had begun only when she met her husband and started her career.

I asked my friend so many questions about his wife's friendlessness that he grew impatient with me. Why was this so interesting? Why did I care? He pointed out that he didn't happen to have any friends, either

– except for me. And that I didn't seem to find this so astounding. (In fact I didn't, although I didn't tell him that. I was afraid that it would hurt his feelings if I told him that I have been the only friend to a rather large number of men.) It struck me that what was unusual was his willingness to *admit* to having no friends. Most men, when asked about friendship, point to the boys they knew as children or in high school. Or in college, two or more decades ago. Some of them even see their college "friends." Vicki's husband used to play basketball with his Queens College buddies once a week, but he never talked to them about anything of consequence, he told her – for that, he said, he had her – and when she was sick, when she was dying, he had no one to talk to. He tried to talk to her about how he was feeling, but she couldn't handle it; she had to ask him to stop. For a while she worked on trying to persuade him to take *me* on as a friend, and I did what I could to help the cause – I'd always liked him, so it wasn't a stretch for me – but when I called or e-mailed him, his response was cautious, even stilted. Vicki gave up but made me promise to keep in touch with him after she died. He would need a friend then, even more than now, she said. And I tried to keep my promise, but once she was gone he stopped answering my e-mails and letters; he didn't return phone messages. I heard from him recently for the first time since right after Vicki died: he let me know that he'd remarried. So now he has a friend again – the only one he needs – and Silas, thank God, has a mother.

The man whose wife had no friends was a very good friend to me. He claimed to be an excellent friend to his wife, too. Perhaps so – why not? But whom does she *talk* to? I wanted to know. Patiently, he said, "She talks to me." But what about when it was he who troubled her, when it was their relationship she needed to talk about? "Especially then," the husband said.

I was impressed but not convinced. What about – well, the kinds of conversation that require another woman? "What kinds would that be?" he asked. "If she had serious problems, she would talk to her priest." That stopped me dead. When people start talking about talking to their priests – or ministers or even rabbis – I am out of my league.

• • •

My mother-in-law (who as it happens is deeply religious) asked me recently what I was writing about these days, and when I told her, she said, dreamily, "You know, I've had one best friend or another all my life." "You *have*?" I said. In the eleven years I've known her, I have never met even one of her friends. All along I've had the idea that there wasn't anybody she felt close to except for her sisters, her daughters, her one daughter-in-law. I was glad for her when she told me this. I was even glad, it occurred to me, that she has kept her friends her own private business. She has very little that is all her own.

My mother has always had friends – two or three close friends at any given time plus a scattering of other, auxiliary friends, and always one *best* friend. Just last night she told me that the other day she'd talked to her first best friend, Millicent, someone she has known for over sixty years. They hadn't talked in a long time – decades, perhaps; my mother wasn't sure. But when Millicent called her, she said, "It was incredible, really. It was like no time at all had passed." They talked for over an hour, catching up, trading news, promising at the end to stay in closer contact, not to let so much time pass again.

"You think you'll do it?"

"I'll try," she said.

Then she asked if I remembered Millicent from my childhood. Of course I did. I couldn't believe she'd even had to ask. In those days, she and Millicent were still very close, almost as close as they had been as children, and although my mother had other friends – young married women with young children, like her – she still referred to Millicent, who was single, as her best friend. The two of them had known each other practically all their lives.

This astonished me, I remember: that Millicent had known my mother when she was a little girl, like me. I remember how jealous I was of her, each time she visited. How much I wished that she would go away.

6

I tell Grace that I am writing about friendship, and she tells me it's about time.

"And why is that?" I ask, amused.

"Because *that's* an important subject," she tells me.

"More important than other things I've written about?"

She tosses her hair (did she learn this gesture from me, or did she inherit it? Or is it simply that those of us with long hair will inevitably toss it?). "It's what I think about all day long."

Does she? This takes me by surprise. What exactly does she think about it?

Well, she says, she thinks about Kristin. Maybe something Kristin had or hadn't said that day – or the way Kristin had spoken to her, or the fact that when she'd come bounding out of the car that morning into the school playground, Kristin had looked at her coolly, and Grace had felt foolish for being so happy to see her. Or Kristin had played with someone else at second recess. Or –

But she is getting agitated, and it is bedtime, so I interrupt her, "All right, we'll talk about this tomorrow." I stroke her hair, kiss her forehead, remind her of what she already knows – that she and Kristin are very different and thus express themselves in different ways – and tell her (for all the good it does) that this is no time to be pondering such weighty manners.

But when I leave her to her thoughts, and her efforts to fall asleep (always arduous for her, something I am sure she has inherited from me), I find that I am thinking about Kristin too now, about her famous reserve, so unlike Grace's naked emotion. That she will hardly ever say what she wants, or how she feels, drives me a little crazy too. And Kristin is affecting Grace, changing her – not completely, of course, but enough. I'll ask if the girls want to go to the pool, and Grace will glance at Kristin to see if it's all right to say "Sure!" the way I know she wants to, and Kristin shrugs and says, "I don't care."

So Grace will say, "It doesn't matter," and then I don't know what to do. Do I say, brightly, "Well, if it's all the same to you guys, then let's go to the pool, because I want to"? If I do, Grace will look worried – does Kristin want to go or doesn't she? – but because she wants to go swimming, she won't argue. She might, however, pretend to feel put upon: my mom is making us go to the pool. This way, she has nothing to lose: if Kristin really didn't want to go, she'd see Grace as an ally; if she did want to, she might even turn her attention now to soothing Grace ("Oh, come on, it won't be so bad. I promise, we'll have fun").

Sometimes I am so irritated by my daughter's refusal to be herself that I respond to her "It doesn't matter" by saying, "Fine," and going back to my study, leaving the girls to continue playing in the air conditioned house – even though I know this disappoints Grace, who not only wants to go to the pool but wants *me* to be able to interpret Kristin's enigmatic responses.

"When she says, 'I don't care,' " Grace has asked me, "is it possible she means she really doesn't care?"

How would I know, I wonder, when I've never "not cared" about anything in my life? I tell Grace I think it's possible that Kristin is trying to be polite – that she thinks it would be rude to say that she really wants something, to "put herself forward."

Grace has never heard of such a thing. "Maybe," she says doubtfully. "But what if it means she *doesn't* want something?"

I have to admit, that's what I always end up assuming it means. But how are we supposed to be sure?

When I go back to check on Grace, to see if she's anywhere close to asleep – because now it's past ten-thirty and she has to be up at seven – she's wide awake. She says:

"Remember the thing I told you about a couple of weeks ago? You know, how Kristin and I hugged for the first time? And I didn't know who started it, and then I got up my nerve to tell her I'd always thought she didn't want to and she said she thought I didn't?"

Sure I remember. It broke my heart.

"Well, I thought that would fix things, that we talked about it. But today when we were playing I kept just wanting to snuggle with her and I didn't know if it was okay. But maybe she wanted to do it too but she didn't know if it was okay with me."

"Can't you talk about it with her?" I ask, but I don't have much hope. She worries too, I know, about driving Kristin away by being too demanding.

"Maybe." She sounds dubious. "Kristin doesn't really like to talk about things."

I end up staying awake for a long time myself, long after Grace is finally asleep, thinking about this – about Kristin's reluctance to express herself, and Grace's usual effusiveness, which I fear is getting dampened. But perhaps it's better for her to dampen herself a little. As she's already learned, this isn't a world that favors complete expression of emotions at all times.

What worries me more, I think, is how this relationship seems to be inviting her to suppress her own personality. Several months ago, she announced that her favorite color was no longer purple, as it had been since she was two years old. It was blue now – blue, Kristin's favorite color. "Really?" I asked. I tried to sound casual. "How did it become blue?"

"It just is. It's the most beautiful color."

And then, a few days after that, she told me she'd changed her mind about getting her ears pierced. Not that her ears were getting pierced anytime soon anyway (her father has said not until she's twenty-one, but Grace and I have agreed privately to reverse the digits: she can do it when she's twelve. I'm sure I had mine done at eleven, though my mother says I was thirteen – so I've split the difference).

But Kristin, Grace reported, thinks pierced ears are vulgar and silly. I told her that the matter was entirely up to her – and I stressed the word her. I had no opinion on the subject of ear-piercing. For once, "I don't care" meant I don't care. Either way was fine with me, for I do think it's kind of silly to punch holes in one's body for the purpose of dangling shiny things from them, but there are lots of silly things we do for similarly silly reasons – after all, I like wearing high heels, too – and the decision about whether or not to pierce her ears, I told her, should be no one's but her own, once her parents feel she's old enough to make it.

But she was fevered on the subject, I suppose because for so long she had been begging to have her ears pierced (too many of the girls she knows already have pierced ears, and she covets their earrings; she likes shiny things that dangle at least as much as I do) and Kristin had thrown her a curve.

"You could just think about it over the next four years," I ventured to say.

"No," she told me. "I've already decided. Kristin would be so shocked if I did it."

I'm glad to say that I kept myself from saying something cluelessly grown-up like, "If she's really your friend, she'll understand." Or, "Best friends don't have to be exactly like each other." Because I know better, on both counts. And I wish I didn't. Friendship should be the most ideal of relationships – the most mutually respectful, loving, empathetic, *real*. But sometimes I wonder. Maybe it is only the most *idealized*.

. . .

In Kristin's family, at Kristin's house, Grace has found her anti-household. Perhaps she hasn't the need to escape that I had (but there is always the need to escape from something, isn't there? In our house it isn't silence, gloom, the pervasive and unnerving sense of being not only unnoticed but unnoticeable, unremarkable – the presence of a mother unmoved by the presence of a lively child – but perhaps its opposite: too little silence from a mother who is much too present and too often moved. Surely Grace must long sometimes to be unnoticed, unremarked upon!); the truth, I think, is just that everybody needs a place to go.

At Kristin's Grace is less a visitor than an extra member of the household. As I was at A——'s. And like A——'s, for me, Grace's second home is utterly unlike her first home, her real home. It is the anti-home, and yet (or thus?) it is a place in which she feels perfectly comfortable. She can imagine herself living there.

It occurs to me that this may be part of the function of these early close friendships between girls – to give them each a place in which to be not just *at home* somewhere else, but to imagine themselves in another life altogether, to try on another life: a place in which they can *be* someone other than who they are (or who they seem to be) at home.

It didn't work reciprocally for A—— and me, because we were almost never able to play in my family's apartment. B—— occasionally spent an evening with us, but it always felt like an event: she and I even bought special foods for it. I remember long strands of red licorice, canned shredded coconut, frozen melon balls – choices made, as we strolled the aisles of the tiny neighborhood grocery store where I was allowed to sign for purchases, entirely on the basis of these being items never before seen in either of our households, and of which both mothers were sure to disapprove (once, I recall, we bought a can of deviled ham, which we found disgusting but ate nonetheless). We would settle ourselves in front of the TV together – something we never did at her house – and watch *The Avengers*, our favorite show, eating our strange food.

For Kristin, I can see that my household serves the same function hers does for Grace. It liberates her; it emboldens her. Our house seems positively wild to her, I know: a certifiable Bohemia. There's the father who works all night and emerges at unpredictable intervals from his studio out back, reeking of paint, his hair in a long braid down his back, and wearing peculiar combinations of clothes he hasn't troubled to match, and which are usually full of holes. There's the mother working in her study with the door open (in theory, so that if the girls need anything, they can just call out; in practice, what it means is that the two of them drift in and out all day for no reason in particular). There's the study itself, jam-packed with everything that hasn't a place elsewhere in the house (my study that used to be sacrosanct! But then it used to be an incontrovertible fact that I couldn't write unless everything was just *so*: silence, uninterrupted hours, desk cleared of everything but the work at hand. In those used-to-be days, I would have found it impossible to believe that I would ever be able to write under the conditions I do now, daily, without even thinking of them as "conditions" or noticing what they are).

There's the *house* itself – Kristin's anti-home – which I have just about given up trying to keep in any kind of order, or even very clean. We live, essentially, in chaos: a trampoline wedged up against the living room couch, a table next to it stacked high with mail that no one's had time to open or even sort, and, beside the mail, a purple glass bowl brimming with forgotten sunglasses and single gloves, used-up disposable cameras, coupons that have expired, bags of candy Grace has brought home from school from someone's birthday party and forgotten. There's a pile of shoes by the front door, and another at the back door – Grace's and Glen's and Grace's friends Anna and Hannah, who are always leaving shoes or clothes behind when they leave us to cross the street to their much tidier homes. (My shoes aren't piled by the door only because I am too respectful of shoes to treat mine that way.)

There are two bikes and two scooters and a hula hoop in the living room, all leaning against a bookcase. The walls of the living room are lined with bookshelves crammed so tight they're sagging (and Glen keeps muttering that they're going to collapse, but they don't, and we don't do anything preventive; on the contrary, we just keep jamming in more books), and all along the top shelf of the bookcase alongside the staircase there are bike helmets and horseback riding helmets and school art projects and more sunglasses (Glen's, because he says if he puts his into the purple glass bowl he'll never see them again).

Every surface in the house is covered with something – papers, books, newspapers, magazines, jars full of markers (some are Grace's, some are Glen's), drawing pads and notebooks (ditto), tapes and records, sheet music, homework, student manuscripts – and on the floor in nearly every room there are baskets of unfolded laundry (who has time to fold? At least it's clean), and on the kitchen table there are pots and pans (clean, dry, just not put away) and more books and papers. In short, *stuff* (and how I swore as a child I wouldn't ever live this way! And I didn't, ever, till I had a family) – stuff everywhere, and the cockatiel flitting around from room to room, landing on somebody's head or shoulder or on top of the refrigerator and then taking off again, chattering. And outside, on the porch, the toy kitchen Grace hasn't played with in at least four years but can't bear to part with, the defunct Wangwriter (mine) and Leading Edge computer (Glen's) that we can't figure out what to do with, and *my* bike (because I draw the line at three bikes in the living room), and the remnants of whatever projects Grace and her friends have been working on outdoors in the last six months. And then there's the "garden" – once a garden, for which I took out my whole front lawn and spent years tending, the years before marriage and motherhood; now a huge patch of groundcover and weeds gone wild, which I make some kind of effort to hack away at several times a year but mostly try to brazen out by calling our "meadow."

Kristin's house and yard are lovely, pleasant, comfortable – not fussy, stiff, ridiculous in the way A——'s house was (not that I thought so then!). It's simply a nice place, tidy and livable and sane. Likewise the front and backyards, expanses of grass, discrete areas of flowers – places kids can play. Grace and Kristin gallop around the yard there as if they were horses (half the time they are pretending to be horses). It's a very *spare* place – not spare as in "extra" (though sometimes I do find myself wondering where they keep the other stuff, the real stuff – as if this *were* an extra house, one just for show) but as in "not liberal or profuse": not dozens of framed photographs, but two (at our house, the mantel is so overcrowded with framed photos that there are some you can't see – *so what good are they?* Glen sometimes asks, because he wishes for *spare*); not twenty, thirty *tchotchkes* (we have Russian nesting dolls I bought in Prague in 1987, a small glass/lead sculpture Glen's ex-girlfriend made and sent four Christmases ago, a scattering of creatures, wood and metal, I've bought at Ohio state fairs in the fourteen years I've been attending every August, a wood folk sculpture from Poland, alabaster eggs from the trip to Mexico I made with Z——, Grace's effort at *retablo*, vases of all sizes and materials, bowls too beautiful to hide in cabinets, my grandfather's *Kiddush* cup and prayer book, my grandmother's *shabbes* candlesticks and the pewter one Glen's mother's Southern Baptist Sunday school group sent us when we married, *and* the Finnish glass one that my all-time favorite English Department colleague Arnie Shapiro gave me for my thirty-fifth birthday – and this is by no means a complete list), but instead two, maybe three such objects. Our house, I realize as I describe it now in detail for the first time ever, is a combination of the junk-piled apartments I grew up in and A——'s place – my anti-home – with all its bric-a-brac and pink brocade.

In Kristin's living room is a single freestanding bookcase with a neat few rows of books and tapes. There are clean, empty surfaces everywhere, and places you can walk. Even Kristin's room, in which there are often toys scattered on the floor, has space to move in it. You are not in danger, as you are in our house, in our daughter's room, of tripping over something or stepping on something if you don't keep your wits about you at all times.

There are no stacks; there is no dust. It looks to me as if when something spills, it is immediately wiped up. Nothing is sticky; nothing is stained.

But then Carolyn has been at home since Kristin was born, and I imagine she must spend a good part of every day keeping the house clean and in order. It's not the very last thing on her priority list, as it has ended up on mine. Carolyn is a soft-spoken, polite, and cautious woman – as reserved as I am outgoing – and in her quiet way, the friendliest, most generous and empathetic of the mother-friends I have accumulated. Our friendship is circumscribed – we don't talk politics or music or love or work – but the connection we've made through our daughters is significant enough to be called a real friendship. We talk about the girls and about being their mothers, and day by day it seems that what binds us is much stronger than what might have kept us at a distance.

Carolyn's husband, Al (curiously enough, that was A——'s father's name too), goes out to work every morning, dressed neatly in clothes that match and fit, and comes home in the evening. That's all it takes, really, to be the anti-Glen. Any one of Grace's friends' fathers would fit the bill.

• • •

"Mama," Grace asks me out of the blue, "don't you wish you had a best friend?"

I am taken aback. It's as if she's been reading my mind, or reading this in progress. But really, why shouldn't she ask? In her world, every-body has a best friend. If you are unfortunate enough to be temporarily without one, you are consumed with longing and loneliness. This is only natural when you're eight – or ten, or twelve. She can't believe that there might come a time when this will change.

I can't either. That's the trouble.

But she has in mind to fix things for me. She squares her shoulders. She says, "What about Carolyn? She's smart and she's nice and you're always recommending books for her to read." It's true, Carolyn is a reader; when she opens the door to us, she is more likely than not to have a novel in her hand, her thumb wedged in it, holding her place. "And the way you talk to her, it's obvious you like her."

"I do," I say. "I like her a lot."

"So why couldn't she be your best friend?"

"It just doesn't work that way," I tell her. "But I appreciate your looking out for me, I really do."

She waves this off. "All right, so then what about Tenara's mother?" But she doesn't even wait for an answer. "Or what about ——? You're always having dinner with her."

"Always" means once a month. And the fact is, although she wants me to have a best friend – or at least she says she does – she hates it when I go out to dinner. She waits up for me, worries that something will happen to me. When I get home, she asks what we talked about. She wants to know how we could have sat talking over food and wine for *three hours* – that doesn't sound like fun at *all* – and I assure her, as I have assured her about so many things, that when she's old enough to do them, these things won't seem boring (or disgusting, as the case may be).

"Well, what about ——," she goes on, "you know, that poet you told me you met when you gave that reading? You talked for a long time and she showed you that she had little plastic people and some fat markers in her purse?"

I smile. I shrug. I say, "Sweetheart, it's just not that simple."

Why isn't it that simple?

We both want to know.

I do know, I think, but I hate the answer, which is that once you've reached a certain age, your life is too complicated and too set in the particulars of its complexity for the kind of fit necessary for best friendship. There are too many different places that need fitting into, and too many irregularly shaped pieces. Finding a match becomes trickier every year until you reach a point at which the chances of finding one are infinitesimally small.

And it may be that, for me, the last time such a fit was possible – all of my puzzle pieces locking into place with someone else's – was with Z—— when she and I were first getting to know each other. When all there was to complicate my life – to complicate *myself* – was what seems quite manageable to me now, in retrospect and by comparison (though none of it seemed manageable at the time): my writing and my teaching, all that falling in and out of love (and the accompanying chronic heartbreak and thrill, both), and my history up to that time – a history of men, boys, family, and childhood – which I handed to Z—— bit by bit, trading my bits for her bits, as if each one were a gift-wrapped package. And how carefully we examined each other's gifts! We asked questions about every single one, exclaimed and murmured over it with pleasure and true interest, looked it over from all angles.

Today, I would hardly know where to begin wrapping. The storage closet is so full and in such a mad jumble – there are so many different kinds of packages stuffed in there every which way – I wouldn't know how to sort them; I wouldn't know how to choose which ones to give, which ones to keep back. Because it's no longer possible to give them all to someone else. "All" is way too much now; it would take forever. And who would want it all? It would be overwhelming; it would crush another person.

Puzzle pieces, birthday gifts, avalanches – these are my friendship metaphors, all mixed up together. Is it any wonder I don't have a best friend?

The trouble is that if the friendship isn't interlocking puzzle pieces, then it's just not interesting enough to be best friendship, and if some of the vast store of stacked-up gifts remain ungiven, what's the point? Because really for me there isn't any point in having a best friend if you're settling for something less than everything. If you settle for anything less, then by definition you don't have it at all. So it's everything, or nothing.

But if the only outcome of *everything* that I can picture is an avalanche, then something's wrong.

And it *isn't* any wonder I can't find a best friend.

• • •

I have other friends, of course. (But why "of course"? This is the question my husband would ask, my husband who is by nature antisocial – indeed, as close to a recluse as it's possible for a man with wife and child to be – and who thinks of my friendships as the exotic, mystifying hobby of an eccentric, something along the lines of Nabokov's butterfly collecting; while, for me, life without a circle of friends – and not just a circle but concentric, ever-larger and more distant circles of friends – is unimaginable. Or if imaginable – because what isn't, if one puts one's mind to it? – then unbearable.)

I even have some nearly best friends – the way Vicki was nearly a best friend (or not *the* way, but in other ways, each in its own way): women of whom I am very fond but with whom the fit is something less than absolutely perfect – because our temperaments don't mesh (which is not to say that they must *match*: just that they have to *fit*), or because I have to explain myself sometimes and sometimes even then I am misunderstood, or because what is central to my life – my work – is a mystery to them, or because the work they do is so thoroughly alien to me I feel I will never truly understand them (I once had a friend who was a soil scientist, and as much as we liked each other, there seemed to be built-in limits to the sense we were able to make of each other), or because we disagree on some basic principle – something I consider a basic principle – or because they love Dickens "for his sensibility" (of all things!) or because they don't understand why being a mother takes up so much time and energy, or because they don't have an analytical bent (or they do, but their analysis only goes so far before they lose interest or patience, and that's long before I've lost interest, or patience – because when it comes to trying to figure things out, my interest and patience are inexhaustible), or because the small and I'm sure mostly harmless lies they tell themselves about their lives – lies that I admit have no bearing on my life; lies that are absolutely none of my business – are intolerable to me (and the other possibility – that they're being honest with themselves but lying to me – is almost as bad). I can't overlook harmless deceit, or self-deceit, or incomplete analysis, or a disapproval of public breastfeeding, or a vote for Bush, or cynicism, or a bit of nastiness toward a child, her own or someone else's, or bad taste in music, or a raised eyebrow over my extensive shoe collection – et cetera. Not in a best friend. I can't overlook anything in a best friend. I give the whole package of myself; I take the whole package of her.

Still, I have a great many other friends – all kind of friends. It never seems to me that I have enough friends. I have writer friends and mother friends, friends I have been close to briefly and then settled into friendly acquaintance with (like the mothers from Grace's creative movement class four years ago) and a few – the jackpot category – who are writers and mothers both, like the dear friend who lives temporarily in Rome, with whom Grace has accused me of "always" having dinner and with whom I exchange daily e-mails, and the new friend I made when I gave a reading at her campus and we showed each other the contents of our purses. I have friends who are my teaching colleagues, friends who've been my students, friends from the pool I used to go to every summer, penpals (friends I "talk" to only over e-mail, and whom I've hardly ever seen in person), friends from my old life – my old lives: from childhood, adolescence, Brooklyn College, the years I spent in the Village after college – "historical friends," I call these, and I am constantly collecting more of them since I won't lose touch with anyone if I can help it (and the Internet has helped immeasurably in these efforts), writer friends from grad school, writer/artist friends from Yaddo and MacDowell, ex-boyfriends who have become my friends, and many of my own ex–best friends (a classification that, for me, as I have noted, has much in common with that of ex-boyfriend, except that there's no name for it, and nothing as obvious as sex to mark the change in status).

With all these friends to call upon, what happened to me in December should not have happened. It should not have been possible that, while making dinner, I would suddenly, *in mitn derinnen*, as my grandmother used to say – right in the middle of everything – feel the need for (and not just feel the need for, but feel overpoweringly in need of) someone to talk to (and not just someone, but someone who understood everything about me, someone to whom I wouldn't have to explain anything, with whom I wouldn't have to *make* conversation, but with whom I could just slip back into our continuous conversation), and that there would have been no one to call.

I was standing at the kitchen counter, chopping green pepper. Kristin was visiting, and she and Grace were busy in another room. I was making dinner for them (spaghetti and the usual plain sauce, and steamed green beans that Kristin wouldn't eat and that Grace would eat three or four of and only under duress) and a separate dinner for Glen and me (same pasta, more complicated sauce, with the green beans mixed right in), and I was hurrying because in half an hour the girls and I, and Kristin's mother, who was due over at six, and the neighbor girls, Anna and Hannah, and *their* mothers, were going to go Christmas caroling on the block. I had already hand-chopped the tomatoes for the grownups' sauce and had just moved on to the green pepper, the garlic was simmering in one cast iron pan and the kids' lump-free sauce was bubbling in another, the pasta was boiling, and it hit me, just like that, out of the blue.

I went to the stove. I stirred the girls' sauce with a wooden spoon; I added the chopped pepper to the garlic and stirred that with the wooden spoon. And I began to go through my mental list. But then I didn't trust myself, and I left the spoon in the spoon rest (the Iowa Writers' Workshop TWF spoon rest made for me in a ceramics class in 1985 by the then-wife of my then–best friend) and dug out my address book from the tower of stuff beside the phone – the phone books, the menu for the only Chinese restaurant in Columbus that delivers, the school papers, the pink While You Were Out message pads that nobody ever remembers to use. All I wanted – "all"! – was to be able to dip into the well of the deepest kind of friendship for a few minutes. While I added chopped tomatoes to the garlic and green pepper. While I filled a pot with water for the green beans. While I stirred, drained, shook with butter, salted, peppered.

I went through every entry and reached the Zs without finding anyone to call. Then I started again – I started from the beginning again, slowly. I paused at the name of the friend who lives in Rome this year, but even if calling Rome made sense (and what time was it in Rome? Six hours earlier or six hours later? Why can I never remember this sort of thing?), we had never done very well on the phone (although, to be fair, we've rarely tried; since both of us have children, the chances of our being free and in the mood to talk at exactly the same time are so small we just don't bother trying) and besides, I didn't even have her phone number in Rome.

I paused at the name of the poet whose purse-contents I'd exclaimed over, and a writer/mother friend who lives right here in town and whom I like very much, with whom I have dinner once a year but otherwise never see (since she has a son, not a daughter, and he goes to another school and he is a year younger than Grace – three strikes against us) and with whom I have never talked on the phone except to confirm or postpone our annual dinner date, and then I paused at the name of a woman from the neighborhood whom I have always liked but haven't seen since our children were babies (back then she hosted a baby play group every Friday morning, which was really a chance for the mothers to get together and talk about things no one else was interested in hearing us talk about: nursing and solid foods and sleep habits – but that wasn't what I wanted now; I wanted something that went deeper than, beyond, our common motherhood), and I even paused at the names of two of my former students whom I think of as friends, but I am so far behind in keeping up my end of our correspondence that it exhausted me just to think about what it would take to get caught up. Besides, there is a certain deference, still, in my ex-students toward me. I didn't want to be looked up to, or respected, or – worse – flattered.

I paused at the entries for each of my ex–best friends, including the friend whose first wife made me the spoon rest (but he is so unpredictable, it's always impossible to tell if he'll be glad to hear from me or irritated, and I knew if he were chilly and dismissive I'd be devastated) and finally I reached the Zs again and that was it, there wasn't anyone, and I took a deep breath and then called Z—— herself – anxiously, a little guiltily, knowing better, without hope – and just as I'd feared, her answering machine picked up, as it always does. For years now she has screened her calls, and she almost never picks up (at least not for me).

By that time it was just as well – it was too late, anyway. I had to get dinner on the table, get the meal eaten and the dishes cleared and be ready to go out for my first-ever Christmas caroling. But even though I couldn't have talked even if I'd had someone to talk to – the moment was lost – I was tearful, fretful, feeling sorry for myself as I finished cooking and spooned pasta and sauce and green beans onto plates, sorry for myself because I didn't have someone I could call while making dinner and know for sure that she would be happy to hear from me and could take five minutes from her own impossibly crammed life to listen and to talk, so that we both would have had five solid minutes of feeling understood, appreciated, *known* – a shorthand for the whole of our friendship.

It's the one thing I am missing – really, the only thing. I don't mind not being famous; I don't mind not having money. I can't even get terribly exercised about being underpaid, the way so many of my teaching colleagues do. I'm still too busy being amazed that anyone pays me *anything* to think about writing, talk about writing, declaim my opinions (which are many and deeply held) – that I am given money to stand in front of a group of people and be as smart and charming and funny as I can possibly be. It's a miracle, really – a blessing.

I am a person who has been greatly blessed. And who is grateful, always, for those blessings.

And yet there is this, which I sometimes find that I can hardly endure: not having one friend, just one, whom I know I can count on, always. That one friend who truly knows me, inside and out.

The one who, when you go there, has to take you in.

• • •

You wouldn't think one would require such a friend in middle age. A spouse, yes. As far as I can tell, it's still considered not just socially acceptable but downright sociable (and possibly patriotic) to complain, in your middle-forties (and as early as your middle-thirties), if you're living alone. It's also acceptable to be stoic, quietly resigned, self-mocking, or genuinely good-humored about it. Or to be none of the above – to be, simply, rather pleased with yourself (even if people are suspicious about your pleasure; even if they're deep-down certain that you're faking it). The only socially unacceptable position I can think of, with regard to being spouseless at the halfway-or-more point, is pure rage. No – either that or despair. Or the two in combination. If you're enraged, or you have given up all hope of happiness, it's hard to complain in a way that won't frighten people.

But what position can a woman my age possibly take with regard to "best friendship" that doesn't seem ridiculous – except perhaps to her own still pre-teenage daughter? (I have no illusions about what Grace will think of me – my thoughts, ideas, requirements, longings – once she hits her teenage stride.) The category of best friend isn't even supposed to have meaning once we are out of our teens.

I might conclude that this is because it's girls and women who have best friends, by and large, not boys and men, and that what's necessary for us isn't going to be considered really necessary (and most assuredly not really important) by the culture at large. But I hate making that kind of assumption. I hate thinking the worst of anyone, and I particularly hate thinking the worst of the general spirit of my time and culture (and to chalk this one up to sexism is just so obvious, and stupid, and small-minded – I really feel I have no choice but to refuse to believe it). So I've decided to assume, first, that it's just a small number of us – some of whom, for all I know, may be men – who continue to have a best friend well past the age of consent, so that (like the needs of any other minority) the requirement for best friendship in adulthood, no matter how heartfelt, is likely to be overlooked by perfectly right-thinking, kind, reasonable people who don't happen to have that requirement themselves (because who isn't guilty of occasionally dismissing something as trivial just because he doesn't happen to need it himself?), and second, that in fact there *is* something wrong with me.

That these two assumptions pretty much cancel each other out doesn't signify. (This is no doubt why I have been accused all my life of being illogical.) I take turns thinking first one way, then the other. And truly, I have no way of knowing which is true.

7

What are friends for? I ask Grace and Kristin. I ask because I realize I have never asked this before – not of the girls, for whom the answer should be fresh in mind. I've read a "landmark UCLA study" on friendship between women that claims that the urge for such friendships is caused by a "cascade of oxytocin," a hormone released as part of the stress response in women, which buffers the fight or flight response found in men and encourages women to take care of their children and seek out other women instead. And when a woman goes ahead and engages in this "tending or befriending," Laura Cousino Klein writes, even more oxytocin is released, "which further counters stress and produces a calming effect." This doesn't happen in men because testosterone, the hormone *men* produce in high levels when they're under stress, actually *reduces* the effects of oxytocin.

Though I'm glad to hear that friendship has a biological basis – I have always found biological bases to be comforting – this doesn't really answer my question.

Nor does the whole book I read on the subject of girls' and women's friendship, which states the infuriatingly obvious, again and again. It tells me, among other self-evident truths, that there is a relationship between psychological health and friendship, and that women have these kinds of friendships but men don't. There was one nice line, one I underlined: "Friends can see the whole of us when we feel lost among the parts." I'm not sure it's true, but it has a lyric feel that pleased me. Plus, it's so idyllic. It makes the real messiness of friendship, the catch-as-catch-can of it – not to mention the yearning and the desperation – sound as if it's all for a higher purpose. Which it very well may be.

But I'm not satisfied. Not by biology and not by lyricism. That's why I go ask the girls.

"You have to have friends to keep you from getting bored," Grace says.

"Right," says Kristin. "And, you know, to keep you company."

"You'd go crazy if you didn't have a friend."

Kristin smiles sweetly at Grace. "Also, if you have a friend, you have someone to tell your secrets to."

"Really?" I say. From Kristin, this is surprising. Grace looks thrilled. "Do you tell your secrets to your friends?" I ask Kristin.

Kristin shrugs. As she so often does. "Sure."

"Do you tell secrets to friends you wouldn't tell anyone else?" I dare to ask. "Like your mother, say?"

Kristin looks shocked. "Well, sure."

Grace explains: "She doesn't tell her mother anything."

This is more than I bargained for – and going afield of the subject, I decide, which I can do well enough on my own – so I redirect. "Okay, what else are friends good for?"

"To keep you from feeling mean," Grace offers.

"To keep you from feeling *mean*?" I say. "How does that work?"

"Oh, you know, if you don't have any friends, you wonder: am I a bad person, a mean person, a stupid person? When you have friends, especially a best friend, then you know that can't be true. Because if you were mean or stupid, this person wouldn't like you, right? You'd be all alone. So if you have a friend, it means you're okay."

"Yeah," Kristin says. But she doesn't look at me, or at Grace. "Better than okay. Maybe even great."

Right. I leave the girls alone – I'm afraid if I stay, I might cry – and go back upstairs to work; it's where I belong. And they're where they belong, together.

Maybe it really isn't any more complicated than that. Even at my age. Company. Secrets. Someone to call and talk to while you're doing dishes or folding laundry or stirring spaghetti sauce, which would otherwise be too boring.

Someone to make you think you're great.

Because otherwise you wouldn't know, would you? And is this so different from my idea about not being misunderstood? Your best friend is the only one who gets it – gets you: who knows how great you really are. The greatest.

Nobody can ever get enough of that – can she?

And most men don't seem to need it . . . because of what? Because they get it somewhere else? From their girlfriends, or their wives – or from their girlfriends *and* their wives, both at the same time? – in a way that women don't. Or won't. Or can't. Men get it from their work – and women do, too, but not *enough*, somehow. Never enough. Not enough from lovers, not enough from work, not enough from our children, from being their mothers. We need it – we need *something*; sometimes it feels like everything – from our friends. We start young. And we don't get over it.

Or *I* didn't. Haven't. And never will, it seems.

I feel about having a best friend the way my friend who is twenty-five years older than I am told me some time ago – she was still in her sixties then – she felt about men, about love. She said she was beginning to be sure she'd never have another man in her life. "Not that I wouldn't like to, but after a certain point you simply know it's not likely to happen again."

Actually, I *don't* feel the way she felt. Or the way she said she felt. The way she sounded. Because she sounded cheerfully resigned. She sounded as if she'd made peace with this, as if she even had a sense of humor about it. And I am neither cheerful nor resigned, peaceful nor amused. There are in fact moments, hours – there have been a few whole days – when I find myself desolate, inconsolable; when I am sure that just like Ringo without George in Grace and Kristin's version of the world, I will continue to be lonely for the rest of my life. That no matter what else I have to call my own in this world, I will feel myself to be all alone.

Bookends

The night before her third birthday, my daughter cries.

She doesn't want to turn three – this is what she says when I ask what's wrong. She likes being two, she says. She is *happy* being two. Why can't she just *stay* two?

She is sobbing, and I am at a loss, as I have been so often in the last three years – one day short of three years. It's not just that the question is hard to answer. It's not even just that it's especially hard for a mother who has taken an oath never to resort to the "Because I say so" or "You think that's unfair? Well, life is unfair" school of parenting – a mother who explains everything, who *enjoys* explaining everything, who is always up for a good healthy debate about her explanation, even with a two-year-old; a mother who has been explaining everything since said two-year-old was two *days* old. Because she wanted to set a precedent. Which she did.

Actually, it's the crying itself that undoes me, as it always is. Compared to my ability to bear my daughter's grief or pain, even the impossibility of explaining the passage of time in a way that will make sense to a nearly-three-year-old seems like no big deal.

When she was a baby, I would cry whenever she cried. I would pick her up, cradle her in my arms, coo and murmur to her, cover the top of her head with kisses, attend to whatever needed attending to – all the while in tears myself.

And Grace at two (as at four, at six, at eight) doesn't just *cry*. She sobs as if her heart is breaking. And once she starts – and she starts often; tears come naturally, too quickly, to her, as they always have to me – she has difficulty stopping. Once, when she was four, I made the mistake of bringing home a video of *The King and I* – a movie I chose because she had so thoroughly enjoyed *The Music Man*, had seen it so many times she knew the dialogue and lyrics all by heart, and because we'd graduated to *My Fair Lady* and then *West Side Story* (the latter of which would soon succeed *The Music Man* as her favorite movie, although what she watched was an adulterated version: fast-forwarded past the rumble, the manhandling of Anita in Doc's store, the shooting of Tony). *The King and I* seemed the logical next step.

I was right to think she'd like it: she watched the whole movie in one sitting with fierce, unswerving concentration, unwilling to take even a two-minute bathroom break. I just hadn't reckoned on her reaction to the king's death at the end. She wept so long and hard she frightened me. Hours later she was still crying on and off, still talking in a hushed, frightened voice about how terrible his death was ("After I got to know him so well!" she kept saying. "After I got to love him too, just like Anna!"). I cried this way after seeing *Camelot* in a movie theater when I was a little girl. I told Grace this. "I cried on and off for *days,*" I said, and she was horrified: "Then let's *never* rent that one."

Even now, almost five years later, she recalls with reverent amazement the day she cried for hours over a movie death.

But at the time I am speaking of she has not yet seen *The King and I*. She is only almost-three and what she is sobbing over is the death of her two-year-old self. I am holding her in my arms, sitting on the edge of her bed. A minute ago she'd been tucked in, ready for sleep – so I had thought – in the "big girl bed" she's been in since shortly after she turned two, not because we had decided it was time to do away with the crib, but because we'd moved to New York for the year and left as much as possible behind in Columbus. I am on sabbatical from my teaching job; Glen has a grant from the Marie Walsh Sharp Foundation that provides him with a large, many-windowed studio in Tribeca – a far cry from the converted circa-1907 one-car garage he works in at home. We are living in a furnished apartment in Brooklyn Heights for which we have bartered (Glen is remodeling it in exchange for our rent). We've brought boxes of books, clothes, toys, cassette tapes, art supplies; no crib.

The apartment belongs to a woman named Pat, who grew up in it, as did her own daughter, Ariel, who is now in her thirties and in whose childhood bed Grace sleeps. Pat is schizophrenic and lives in a group home upstate, near Ariel but not with her. The husband of my old friend Vicki has made these arrangements for us. Vicki and her family live in the building next door, and the two buildings together form a co-op. Everyone in the co-op is pleased to have us living in Pat's apartment, which has been empty since she was first hospitalized.

We have put most of Pat's furniture and other belongings in storage for the year. We keep out just what we absolutely need – a bed for Grace, a bed for us, bedding and towels, two dressers and a couch, a kitchen table and three chairs, pots and pans and dishes and flatware. Everything else – hundreds of books and records and magazines, closets and drawers full of clothes, a lifetime's worth of papers, Ariel's childhood things, the contents of junk drawers and desks – everything else is packed up, taken away. We pay the monthly fee to keep most of Pat's things safe, and live with the rest of them, as gently as we can.

But now our year in New York is almost up. It has been a wonderful, strange, idyllic year: a year without day care or babysitters; a year in which I divide my days between writing and outings with Grace. Glen is with her in the morning, from nine a.m. till noon or one – building with blocks or making paintings or drawings, or else out at a playground – while I write, and then we three have a lavish lunch together, our one family meal (ordered in from the Middle Eastern place just off Atlantic Avenue, or from the Vietnamese place on Remsen – one container after another of different kinds of noodle soups), and after lunch, Glen will leave for his studio and won't be home until Grace and I are asleep.

In the afternoon, Grace and I explore the city. By this time – mid-June 1996 – she knows every inch of the Metropolitan Museum. And while six years later it will be almost impossible to drag her into an art museum (she will fold her arms and insist that she has already seen enough art for a lifetime), at two, at three, there is nothing she enjoys more. She is crazy about the Guggenheim Museum and MOMA, but best of all is the Met, for the Temple of Dendur and the rooms full of furniture, which captivate her ("This would be good to have," she says thoughtfully, standing before an ornately gilded dressing table), and also for its twentieth-century wing. Sometimes, while we are wandering through European paintings or in a nineteenth-century room in the American wing, she will suddenly shriek, "Get me to the twentieth century!" – for when it comes to paintings, it is only the modern that is of interest to her, the more abstract the better. She likes to talk about what she sees in the paintings and make up titles for them: *Bang!* and *Some Smokestacks* and *The Bluest Blue*.

We also spend a day or two each month at the natural history museum and have made a dozen visits to the Transit Museum (which is in walking distance from our apartment on Willow Place, and features a real city bus Grace can pretend to drive and subway cars from every era – so that I have the pleasure of sitting with my daughter on the hard wicker seat of a D train car, possibly one of the very ones in which I traveled with my mother and grandmother when I was no older than Grace) and at least as many visits to the Brooklyn Botanical Gardens. She has been to the Aquarium in Coney Island and the Hall of Science on the old World's Fair Grounds in Flushing, and the Brooklyn Museum and the Brooklyn Children's Museum and the Soho Children's Art Museum and Sheepshead Bay to eat lobster at Lundy's, as I did as a child, and Brighton Beach and the bead district on Fifth Avenue to buy necklace-making supplies and up and down every street in the Village, and if not every playground in Central Park then damn near, and we have recently discovered the best playground in all of New York, the one at the end of the Battery Park Esplanade, Hudson River Playground, which has its own squad of Battery Park City servicemen who patrol nonstop with tool belts, and sculpture everywhere by Tom Otterness on which the children can climb (a giant foot, a head in profile, bulldogs they can use as footstools in order to reach the drinking fountains, dodo birds that spit water from their beaks).

Sometimes we don't get back to the apartment till bedtime. We'll stop at a restaurant on our way home and she'll share whatever I'm having for dinner – a cheap date – and order water in a wine glass for herself. Over the course of this year, Grace has learned to love restaurants, to take the subway for granted; she has learned how to hail a cab. She speaks with enough of a New York accent to ensure that she will not grow up to pronounce "merry," "marry," and "Mary" as if they are all the same word, the way my undergraduates do (and when she points at a passing dog and declares, "Dawgie!" for the first time, early in our New York year, I am dizzy with relief).

Weekends, Glen and I both take breaks from our work: he plasters and paints the apartment and Grace and I visit my parents on the Upper East Side, sleeping together in a fold-out sofa bed in their den

– the room that was my brother's when my parents first moved in to this apartment, in the late 1970s. Saturday nights, I cook – for my daughter and for my parents, who otherwise order in their dinners every night. Sometimes I leave Grace with my mother and spend hours walking around the city alone, happy because I am home, because I am always happier in New York than in Columbus, and because Grace is getting to know her grandmother better than she ever would otherwise.

And Pat's apartment is becoming beautiful, thanks to Glen. And Vicki's son and Grace are becoming as comfortable in each other's company as siblings. Vicki and Silas accompany Grace and me on many of our non-museum outings (Vicki's convinced that Silas would run around like a maniac, bellowing at the top of his lungs, in an art museum), and the children play at home together, too, most evenings for at least a little while before bed. Grace teaches Silas the joys of playing dress-up, and the two of them "take the subway" sitting on her bed side by side, in shawls and crocheted hats, wearing necklaces and bracelets and clutching their purses; Silas introduces Grace to a game he calls "money money money," which involves diving off his playroom sofa into a combination of sofa cushions and thousands of pennies, spread out all over the playroom floor. Vicki and I give the children their evening baths together, and we talk and talk.

Our kitchen window looks out on the Statue of Liberty. Every day Grace says good morning to it.

And I have just about finished a new manuscript, and Glen has had a dealer visit his studio and offer to take him on. All in all, it has been as perfect a year as we could possibly have hoped for – as we hadn't dared hope for.

We arrived in New York just after Grace turned two; soon after her third birthday it will be time to leave. She can't even remember our house back in Columbus (and when we do return in August, she will be puzzled by it for the first few days, repeatedly forgetting where the staircase is that leads to the second floor and her bedroom), but she does remember the people of whom she was fondest there. Sometimes when she's playing in our Willow Place apartment she'll pick up her toy phone and call Amira Silver-Swartz, who is three and a half years older and the child she likes best in Columbus. "Hello, Amira? It's me, Grace Jane. I'm still in New York. Everything's fine here. How are things in Columbus?"

In Brooklyn Heights on this birthday eve, things are far from fine. Grace is in my lap, sobbing, begging not to be dragged forward in time, and I am tearfully doing my best to reassure her, as I have been doing since she was a baby, when I'd pat and rub her back and murmur, "I know, I know," saying this so often that the two words ran together for her, became one, a magic word, so that by the time she was ten months old, I'd hear her muttering, *IknowIknowIknow* to reassure *herself* when she was feeling bad.

By this time, with Grace just hours shy of three, "I know" has been expanded to take into account the particulars of each unhappy situation, and as I hold her on my lap, I stroke her hair and murmur that change is difficult for everyone, even for grownups, that going forward is always hard and scary, and leaving things behind is sad, but that she has lots of things to look forward to, that not knowing what's ahead is part of what makes life interesting and exciting. And I promise her that three will be fun, even better than two. That there are joys and adventures ahead, things she will be able to do that she can't even imagine right now. *You'll learn to read. You'll learn to swim. You'll learn to ride a bike.* And all the while, I am doing my best to hide from her not only my tears but also my surprise. Who ever heard of a child who doesn't want to get older?

I don't care! I'm not turning three. I'm staying two forever.

What I have no way of knowing is that this crisis will be repeated in a year, on the eve of three about to turn four, when we are back in Columbus, when she has forgotten all about the room she lived in in New York, and what she remembers about the year itself is patchy and vague, mixed up with what I have told her about it.

When the crisis occurs again, in exactly the same way, the night before she turns five, I am ready for it. Likewise on the eve of five about to turn six. Six turning seven. Seven turning eight. At some point along the way she becomes too grown-up to climb into my lap for a routine crisis like this one, and she sits by herself with her knees to her chest, her head in her hands, sobbing into them, and I sit on the edge of the bed, reminding her that the year to come will bring undreamed-of pleasures. I list for her – ticking them off on my fingers

– the things she has accomplished in the last year: *You taught yourself to swim, you read a chapter book, you learned to sew.* I mention a few of the things I know for sure are shimmering in the future just ahead: *piano lessons, New York in the spring for Daddy's next opening, Girl Scout camp.*

She doesn't want to hear about it.

You jumped off the diving board. You wrote your own story about a horse. You'll learn to ride a horse.

I don't care, she says. *I hate time. I hate the way it never stays now, the way you can't even keep it still for a second. It's already then.*

I am amazed that she has figured this out. It is the night before she turns eight.

And so I have to ask her – I have to; I really want to know – *If you could run the universe, what would you do? Banish time?*

I'd do anything to make her feel better, and I'd never purposely do anything to make her feel worse, so I'm shocked when this question causes her to sob harder. *No, I couldn't. That's the problem. That's why I hate it. If time stopped, everything would stop. But it just keeps coming and coming. And it's so terrible.*

• • •

But it's not so terrible – or it's not *only* terrible – she has decided this year. As I write this, a little more than two weeks remain before her ninth birthday, and, like everything else about her (like everything else about motherhood), change has kicked in just when I have become complacent. Now that I have grown habituated to our annual ritual of grief and ineffective reassurance, it appears that no grief, no heaving sobs, no terror, and no ineffectual yet vaguely soothing reassurance are on the horizon.

This year, she says, she is *ambivalent.* She has just learned this word and it has become a favorite.

Grace, your bird is out of seeds. Do you want to go with me to the pet store?

I don't know, Mama, I'm ambivalent about it.

I'm tempted to point out that Cody is supposed to be her bird, not mine, that it's her responsibility to keep the bird in seeds. But if I enforced *whose-bird-is-this,* I might have to give up keeping Cody on my shoulder or ankle (the latter is where she's perched at this very minute) while I work, and I'm not sure I can, I've become so accustomed to her company, so I don't say anything, and Grace interprets my silence as a request for elaboration.

Naturally I'd love to have the chance to play with some guinea pigs at the pet store, but I also really want to stay here and finish this game. She waves her hand at the lineup of American Girl dolls in the hallway outside her room: one in a brass bed, one in a wheelchair, one on a horse. What kind of game can that be? I wonder. But for once I don't let myself get sidetracked. I ask her to make a choice, and make it quick, please, and then I sigh, because ever since she learned about ambivalence (and it's not just the word that's new, but the state of mind it describes, which she had no idea existed – or rather, she had no idea it was allowed), quick decisions of any kind are extremely difficult for her to make.

(For the record: neither of us ended up at the pet store that day, and Cody ate Grape Nuts and sugar snap peas and pasta, which she prefers anyway.)

About getting older, Grace tells me, she finds herself now of two minds. *Equally* of two minds, she adds. One part of her mind, she says, keeps tugging to stay in place, and there are days when she is so enjoying being eight, so sad to see eight go and click over into nine, and so nervous about fourth grade come fall and what lies ahead of *that*, that she seems positively mournful. She waxes nostalgic about the great events of this past year – a new friend made, new skills learned she never thought she'd master, parties attended, books read (in this way, she sounds like me, making our annual birthday eve list).

But there are other days on which the future beckons, glimmering, and the other part of her mind is saying, "Let's *go!*" While she is not in the kind of breakneck hurry her friend Anna is (Anna who shows up at our door on Sunday mornings at nine o'clock with dark purple lips, glitter on her cheekbones, blue-shadowed and mascaraed eyes – an eight-year-old vamp in platform shoes, short-shorts and tube top, flashing her bejeweled blue artificial fingernails), she is *interested*, she says, in being older. "Maybe more than interested. Fascinated?" – she tries out this word, another favorite – and adds, "Sometimes it's like I'm in love with the whole idea."

It has crossed my mind that she is moving backwards through emotion: that having outgrown birthday grief and moved into uneasy equilibrium – a balance of anxiety and interest/fascination/love that teeters from one end to the other, day by day – by the time she is my age she will look forward to each birthday with pure pleasure of the kind she missed in early childhood.

(I don't really believe this. I'm an idealist, an optimist, not a fantasist.)

Anyway, for her, the pain of each year's passing has not been just about time elapsed – this much of a life already lived, this much likely to be left. It has nothing of the character of panic that for me kicked in at thirty: *how little I've accomplished! And what if it turns out I never do anything else?*

Her greatest fear, each birthday, has been change itself, and her unwillingness to let go and leave behind what she already knows, what she has *been*.

It seems to me in fact that this is what we all fear with each passing year. Change, the inexorable moving forward, the leaving-behind, the potential for the shedding of skin. Never mind that there may be wonderful things ahead – and there always are, at any age. Life is full of wonders. At thirty I was sure I'd never have a child and almost as sure I'd never publish a book. I gave myself a birthday party – a big one, in consolation, in lieu of what I thought I'd never have, never do.

We are so attached to what we know, to what we have cozily, if miserably, become accustomed. We are such fearful creatures.

My daughter, I believe, is fighting her fearfulness with all her heart.

• • •

I was a fearful child too, but I had no weapons with which to fight it – by which I mean that even if I'd been encouraged to fight with all my heart (if anyone had had any idea how fearful I was; if I'd ever spoken of my fears, or allowed myself to show them, as Grace does), my heart wasn't strong enough for battle, anyway. Or at least I didn't think it was.

By the time I was fifteen, I found ways to circumvent the battle: bad boyfriends, misbehavior, drugs – the fear-circumventer of choice in 1970 – but in the interstice between childhood and adolescence I crawled into my bunker and hid, trying just to wait it out.

I knew this much: that my grandmother, on whom I had counted most for comfort for the first twelve, thirteen years of my life, and my father, on whom I'd counted for protection, were of no use to me. I was changing in ways even I didn't understand, and yet the way they treated me didn't change at all. Their attitude toward me – the same attitude they'd always had toward me – made me irritable. I found myself shrugging them off, snapping at them. And although my mother and I began to get to know each other then – she was coming out of hiding just as I was going in – this was too tentative and new a relationship to do me much good.

I went to my room, with its red-and-black shag carpeting and red corduroy bedspread, or to my best friend B——'s room (which had no color scheme to speak of, and therefore seemed both homier and more grown-up to me) and found the solace I had always found in books (but now it wasn't Edward Eager and the Betsy-Tacy books and the hundredth reading of A Wrinkle in Time, but The Catcher in the Rye and Joy in the Morning and Catch 22 and and the romantic historical mysteries to which B—— introduced me, and Vonnegut, and trashy novels with semi-detailed sex scenes, like The Carpetbaggers, which I found on my parents' bookshelves) and, for the first time, the year I was thirteen, in music.

I'd been listening to music all my life: to my mother's albums of show tunes and my father's collection of Al Jolson since I was hardly more than a baby, and to more show tunes and the pop songs of A——'s and my parents' generation – the Sinatra and Judy Garland and Tony Bennett and Barbra Streisand albums A—— and I listened to together – and to the pop songs of my own generation since I was nine and the Beatles hit the Ed Sullivan show. I arrived at thirteen with both Monkees albums and a stack of 45s that included "Leader of the Pack" and "This Diamond Ring," which I'd paid for myself out of my allowance, and copies of December's Children and Rubber Soul that I'd been given as gifts from classmates for my twelfth birthday, when I actually had a party, the first year I can remember my mother being well enough to manage it. Besides, I had been taking piano lessons since before I was tall enough to reach the pedals, so I knew Chopin, Beethoven, Mozart. My mother and I had played a duet of Schubert's "March Militaire" at my most recent recital (my piano teacher had been my mother's piano teacher when she was a child, and my mother had been my teacher's daughter's teacher for a while, before I was born and she retired to her room). But my relationship with music changed completely in 1968, when for the first time – and apparently overnight – it wasn't casual diversion or the background to games of imagination or a hand-me-down from either of my parents, or an obligation, but a pure necessity. Suddenly I couldn't live without it. And for the first time I found that listening required my complete concentration the same way reading did. I felt the same way, listening to music, that I'd felt for years, reading: alone but not lonely. Alone and yet connected to something else, something outside myself.

Thirteen: the year I changed schools, changed best friends, fell in love and was loved back (the former nothing new, the latter so new and surprising that for a long time I couldn't believe it. I kept asking the boy, Howie, to tell me *again*). The year I was startled every day by the sight of myself in the mirror. I lost weight that year, and I became pretty for the first time since I was very young (my mother would argue with this – so would my grandmother if she were still alive – but I remember myself at ten, at twelve: chubby, wearing clothes my mother had picked out for me, in pale pink, pale blue, gingham, skirts and jumpers with pleats and puckers and smocking and ribbons – or, worse, in A——'s ill-fitting, too-sophisticated hand-me-downs – and those gold-flecked pink eyeglasses, my hair cut short in a "Sassoon" with question-mark curled "sideburns" that had to be Scotch-taped to my cheeks at night).

The summer after I turned thirteen I wasn't chubby anymore. I picked out new glasses and I let my hair grow (*It's my hair, I'll do what I want with it!*). I insisted for the first time on choosing my own clothes (*They're my clothes, I'll wear what I want!*).

And alone in my room, I listened to Janis Joplin, Leonard Cohen, Cream, Marvin Gaye, the Beatles. It wasn't that I was indiscriminate – what I loved, I truly loved, and there was plenty that I hated, too – but that I loved so many different kinds of things, "Wichita Lineman" every bit as much as "Crown of Creation."

But it was an album by Simon and Garfunkel, *Bookends*, that I loved most that year. I listened to it dozens of times a day, every day, on the phonograph (red and white, to match my room) I'd had since I was very young. It would be nearly two years before I'd save up enough money, working as my father's secretary all one summer, to buy my own stereo system.

After thirty-four years, I can still put *Bookends* on the turntable – as I did on this May morning, before I came upstairs to work – and sing along without looking at the back of the album cover, where the lyrics I contemplated endlessly when I was thirteen are printed. I can sing from memory all about how empty I feel, how I ache but I don't know why, and oh what a time it was, and when I go, I'm gone – and *Oh, my Grace, I got no hiding place.*

2

She has been thinking, my daughter says, and she has decided: thirteen is the perfect age.

Which I suppose makes a kind of sense, given the teeter-totter she's been on these last few months. Thirteen is the age of ambivalence itself. Still, I ask her, "What makes you think thirteen will be so great?"

"Did I say I thought it would be *great?*" she says. "It'll be difficult, I know that. But also – I don't know – exciting."

Well, that about sums it up. But how on earth does *she* know? I wonder.

"Oh, come on," she says when I ask. "Remember Erika? Remember Blanche?"

I do, but I'm surprised she's thinking of them. Eight and nine years older, respectively, than Grace, she loved and admired them when she was very small and we saw them every day at the pool we used to go to in the summertime each year, before it was bulldozed and replaced with townhouses.

Those summers! Mornings, I would write while Grace played with Glen. In the afternoon, he'd go out to the studio and she and I would walk over to the pool at Olentangy Village, loaded down with towels and snacks and swim toys, and we'd stay till dinnertime. We made friends there – good friends. There were no children Grace's age, but it didn't matter. Blanche and Erika more than made up for that.

Grace and the girls were close both before the "big girls" turned thirteen and after. She witnessed and filed away their changes.

Both girls, at thirteen, would bounce back and forth – sometimes within minutes – between childhood and adolescence. In and around the pool every afternoon, and often enough in the evening, too, at our house, they would play with Grace. They would "make the animals talk" or play "going to New York for Daddy's opening" or pretend they were having a birthday party or arrange the model dinosaurs into groups and relationships. They would dress Grace's Barbies and put the dolls through the elaborate paces of games they'd work out along with her – complex stories that required many changes of clothes. They would sometimes remember to be ironic about this play – using Barbie shirts as turbans and leopard-patterned pants as sashes, dressing Ken in drag, and Stacey in Ken's clothes (which hung on her so that she looked like a suburban teenage boy trying to look like a gangsta); using Legos to build postmodern structures in which no one could possibly live ("It's not supposed to have doors or windows, that's what makes it interesting"); and making jokes about the dinosaurs (I remember the questions four-year-old Grace would ask after Blanche and Erika went home: "What does it mean that a dinosaur 'committed suicide'?") – but mostly they were just having fun, doing something they felt sure they were too old to be doing, taking advantage of the excuse of keeping Grace amused to do something that still gave them pleasure.

I used to watch the girls with their own mothers: Erika and Stefania tense, ready to argue at the slightest justification; Blanche and Amy teetering, always, between adoring and edgy with each other. Blanche was an only child, and she and Amy were driving each other crazy by then: they couldn't be together as they'd been before, but they couldn't be apart, either.

Blanche was less self-conscious than Erika, needed less irony to lean on in her relationship with Grace. But she was also interested in boys long before Erika was, and not just because she was a year older. The summer Blanche was thirteen, she would stop talking to Grace midsentence, wander away from the place on the cement where they'd set up the dinosaurs, when Andrew showed up, threatening to dunk her.

Erika at thirteen, the following year, still thought boys were icky. She would dissolve into tears over what seemed even to five-year-old

Grace to be nothing (a cheap toy broken, an insult flung at her by her little brother, something in her mother's tone of voice that struck her as especially provoking) and her moods swung dramatically from ecstatically high to so low she would speak to Grace in monosyllables if she could bring herself to speak at all.

Blanche sometimes grew sulky, and would sit on the end of her mother's chaise longue staring into space, her hand moving reflexively in and out of a bag of chips.

But when they came to life, everything was an adventure for these girls, and the excitement they generated – the electric buzz around them – affected Grace so strongly sometimes it seemed to lift her off the ground. They would carry her off with them to their "secret place" behind the cottage that housed the showers; they would make a picnic of snack foods – nothing but chips and dip and cookies and pretzels – and "talk things over."

Grace would tell me that much, but if I asked *what* they'd talked about for so long – for sometimes they'd be gone for hours, and all I could see was a flash of my daughter's long red hair as she galloped in and out of my line of sight (and all I could hear were shrieks and giggles) – she'd shrug and say, "Just big girl things, you know." Did she understand all of it? I asked. No, but she didn't care. That wasn't what was important, she told me. Besides, if she really wanted to know, she could ask and they would explain. She said this confidently.

Oddly enough, just a day after Grace mentioned Blanche's name for the first time in years, the mail brought an invitation to a party in celebration of her high school graduation. I knew we wouldn't be able to attend – our next-door neighbors were getting married the same day – and I called Blanche to tell her that. She sounded very grown-up. But of course she does, I told myself. She's eighteen now, a young woman.

And she was gracious, charming – not *polite* but genuinely warm, wonderful to talk to. She told me all about the college she'd decided on, and what she was interested in (chemistry, creative writing, and theater – and I bit my tongue and didn't mention that I'd double-majored in chemistry and English myself, because that wasn't the point at all: this is her new life, the first such life anyone has ever lived). After we talked for a while, she put her mother on, and Amy and I talked for a long time, too – long enough for her to confess that she was "having a nervous breakdown" over Blanche's imminent departure. I assured her that I would too, when Grace grew up and went away to college. I said it laughing – and Amy was laughing too, just two middle-aged women talking about their only children, the daughters they are closer to than they have ever been to anyone else in their whole lives – but a shiver went through me.

. . .

Amy is only a few years older than I am, but it'll be a decade before I have to face what she's facing. I've been thinking of this – how lucky I am, how much wiser and saner I hope to be eight or nine years from now – which makes me think about the other hidden benefits of being an "older mother." I think of all those mothers whose daughters start menstruating just as *they* are reaching menopause – the beginnings and the endings elbowing each other out. I'm two, three – maybe four – years away from Grace's first period, and there's no danger that simultaneous hormone detonations will occur in our house, because I'm already having mine, and by the time Grace's comes around I should be safely out the other end.

It's a benefit of late motherhood I hadn't anticipated, mainly because – somehow or other – I hadn't anticipated menopause at all. I knew it was coming, obviously, but only in the vaguest, most abstract, *someday* kind of way. I never thought about it. Not until I had to, because it began.

And even then, not right away. Never mind that I hadn't had a period in months: I was "irregular," that was all – payback for all those years, decades, of perfectly predictable regularity. (Still, just to be sure, I took a home pregnancy test. Twice.)

And never mind the hot flashes. It never crossed my mind that they *were* "hot flashes" (I even had one while sitting on the edge of the bathtub waiting for the results of my second home pregnancy test). I thought I was getting sick (I complained to Glen that I was feverish, on and off, all night long. Every night. For a week. For ten days. For two weeks). I took Echinacea and sucked on zinc lozenges, rested whenever I could, drank a lot of water. I felt I was putting up a good fight, since no other cold or flu symptoms kicked in.

Like Z——, of whom, last night over dinner, I asked if she'd had any hot flashes yet ("Me?" she said, startled, "don't be silly! I'm still a young woman"), I didn't let the possibility that I was "old enough" float to the surface. Like Z—— – who laughed again in the pocket of silence that followed her protest (laughed self-consciously this time, turning the laughter into scare quotes around the phrase she'd used, because she's only three years younger than I am, and we'd just been talking about my menopause, and she didn't mean to insult or upset me) – I couldn't look it in the face. Not yet, not until I had no choice.

But even after I had no choice, even after I knew what was going on, I would sometimes be fooled, or – more to the point – I would fool myself. It's easy to do, because "hot flash" is a phrase that doesn't do justice to what it's meant to describe. "Hot flash" makes it sound so snazzy, as if you're lit up for little while with a flame-colored halo. It makes it sound like a sports car. A man's midlife crisis car, small and red and sexy.

Once, in a restaurant, I was suddenly so hot I was afraid I was going to faint. I looked around for the heat register I was sure was either in the floor under the table or in the wall beside my legs, and when I didn't find it, I asked the two women I was with (both middle-aged, but neither yet menopausal; thus neither knew to point out the obvious) if they could see the source of the heat that was blasting out at me ("I must be directly in its path," I said, which I suppose I was), and they looked – they both bent down and looked under their side of the table, where the two of them were sitting across from me – but they didn't see anything either.

And this was *after* I'd been to the gynecologist for my annual exam and she'd chuckled when I told her about the missed periods and the home pregnancy tests (it was the first strike against her in years, but it brought me back with a jolt to the last time I'd been going through something she didn't understand, when Grace was a baby – and she, my doctor, was still childless – and she said, "Look, if you can't sleep and you're exhausted and feeling crappy all the time, just wean her and take Zoloft for a few months"). She was the one who raised the specter of hot flashes and night sweats (the latter a phrase that captures the experience perfectly, but indelicately): she named what I'd been experiencing, and I said, "You're kidding me."

"Not kidding," she said cheerfully. "It happens to the best of us, sooner or later." (She has a couple of children now, and I hope she's not still telling new mothers to quit breastfeeding and blithely pushing antidepressants on them, but you'd think she would have learned a lesson from the years before her children were born. Something like: never be blithe about something you don't really know a damn thing about yet. She's at least ten years younger than I am: menopause must feel very, very far off to her.)

I took a blood test. I wouldn't have believed it otherwise, because the experiential questions she asked me weren't helpful at all.

Mood swings?

How would I know?

Any insomnia?

All my life.

Tearfulness?

Ditto.

I have since learned that the test I took – of the level of FSH, or follicle-stimulating hormone, in my blood – isn't the best way to find out if you're menopausal, that FSH levels fluctuate from month to month. But mine was so high (well over sixty, when an FSH level of thirty, my doctor said, is considered postmenopausal; and, while women with FSH levels of sixteen are considered still to be ovulating, those who are considered the best candidates for pregnancy have levels between one and ten) that it served its purpose: it convinced me, the way only specific, concrete things – numbers, "facts" with sources cited – can.

And once I was convinced, I wept.

"Why so sad?" my doctor asked. "You weren't planning on having any more kids, anyhow."

I wasn't, it's true. I wasn't planning. I wasn't even *wanting*. I had, for a while, when Grace was much younger, when I was still in the throes of amazement that I so enjoyed being a mother. But what with one thing and another – Glen's incredulity when I mentioned it for the first time (But we're just now getting back to work!) and Grace's declaration shortly after she turned two that she didn't "want any sucked-on milk" or have any interest *whatsoever* in sharing my attention "with some other kid I don't even know yet and might not even like," plus my own feeling that if I were going to do it, I'd want to wait a few years so I could give my full attention to both children while they were still very young (and I didn't *have* a few years, I knew, so this was a moot point) – I let it go, and eventually I got over even the wanting.

Still – the difference between not wanting and not being able: that made me cry.

What's taking longer to get over is the other part of my sadness, which comes from how much my sense of myself has been tied up with being a *girl* – even now, even as I indisputably move from my mid- to my late-forties. It's crazy, I know it, to think *girl* at forty-seven.

(But it may be crazier still to think that menopause forces you to *stop* thinking *girl* if that's what you've been doing anyway, past the age of twenty-one.)

When I say "girl" I don't mean any disrespect to myself, tenets of sisterhood notwithstanding (I know better than to call my college students *girls*, much less my friends and colleagues; I've known that since 1972). I mean something like: I still listen to music every day, every minute I'm not working or sleeping. I listen to the music of my youth – Judy Collins (on vinyl, in mono), The Band, the Dead, Fairport Convention, Janis – and to the music of the first years after I grew up and left home, the soundtrack of my early twenties – Ry Cooder, Elvis Costello, Al Green. I listen to the music of my no-longer youth, my holding-on-to youth, somebody else's youth (Katrina and the Waves, the Romantics, the Psychedelic Furs, and – it should go without saying – the Clash) and to music to which I have no youthful rights at all, no matter how remote – the music that would by rights belong to my children if I'd had children in my twenties: Old 97's, Belle and Sebastian.

Pop music is as essential to me now as it was thirty years ago. Or more essential, after all these years. Because everything I love, I love more as time passes. It's possible that this is something I should be embarrassed about. A clever student of mine once wrote, of a vain, middle-aged fictional character: "More and more he loves the things he loves." She was mocking him, mocking middle age itself – its pointless vanities. I didn't take it personally (or, rather, I did take it personally, but I wasn't insulted). More and more I love the things I love, and I am grateful that I do.

As I age, everything and everyone has become more precious to me. Even my *self*.

Which brings me back to being a girl – *and by me that's only great* (a line from "I Enjoy Being a Girl," one of two show tunes I sang at a talent show in the Catskills when I was Grace's age; the other was "Wouldn't It Be Loverly?" – a performance for which I won second prize, a brush-and-mirror set, backed with pink and gold enamel. First prize went to my own father, for lip-synching to two Al Jolson songs).

I still think like a girl, when it comes to some of what matters most to me – my friendships with other "girls," say – and it's never hard for me to imagine, or remember, what's going through the minds of Grace and *her* girlfriends when there's trouble between them. I'm well-known for being the mother who "gets it," and I'm proud of this and hope it lasts through adolescence (despite the times it's been a dubious honor, like when three of the girls were over here with Grace and they made penises out of a substance called Model Magic and danced around our playroom holding them against the front of their jeans, calling me in to watch the show, and later when the other mothers came to pick up their daughters, they showed *them* their sculptures but said they were microphones, because – or so Grace explained when everyone was gone – I was the only mother they could count on not to get mad).

I still dress like a girl, although I cover a lot more of myself than I did at sixteen (my one sober concession to my advanced age. If I were slimmer, I doubt I'd concede even that). I still wear my hair the same way, long and messy. When I have it "done," I have it flat-ironed stick-straight and limp, the look I longed for in my teens, before the invention of the flat iron (I achieved an approximation of the look then by sleeping with my hair rolled up in coffee cans, and it lasted only for an hour at best, and even for that hour was too bouncy to suit me). I still wear jewelry draped over every part of me that can hold it up, as I have since I was fifteen. I still flirt like a girl, too – meaninglessly, cheerfully, heedlessly, unselfconsciously.

It's not that I'm "immature." I'm *famously* mature. I'm the most mature person in almost every group I've ever been a part of, including my own family (including both of my own families: the one I'm from, and the one I've made).

No doubt it's this famous maturity that has finally begun to kick in and get me thinking that none of the above – except the ability to bear a child – is going to change because I'm not a round-the-clock estrogen factory anymore, that I am still myself, the same old (if older) self I've been nearly all my life. But the "nearly" came damn close to throwing me, I confess.

If I started to become the self I recognize when I was thirteen – when I "became a woman," as they told us in Girl Scouts – then coming to the end of this ride could very well mean I would cease to be the person I'd become then. The one I *am*.

But I was already on my way to becoming her – that girl, that woman – from the minute I was born. That the marker for girls, for women, is so clear – that it's a mark made by blood – just confuses things. Or so it seems to me now. That men don't have such big, looming, obvious symbols to mark their transitions, that every change for them is subtle compared to ours (their voices shift register; we *bleed*), you'd think would make them the more subtle gender overall, instead of the more flat-footed, heavy-handed, obvious one.

The fact is, I am a little bit ashamed of myself for having been, for a moment – a months-long moment – so flat-footed myself, so unsubtle, so male. Perhaps it was the slowdown of estrogen production.

But at least I didn't buy a fast red car or stumble into a ruinous affair.

• • •

Nevertheless, I get sad when the signs of age jump out of the bushes and ambush me, as one did recently when I sprained my thumb, typing. How pathetic is that? I asked everyone I know. (My students said, *Not pathetic! Impressive! Working hard enough to sprain your thumb! Wow!* Which was what I had longed to hear. *Pretty pathetic*, said my forty-three-year-old little brother, the voice of my heart.)

I used to be able to work all day, every day, for weeks, months – *years* – on end without hurting myself. And (I tell myself, as if this matters where the thumb is concerned) I'm fitter than I was when I was in my thirties, because I've started exercising again, at last, in my mid-forties. Not as fervently as I did in my twenties, when a daily aerobics class taught by a dancer gave me a place to take a shower – at home I had just a tub in the kitchen – but that's probably a good thing on the whole (those leaps he had us do! those triple-time calisthenics to the Talking Heads, the Gap Band, Prince!), for it seems that although exercise serves many useful purposes, one of them is *not* fooling the body into thinking it's still a relatively new piece of equipment. I may be stronger than I was a decade ago, and I may have slowed the arthritis that has begun creeping into my ankles and toes – and I may be helping to stave off bone loss and sleeping better and feeling less tense and tired – but all of my joints and nerves and muscles are still supporting a machine that's nearly five decades old.

I am typing these words while wearing a custom-made splint to allow me to keep working while holding all but one joint of my right thumb still. But I am worried now about my index finger, which has taken over the work of my thumb and has begun to tremble when it's poised over the keyboard, and I am worried about the padded part of my hand just below my thumb, which is throbbing. The smallest finger has begun to ache too.

This is simply not something that could have happened ten years ago.

Nor this: sometimes in the morning when I walk from bed to bathroom, I have to clutch the wall, my ankles hurt so much.

Or, more superficially but no less shocking to me: if I don't use moisturizer on my face, it *hurts*. And around my chin I seem to be developing a jowly look.

When I go to the salon to get my hair trimmed of split ends, or to have it flat-ironed for a special occasion, the handsome, sweet young man who holds the scissors or the iron says, in response to everything I tell him, "Yeah, that's what my mother says, too."

I ended up joining a women-only gym after my one-week free try-out period at an ordinary, everyone-who-pays-is-welcome gym that's part of a national chain, not only because the handsome young man working there kept saying, while filling in the answers to the list of questions on the form in front of him (*What are your primary reasons for joining? What do you hope to accomplish by exercising?*), "Yeah, same with my mother," but also because I discovered I was invisible to the crowd of young men and women working out all around me, so invisible that as they made their way from treadmills to Nautilus machines, Stairmasters to dumbbells, they would *bump into me*.

I didn't mind so much not being sized up, looked over, admired (every time I return to New York for a visit and find that nowadays, for the first time in thirty years, I can walk by a construction site without flinching, I am reminded that the sacrifice of anonymous admiration has its compensations), but I hate having become aesthetically insignificant enough so that to a certain segment of the population I have vanished altogether – something even more inconsequential than Muzak or the "paintings" one finds in hotel rooms, which at least people complain about.

What my grandmother complained about in the last two decades of her life was that no one could really see her anymore. Not that she was invisible, but that she was visible as something everybody thought they understood, which is perhaps the next stage: from invisible middle age to a *pretense* of visibility. She would say bitterly that almost no one saw how she was "inside," that even people she'd imagined knew her well assumed that she was not herself anymore because she looked so old. I was in my early twenties when she first said this to me, but I think even then I understood and was troubled by it, on my grandmother's behalf if not my future own. I saw the way people treated *old* as apart from *us*, the regular people – the real people. Even when it was meant "positively," the way "some of my best friends are . . ." is meant positively – "I get along marvelously with old people," "I just love being around the elderly" – it isolates the old from the still-young.

You hear the same sort of thing about children. People are always claiming to "love children" as if the category itself meant anything, as if every single child weren't entirely different from every other child, setting children apart from the rest of us, making a group of them as if they *aren't* us.

As if we weren't children once; as if we'll never be old.

No wonder "getting old" feels like entering another universe – the universe of the Others. The one in which you leave your old useful, normal, *real* self behind. Where you assume a false self, a mask and a costume, so you can conveniently be set aside.

The hell with that. I'm taking myself with me, just like my grandma did.

3

If Blanche is graduating, that means that Erika will be starting her senior year. I report these developments to Grace, whose response was what my grandmother's would have been, if she were still here to say it. *Where have the years gone?*

I laugh, but I am close to tears. At closing in on nine, there are times when Grace sounds just like my grandmother at eighty-nine. *Where do the days go?* Grace will say on Friday morning when I wake her for school. Clicking her tongue, shaking her head. *How can it be Friday already when it was just Monday?*

Sometimes, at these moments, I almost expect her to speak to me in Yiddish. *Mamaleh*, she might say, *isn't it something, the way time flies? Amol iz geven un haynt iz nito.* Once it was; today no more.

She has no idea that she sounds like my grandmother. She has no idea what my grandmother sounded like. They never knew each other. My grandmother had the chance to hold her once, but she was fading by then, almost gone.

By the time she died she had lost everything: she couldn't walk – a development of only the very last weeks of her life – and she couldn't hold on to a memory for more than a few minutes (which had been coming for months, maybe even years, but I hadn't been able to let myself see it); she no longer knew any of us with any certainty. She had finally become elderly, truly frail, tiny, in all sorts of pain. She had stopped eating anything but white bread smeared with Tabasco sauce, according to the young woman who took care of her – who loved her, and would have given her anything to eat, anything at all that she asked for. Grandma said this was the only thing she could taste anymore.

Still, until that last year she had been fine – relatively fine: not ancient, as she was near the end; still sharp; still *herself.* Until she was ninety, there wasn't even any serious physical decline, or nothing worse than there had been over the twenty years before that (that is, there were all kinds of things wrong with her, but nothing held her down). Then, at ninety, it was as if a bell went off inside her. She began to seem fragile for the first time; she began to shrink. For the first time, she was thin – then skinny; finally, she was a wisp. Before, she had been downright sturdy-looking, stout, with soft white hair down to her shoulders, dressed in bright-colored stretch pants and blouses, crocheted vests and shawls she'd made herself years before. Her skin, with its "peaches and cream" complexion (a phrase she'd taught me, which she must have learned from ladies magazines), was still unwrinkled, so soft I'd touch her cheek just to marvel over it, which had always pleased her. *Ivory soap*, she'd say, *nothing but Ivory soap for all these years! And a wash with snow in the winter is always good, too.*

She was old, of course, and she looked old, despite being wrinkle-free. But she had been old all my life.

When I was a child it saddened me that I had never known her young, by which I didn't mean *as a child* but as a young woman – a woman in her twenties, pretty, slender, hair still brown.

What I wished for, although I didn't understand this then, was that she was my mother, who *was* in her twenties, and pretty and slim. My grandmother was full of energy, apparently tireless, busy, talkative – all that I suppose I wished my mother to be. But my mother was exhausted, shy, sad, tearful, silent. I wanted a mother who would play with me, talk to me, tell me stories, ask me questions, make demands, bustle around the apartment while I trailed her, let me help with the cooking. I had all of this from my grandmother except the first, and I think I must have imagined that if only she were younger, she would have gotten down on the floor to play with me. The truth is she never would have, not even if she had been much younger. It wasn't her style.

Her style – I can see it myself in the photographs I have of her as a teenager – was dignified, grown-up. Or maybe just trying to be. She had picked out her style, determined what she could carry off, or *should* be like, and she kept her eye on that always. Even at the end she had ideas about how she should behave – indeed, how we all should behave. Every one of us had a niche: my mother delicate, "too good for this world"; my father loud and bossy but "a good man," the one she could depend on (a judgment she made late, too late to satisfy him);

each of her sons fitting somewhere too, though not always where they belonged if you observed them objectively.

My grandmother knew what she was supposed to be long before she'd collected the rights to *be* it. But by the time I was born she had met her destiny. Her hair had already been white for a long time (as she told it, it had turned white overnight when all three of her sons left home for various armed forces). By the time she clicks clearly into focus in my memory, everything physical about her was about old age: false teeth, hot water bottles, support hose I watched her grunt and groan herself into, bifocals that made her eyes look wobbly, cups of hot water with lemon.

I was so familiar with the sights and smells of old age that they weren't scary or even unpleasant to me, as they might have been to a child who spent less time with – or who didn't so thoroughly approve of and marvel at – her grandmother. In the morning, the teeth in a glass of water beside the hot water tap on the bathroom sink didn't faze me. Nor did her body, which I was used to, and with which I was on friendly terms: the huge floppy breasts she dangled into gigantic white bras; the scars from all her surgeries; the varicose veins; the pouchy belly she would rub and say, with a sigh, was the gift her four children had left her.

All of this was part of normal, ordinary life. My mother's body, on the other hand, and all of its accoutrements – the pointy bras and pointy high-heeled shoes she'd put on when she was feeling well enough to go out (shoes with vamps cut so low that only her toenails were covered – a style that to this day strikes me as sexily, youthfully *adult*, something I couldn't possibly pull off); her wedding ring, a wide band sparkling with marcasite chips (my grandmother's was just a thin, plain gold circle: another sign of the difference between young women and old, glamorous and workaday, that I tucked away in my memory); my mother's mah-jongg games, her weekly trips to the hairdresser, the scarves tied under her chin that protected her teased-up hairdo, the wide elastic cinch belts she put on when she got dressed up, and even the "housedresses" she wore when she wasn't up to going anywhere, shapeless flowered garments that seemed to have been invented especially for women like my mother, clothes meant to be worn in the daytime, at home, but perfect for sleeping or "just resting" in – all of these were extraordinary to me, glamorous symbols of adulthood, of *womanhood*. And I aspired to this version of womanhood the way some children dream of being firemen or ballet dancers – something real in the world but still thrilling and distant, something only the lucky few would get to do, to be, but which it stood to reason almost anyone would want.

I have my mother's wedding ring now – she replaced it with a platinum and diamond band years ago – and I wear it along with seven other rings, including my own wedding band, which looks a lot like my grandmother's. But despite all the rings – and all the bracelets (four on a slow day, but otherwise as many as ten) – and the high heels I love, and plenty of other loud and clear call-and-response symbols, I never feel I have attained that grown-up female glamour that my mother emanated. I feel much more like my grandmother, even though I'm ten years younger now than she was when I was born, and despite my still wild, still long, still-dark-brown hair – streaked blond these days, thanks to Chris, the young man who's always telling me I sound just like his mother (he highlighted her hair, too, he reported happily) – and my readiness to get down on the floor to play with my daughter. Not to mention all my own teeth and the fact that I wear my progressive multifocals in cool black frames. I'm energetic and busy and competent and bossy (my grandmother calling my father bossy was the pot calling the kettle black); there's nothing delicate about me that anyone can *see*.

Anyway, I was never a young mother, as my mother was. When my daughter was born, I was the age my mother was when I was sixteen. I'd been living alone since I'd left my parents' house at twenty. By the time Grace came along, I'd been supporting myself and looking after myself for eighteen years. I could cook like my grandmother. I could, I thought, do anything my grandmother had done. She thought so too, and she was proud of me. *Balebusteh*, she called me – a real homemaker. And I was, even though the home I was making was only for myself. She would have enjoyed seeing me turn it into a home for a husband and a child, too. But by the time I married she was beginning to drift away, and by the time she felt the baby kick – she was in the hospital then, for the second time since the start of my pregnancy, and I stood as close to her bed as I could and held her hand on my belly – she wasn't really with me.

I was grateful then that I had told her I was pregnant before I let almost anyone else know, less than a week after my first missed period, because that moment between us, so early in my pregnancy, turned out to be one of her last entirely lucid ones, and she had been so joyful in it.

Grace was fourteen weeks old when Glen and I flew with her to New York and I put her in my grandmother's arms. She had been in and out of the hospital for months; there was almost nothing left of her, and it was too late for her and Grace. She didn't know whose baby she was holding, and the day after our visit she didn't remember that anyone had been there.

That was on October first. On January tenth, she died in her sleep, in the middle of the day, in her own apartment. She had just asked the young woman who took care of her to bring her a glass of water, and – as she did so often then – she fell asleep as soon as she had spoken. Her caretaker stood watching her breathe for a minute, then went to the kitchen to fill a glass. When she came back with it, Grandma was gone.

She would have been ninety-six on her next birthday. In two months – two months minus one day – I would be thirty-nine. Grace was five days short of seven months.

. . .

These numbers matter to me in a sort of magical way.

The age my grandmother was in 1955, the year I was born – this is a magic number, the kind of magic most people recognize. You hear it all the time: "I can't believe I'm now the age my mother was when she got married!" or "This is how old my father was when I was born" or " . . . when I turned sixteen" or " . . . when he died."

When I turned twenty-two, I couldn't help thinking, marveling, "This is how old my mother was when I was born!" But really I have never felt the age my mother was the way she *was* it; that is, I was never nineteen – my mother's age when she married my father – the way she was nineteen. At nineteen I was finishing up at Brooklyn College and writing poetry and seeing three different people at the same time, juggling dates and hoping not to screw up, plotting my escape to freedom, to the Village, to be a starving artist – my single-minded goal. I was never twenty-two, her kind of twenty-two, either: by then I'd been living in the Village in the garret of my dreams for two years; I had already worked at and quit three jobs – I'd worked in publishing and as a wire service reporter – and I was writing short stories no one wanted to publish and earning a living as a freelance copyeditor. I was taking care of myself. I cooked rice and beans for dinner, I made coffee every morning in a percolator (back home, in Brooklyn, my mother was still using instant) and I had a much-older boyfriend, a writer, whom I had no intention of marrying. I had no intention of marrying anyone, ever. I told this to my grandmother, who worried, and who kept worrying for years – until I was in my late thirties and finally did marry, surprising both of us. She had been talking for years by then about how it was *no good to be alone in old age*, wondering aloud how my grandfather could have been thoughtless enough to leave her. She was eighty-five when he died, suddenly, of a massive stroke (and he was probably at least ninety-five, though we never knew for sure, since his age was a secret he'd kept when he was first courting her, certain that her family would disapprove, and felt obliged to stick by through all the decades that followed).

You'd think it would be just as hard for me to identify with my grandmother, who after all was married at fifteen and a mother a year later, but it's always been much easier, because even at fifteen she seemed grown-up – the way she told it, the way she looks in photographs, the way I think of her – in a way my mother didn't, even in her twenties. Married at fifteen, she seemed independent, tough, taking care of things and taking charge of things. She'd arrived alone in this country two years earlier – she made her way here alone, on "the boat," as she called it, seasick the whole time and still courted by boys. One of them gave her a handkerchief, which she still had, and showed me when I was a child, more than five decades later.

In my twenties, living in New York, getting by on freelance work, eating cheap meals, I spent hours on the phone with my grandmother. We talked the way I never talked to my mother; the way my mother never talked to her.

These were the years we were closest. She was in her early eighties, a great-grandmother already many times over, my grandfather still alive and keeping her company in his abstracted way. I was single, figuring I'd stay that way, and six decades younger, but somehow the gaps and differences between us seemed too small to mean anything. Late at night, when my grandfather was asleep, we would exchange stories, confessions, secrets, advice.

It was a complex friendship, not just because we were grandmother and granddaughter – that is, not just because we were *any* grandmother and granddaughter – but because, for starters, I was becoming the one who took care of her and my grandfather when they needed care taken. I was the one who took them to the doctor and made charts to help them remember when to take which medicine. But I never felt that shift of power adult children are said to feel with their aging parents: she was still the wiser one, the one who knew things, the one I turned to. I was just the practical assistant. The ways I could help her were of much less consequence than the ways she could help me.

What she felt, I know, was that the practical help I offered was less important and less meaningful than our conversations. What she required of me that mattered was my listening when she complained or worried about my grandfather; or complained or worried about one of her children, or one of the other grandchildren. Or when she confessed that she was angry, still, with her own mother, dead since my mother's childhood; or when she went back over – slowly, adding a detail here or there – a choice she'd made as a young wife, a young mother, a daughter trying to do right by the mother she disliked and feared. *I did the best I could*, she would insist finally, although I never said she hadn't.

Also complicated: that we had my childhood in common, a childhood no one else seemed to remember. If I tried to talk about it with my mother, she would cry. But my grandmother was matter-of-fact about those years: she'd been there, I'd been there, we'd been through it together. That she was willing to talk about it, as often and as thoroughly as I needed her to, mattered as much to me as anything else about our conversations, as anything else about *her*. If she sometimes saw things differently than I did, if she had her own theories about what had happened, and why, this meant less to me than her willingness to talk about them.

But there was a further complication. By this time I held her largely responsible for the shape my mother was in in my childhood. That I knew she hadn't done my mother harm on purpose meant that holding her responsible didn't equal hating her for it. I knew she *had* done the best she could. I knew this in a way I couldn't know it about my own mother – not because my mother hadn't done her best, but because her mistakes were made on me. That I couldn't quite forgive her as I could forgive my grandmother is testimony to the ferocious need of a child for her mother, more ferocious than understanding, insight, wisdom, sense.

For my mother, then, I could feel compassion only when I imagined her as a child. But this could lead to trouble – yet another complication – since my anger, if I concentrated on my mother's childhood, might turn toward my grandmother, whom I loved too much and to whom I was too grateful to allow myself to become angry. And even though I tried sometimes, I couldn't keep flipping back through the generations, locating my anger with her mother, say – who had neglected *her*, I knew – because I couldn't ever fully imagine my grandmother as a child. It was inconceivable to me that she had ever been one.

My mother, on the other hand, I could easily imagine at four, at eight, at twelve. Not only were there photographs to back up the stories my grandmother told, but the stories themselves were so detailed, so specific and concrete and elaborate, I thought of them the way I thought of the books I loved, which is to say: real, true, alive. My mother as a little girl – my grandmother's version of my mother as a little girl – was realer and more alive to me than my mother as a mother in her twenties and early thirties.

I knew my grandmother had to have been a child once too, but the stories she told me about life in the *shtetl* were general and vague – *life was hard, the Cossacks would come sometimes and we'd hide (Were you poor?* I'd ask and she'd nod, *Poor? Sure, everyone was poor)* – nothing like the stories that began on the ship, on the crossing. The oldest extant photograph of her was taken not long after she arrived in the U.S., and in her big feathered hat and long dress, her big bosom and fluffy hair, she looked to me like a middle-aged woman (and if I did try to imagine her as a child, what I saw in my mind was just a smaller, not a younger, version of this bosomy, solemn-looking, middle-aged teenager. It was hopeless. I couldn't make her young).

For my first book, a novel about an old woman contemplating the end of her life and casting back over nine decades to piece together something that will make sense to her, I had to invent a childhood for the protagonist, whose biography bore certain resemblances to my grandmother's. The pleasure I took in this – in creating my character's childhood – was almost shocking to me. But then I suppose it was shocking, in a way, that my first book should have been about someone over sixty years older than I. This never occurred to me. I spent long days inhabiting the world of an eighty-nine-year-old woman – thinking her thoughts, worrying her worries, reliving the past I'd invented for her. I would get up from my desk chair at the end of the day bent and aching, and not only from having sat for so long. I had become my old woman, Rivke – some combination of my grandmother and myself, or myself as I imagined I might have turned out had I been born in Poland in the nineteenth century, had never been educated, had been faced with some of my grandmother's choices. I slipped into her skin; for months and months – for two years – I lived in her head.

When I finished writing it and told my agent that I was weary of this, exhausted and heartsick, glad to be done with it at last, ready to turn my attention to writing about young people, Marian – who has been my friend for many years – laughed at me. She said, "What do you know about young people?"

· · ·

The contradiction is perplexing: a woman who thinks of herself as a girl and yet knows nothing about being young – who was comfortable writing her way through the mind and heart of an old, old woman.

My grandmother considered that book – rightly   a tribute to her. She understood instinctively and thoroughly what it meant to make fiction of the bits and pieces of "real" life. She would come to my readings in New York the year the book came out and listen to me reading aloud the made-up details of my character's childhood and youth, her marriage and motherhood, and she would murmur, loud enough to make the people around her laugh, "It's true, it's all true."

Later she would wonder – the way I have wondered about my own life, after writing stories that took and twisted parts of it, made characters and places up out of whole cloth, discarded people who had "really" been there – "Did that happen or is that something from your book?" and "Was that me or was that Rivke who did this?"

To say that my grandmother and I were close doesn't begin to account for our relationship. We were co-conspirators.

My grandmother, who never went to school – not in Poland and not in the U.S. – and spoke a mixture of English and Yiddish (often slipping from one to the other without noticing, even after eighty years here), whose knowledge of literature was limited to The Forward's printing of Isaac Bashevis Singer's stories in Yiddish, was for years my staunchest supporter in my determination to live as a writer, to spend my days at it whether I was successful or not.

My parents were too worried about me to encourage me in this plan. My father wanted me to get a job and write in my spare time – he was always naming writers who'd lived this way – and although later on he changed his mind (and, in the way my father does everything, he changed his mind wholeheartedly, decreeing that I had to make writing my main occupation, and offered help of every kind he could think of so that I could do just that), when I was in my early and mid-twenties, living on Christopher Street and digging through the pockets of all my clothes for change I might have overlooked, only my grandmother supported me.

Sometimes literally supported me, for from time to time she would slip me money from the savings accounts she'd scrimped all her life to build up. Once she cashed in a CD when it came due and gave it to me – thousands of dollars, the most money I had ever had at once and ever would have until I got my first grant. She told me to take some time off from freelancing and concentrate only on my writing for as long as the money lasted – something no one else has ever done for me (unless you count an institution, the NEA or the Ohio Arts Council or any other foundation that has sent me a check, as someone).

It is perfectly fair to say that I would not be who and what I am without my grandmother's involvement in my life. That old woman –

old, as I saw her, every day of my life – helped to *make* me myself. Why should it be surprising then that it is she with whom I identify, she I use as my marker – my magic marker! – of each milestone. And of every stone between.

Here is what I tell myself when I start to feel uneasy about my advancing age: that forty-seven is nothing. *Nothing.* My grandmother, Yetta Weingrovitz Weiss, was interesting, lively – a *force* – for close to five decades *after* that marker.

Besides, I have Grace, who has helped me become myself in another way, who is a force as powerful as my grandmother's in my life – and who says, when I start muttering about getting old: "You're not even fifty. You're in the middle."

"So what's old?" I ask her.

"Seventy," she says with confidence. "You're not old till you're seventy."

• • •

My mother is going to be seventy next year, but for a change it doesn't matter what Grace says. I don't, can't, think of her as old. She has been young my whole life. Just as my grandmother was always old.

It is as impossible for me to believe that she will be seventy in March as it was for me to believe my grandmother had ever been a little girl. That is, I know it's true, but I can't *feel* it to be true – I can't feel it in my bones – which makes it unimaginable and thus impossible.

I don't have to imagine my mother as a very young woman, an innocent, just starting out in her life, for not only was she precisely that in my childhood, but there are times she seems that way to me even now. She has been just starting out in her life for as long as I can remember.

In my childhood, my mother seemed to me younger than anybody else's mother (though she couldn't have been, I'm sure, at a time when so many women had their children in their early twenties; nevertheless, I remember very well that that was how it *seemed,* and that I was proud of it). I remember her twenty-ninth birthday, two weeks after my seventh. I remember telling everyone at school that it was my mother's birthday, and I remember the children who laughed at me, and the ones who looked at me with pity because I thought my mother's birthday was an occasion worth a fuss. I don't remember why I thought it *was*, except that it seemed marvelous to me that she was still in her twenties, "still young."

Perhaps what I was marveling over was that, at twenty-nine, my mother was still in her cocoon, and that I understood this to be unusual, even extraordinary. "Understood" in a way that had nothing to do with knowledge. There was so little I knew then! Unlike my daughter, as a child I felt I was always in the dark. The adults – my father and my grandmother – told me as little as they could manage. That's how it seemed then; I always felt that they were holding something back, that there were secrets. But it's possible they told me all they knew, that they were in the dark too.

Perhaps when I say "marvelous" I mean "full of wonder, amazing," not "glorious." Because it *was* a wonder, it *was* amazing: how hard it must have been for my mother, almost three full decades along in her life, to be still tucked away, not yet ready for flight. Still not fully formed into the being she would ultimately become, the ready-for-the-world creature that she must have known (I am sure she knew, and sure that was part of what kept her hidden, silent, sleeping, and in tears much of the time when she was awake) she would have to emerge as, eventually. She must have been frightened.

What kept her in the cocoon for so long? My grandmother, protecting the delicate little creature within, but failing to let her catch a glimpse of light, a breath of air?

My grandfather, by omission – by his benign absence, leaving my grandmother to do as she wished, or as she thought right?

My father, whom my mother married at nineteen, emerging only halfway – if that – and blinking in the light, then doing her best to slip back inside where it was safe?

But after all, sooner or later, the cocoon is made to wither away, and finally to disintegrate.

As it did. As my mother worked her way out slowly, bit by bit.

At twenty-two, she had a daughter, and in the home movie that charts our path from hospital to car, and car to home, it is my grandmother who carries me. My father and my grandmother must not have trusted her with the baby. Or she didn't trust herself. She told me years ago that she confided in her doctor her fear that she wouldn't know how to take care of a baby, and that he said, "Any moron could take care of a baby." She wept for days over this, and she believed him: believed she must be something less than a moron.

Throughout her twenties and half of her thirties she was severely depressed, on and off medication, in and out of what we thought of as remissions though we didn't use the word. We'd count the days, then weeks, between episodes of the worst depressions, the ones that drove her back into her room, into the dark, under the covers, into silence.

The second half of her thirties she spent looking around, trying to make sense of the world. It was as if she were a newborn. She was tentative with me; she wasn't quite sure what to do with herself. She'd been in college briefly before she had married; she'd done a little office work, taught piano – she hadn't imagined her way into a life. She didn't keep house or cook. She seemed puzzled, curious and doubtful – this is mostly how I remember her from my teens. As a new friend to me, interested in me for what seemed to me the first time, but surprised by everything, and entirely innocent.

I started college, still living at home, at sixteen. And she began to work, first as a volunteer and then for pay, at a school for "special needs" children. She was good at it, and she enjoyed the work – she loved being with the children, and she threw herself into it, this first real work she'd ever had. The pay, once she was paid anything, was hardly more than minimum wage. She was the "assistant teacher," the one without a degree, without experience.

By the time I was in my junior year, my mother had joined me at Brooklyn College. We would wave to each other across the Quad. Her friends would always be taken aback to find out – and I made sure they did – that she had a daughter my age. They knew she was "a little older," but she looked and seemed so young, they thought the gap was a much smaller one. And when I look at photographs from then, it surprises me too: she does look like a college student; she doesn't look a bit out of place with her shoulder-length hair neatly parted in the center, her big sunglasses, her crocheted purse on her shoulder.

She was not invisible. She was middle-aged by then, but she had the untouched look that only someone who has spent most of her life inside a cocoon could have. She was beautiful, and she was full of enthusiasm. She was just getting started.

She was a straight-A student at Brooklyn College, studying psychology. She had intended to study Special Ed, but once she started school, her ambitions enlarged. And enlarged again. After graduating, she decided against applying to grad school in clinical psych, on which she had been focusing: she would go to medical school, she decided, and become a psychiatrist like those who'd helped to inch her out into the light.

She was younger then, with her brand-new B.S. in psychology, than I am now, and she was younger still, inside and out, than her chronological age would suggest – but she was ancient by U.S. med schools' standards. She made a leap then, which was inconceivable if you pondered the place she'd been in a decade before, and decided to go to school in Mexico.

She took a "complete immersion" Spanish class, because her courses – and her textbooks and her tests – would all be in Spanish. She took a deep breath and she went – off to Mexico, to live all by herself for the first time in her life, a butterfly set free.

My father, bless him, paid her way, found her an apartment, phoned her every day and visited every couple of weeks. She did very well in school, which surprised no one.

There were key ways in which those of us who knew, knew that she hadn't flown entirely free: it was my father who bought the groceries, during his visits; she never spoke the Spanish she knew so well – she would only nod to her landlady, to show that she understood every word she said. There were plenty of American students around to talk to, so she didn't live in silence – but she never fully lived in the world around her, either.

Still, back in the U.S., back in New York City, where she did her "externship" years in one hospital after another – the clinical portion of her training – and then, after a while, her residency in psychiatry, she did fine. Better than fine. She was chief resident at her hospital in Manhattan. She won awards for best patient care. And at the graduation banquet for psychiatric residents, for which Glen and Grace and I flew in to New York, everyone involved in the program came to our table to let me know, and to tell my father once again – as they had told him every time they'd met him over the last few years – how valued my mother was, and how loved.

In order to practice, my mother, like all graduates of foreign medical schools, still needs to pass certain exams – and she has yet to pass one that stands between her and her future. It is impossible to think of her as old when she is planning for this future, when she spends all of her time studying.

But she no longer looks young: at sixty-nine, at last, she looks middle-aged. These days she dyes her hair, which would otherwise be gray, we assume, though we don't know for sure, since she has been dying it since the first few gray hairs began to show up, when she was about the age that I am now. My own first stray gray hairs have turned up, and I regard them with pride (I told Chris not to mess with them when he put in the blond highlights, which made him laugh and shake his head): the gray in my hair is the one sign of aging I don't mind. I find myself wishing I could point them out to my grandmother (*see? I'm catching up with you*).

My mother looks middle-aged but she's not really even in the middle yet – she's still near the beginning, catching up to herself.

Like Grace, working her way from grief through ambivalence to the occasional flash of joy over her birthdays, my mother has worked her way backward through the expected passages of time: she has gone backward by going forward. She is living proof that time doesn't have to be the enemy.

4

It is now one week before her birthday, and Grace's ambivalence is tipping back toward terror. She doesn't want to be away from me. She says when I leave her at a friend's house and walk out the door, she feels she's "hanging off the edge of a cliff and you're not going to be there to catch me." And what's the cliff? I ask her. "My own life," she says.

But you want your own life, I remind her.

"I do. I really do," she says. "I want to grow up. But" she lunges forward, throws her arms around me – "I want my life with you too. That's what I *need*."

Part of this, I know, is that school has just ended, and the days without structure loom ahead – days without structure she's been looking forward to all year. But like growing up, the chance to fill her own days as she wishes is both thrilling and alarming. In an effort to help, I've built in a little structure for her. I let her choose two week-long day camps, and so she's spending a week at the humane society, in a program called "Humanitarians of the Future," and a week doing Kabuki theater. Then there are her guitar lessons, swimming, horseback riding, twice-weekly standing dates with Kristin.

Still, her anxiety is palpable. Ambivalence, it turns out, makes things more difficult.

But of course this should not be news to me.

· · ·

This should not be news is an understatement. The times of greatest upheaval in my life have been the times when I was being pulled in two directions at once.

Ambivalence sounds like something in the middle, the calm, the gray area where two ideas or feelings meet to have a reasonable conversation – but it's a battleground. The only thing it's the middle of is a war between yourself and yourself. And war, as we all know, is hell. Or rather – as my daughter the phrasemaker has noted – it's *difficult and exciting.*

I remember very well the feeling I had at thirteen that I was at the beginning of something, staring into the face of mysteries and restlessly, tensely ready for them to unveil themselves to me. It seemed obvious that there was a great drama ahead, that my first steps into this drama, my life as a woman, would be announced by the sounding of trumpets – that the path I was to take through it would unspool like a strip of carpet rolling out as I put one foot in front of the other.

But at the same time, even as I imagined this beginning, with anxiety and something that was not quite longing – enthrallment? anticipation? – I saw I was also at the beginning of the *end* of something else. Once I set foot on that red carpet, heard that fanfare blow, I would be leaving behind something I wasn't sure I was quite ready to leave.

That place of *almost* ready – that precipice between beginnings – I think of now as the first Change.

But it wasn't until I actually began menopause myself that I saw how much the two Changes are alike, and recognized that it's no accident of nature that these two major female rites of transition are said to be marked by violent swings of moods, rages and gloom, giddiness and irritability, dissatisfaction, tears, heat that comes on suddenly and just as suddenly passes, skin and hair changing their texture, aches that can't be explained, tenderness and ferocity.

My "childbearing years" – as that long period of variously reliable fertility is so absurdly called, even in a woman who doesn't bear a child until twenty-five such years have passed, and has no intention of doing so again during the nine years before they grind to a halt; even for a woman who never bears a child, by circumstance or choice (and so many women I know have found the choice itself so agonizing!) – began when I was thirteen: thirty-four years of estrogen pumping through my veins, estrogen manufactured here at the home factory, strictly kosher and one hundred percent natural and organic but nevertheless mind- and body-altering. Thirty-four years under the influence.

Christiane Northrup, the author of *The Wisdom of Menopause*, suggests that the "symptoms" of menopause have to do with the shedding of states of mind that are necessary during the childbearing years – states of mind that are fueled by estrogen as surely as estrogen supports cell growth. Estrogen, Northrup says, is all about the biological imperative toward caretaking.

As I write this, it strikes me for the first time that my mother was menopausal right around the time she decided to go to med school – that for my mother, menopause was freeing in a way she was not even aware of. Whatever had been tugging on her – the sense that she should be taking care of other people, whether she had or could, or hadn't and couldn't – was lifted, finally. She was coming into herself at last.

I know it's more complicated than that, and not just for my mother. But the freeing up from that biological imperative has to play a part – and Northrup remarks in passing that it shouldn't be surprising that many women get cranky postmenopausally: their families expect them to continue to take care of them – to take care of everything – at a time when estrogen production is slowing down, the fuel is running out. And nearly out of fuel, we are expected to keep chugging along in the same old way.

Perhaps the first Change, from girlhood to earliest womanhood, is "about hormones" in more than the simple ways we've always assumed. Yes, our bodies are changing and we're separating from our parents. But we're also getting a hormonal glimpse at what's ahead, and why wouldn't that make us moody, angry, hard to get along with?

I've been thinking a lot lately about what it was like when estrogen first kicked in for me, at the beginning of that long haul: the year I listened to *Bookends* every day, the year I began to argue with my father, to whom I had never once before "talked back." He handled this maturely, as so many fathers do: he stopped talking to me. And so I became friends with my mother, which was also new.

It would be a while yet before I'd figure out that I could break my parents' rules (*what can they do, anyway?* I asked myself at fifteen, as I broke rule after rule – ignored curfews, rode on the back of Steve Schecter's motorcycle, went places I had been forbidden to go, saw people I'd been forbidden to see, stayed out all night or nearly all night and then came home barefoot, long dress dragging along the sidewalk, shoes and house keys lost, singing the songs I'd been listening to all night by Poco or the Dead or the Airplane or Hot Tuna – *what are they going to do? kill me?*). At thirteen, though, I began to test the rules a little, to see how far I could push them. Not very far, I found out. Not yet, not then. But each time I pushed, I pushed a little harder – talked back a little more, dressed a little more provocatively, flaunted my new self, my *womanhood*, just a little more aggressively.

What was just ahead was an explosion, but this was the tinderbox. I was only beginning to find out how combustible it – I – was. By seventeen I would have made my historic trip ("running off," as my father still calls it) to Europe with Russell. By then I had a hundred and fifty rock concerts under my belt – by then I was even singing in a band myself, at the occasional Sweet Sixteen party but mostly just for fun in Russell's basement room, wearing tiny blue jean cut-off shorts and a hot pink stretchy halter top, looking for all the world (it seems to me now; it seemed to my father then) like a teenage hooker, or else transparent peasant blouses and skirts that looked like (and maybe really were) petticoats. The entries in the journal I kept then (the only time in my life, other than during my pregnancy and Grace's infancy and early childhood, that I have kept a journal) can break my heart for my young, endangered, foolish, brutally unhappy self, and make me gasp as I never would have in the years before I became a mother: how did my parents live through it? Surely it would kill me if Grace behaved as I did.

But that was later, the explosion – and later still, the explosion over, when the smoke settled, remarkably enough, everyone was still alive.

. . .

Grace is better prepared than I was for what's ahead. Much better. I was as ill-prepared for the first Change as I was for this second one. It wasn't that I didn't know, by the time I was ten or eleven, that I'd get my period, grow breasts, "become a woman" – I'd heard all about it: there'd been a movie, either in Girl Scouts or in school, maybe both. My mother and I had had a talk, and there was a box of Junior Kotex in the linen closet, ready for me. It was a year before I had to get the box out, which was embarrassing. By then – when I was thirteen – all the girls I knew already had their periods.

But even though I was "ready," waiting impatiently, I had no idea what was ahead, how much things were going to change. Nobody tells you that, not in a way that means anything, anyway – the same way no one prepares you for the other Change. I know I felt about menopause the way I felt about menstruation. I was aware that it was coming, I even knew what the "symptoms" would be, and I knew it would feel symbolically important, but it all seemed so theoretical to me. It was as if I didn't believe it was going to happen to *me*, not to the me I already knew.

You'd think I would have known better (that is, I didn't have the excuse of extreme youth and ignorance this time around), but I suppose I imagined that by the time menopause "hit" – that was how I thought of it, as an attack – I would be someone else. Despite the lesson of my grandmother, despite my own convictions, I believed in the universe of the Others.

Just as I believed that about entering puberty.

There may be no help for this. No one can be well-enough prepared for either Change, the one that ushers in your "childbearing years" or the one that ushers you out of them. There are plenty of experiences that you can be prepared for only if you have already been through them. I remember thinking, when I was pregnant, after I knew for sure, at twenty weeks, that I had felt Grace moving inside me – Ah, if I ever do this again, I'll know what it is the first time it happens, because I was certain then that for weeks I had been feeling something I had not been able to identify, waiting for the feeling to become more obvious, so I could name it. This happened when I felt my first labor pains, too. I thought, Oh, so this is what it's like, and promised myself that if I ever had a baby again, I'd remember that this pain feels different from any other kind of pain, feels like this (a hollow promise, since I had no intention of having another child). Really what I meant – though I lied even to myself, because it seemed so crass – was that I'd remember what it felt like well enough to write about it, that maybe I'd be the one who would finally describe it so that someone who hadn't felt it would really and truly know what it was like.

I was not the one. As it turns out, I haven't even tried. I've come to believe that there are some things that really are beyond words – even unerringly chosen words, strung together beautifully, strung together perfectly (as if there were a mathematical equation that dictated the perfection – the possibility of which I have put so much faith in for so much of my life).

When Grace and I talk about what it will be like for her to be a teenager, I don't tell her that there are some things that are going to take her completely by surprise, that she will feel out of control, that her own emotions will constantly surprise her. That sometimes she won't even know herself.

I don't tell her that she will have to ride this change like a wave, rolling in as she stands waist-deep in the ocean watching for waves, ready to ride them. That she will have to ride this one even though this one – she'll see for herself when it's upon her – is too big to handle; that she'll have no choice but to trust that her instincts will carry her, or else trust the wave, big as it is – trust that it won't do her any harm, will just knock her about a bit, maybe even turn her upside down, smack the wind out of her, scare her half to death before she lands on her feet, shaken. I can't tell her that both kinds of trust – in herself, in the wave – have to do more with hope and luck than with anything she can really count on.

But at least she knows it's coming. I had no idea. I wasn't watching for a wave; I wasn't even in the ocean – I was still on the sand, daydreaming. And it just came at me.

• • •

Six weeks ago, I wrote a note to myself about the way I thought I might begin this section, these last few pages of the part of this book that's about aging, both Grace's and mine.

Start here? I wrote. *Something like: My next birthday will be my first officially postmenopausal one, since a woman is not considered postmenopausal, no matter what her hormone levels suggest, until she has passed twelve months without a period.*

But two weeks later, while I was writing about Grace's ambivalence toward her approaching ninth birthday, I had an "episode of bleeding" – the term invoked by the nurse practitioner who answered my call to the doctor. Because of my FSH levels and because it had been many months since my last period – I wasn't sure exactly how many (for which I was scolded by the nurse), but I thought eight or nine and maybe even ten – and because I was "insisting on going natural" (the nurse practitioner again), which meant the bleeding was much more surprising (women on hormone replacement therapy often bleed postmenopausally), an endometrial biopsy was ordered. For ten days after the biopsy, I worried that there *was* something wrong, and even though I didn't say a word to Grace about my worry (which must in itself have seemed alarming to her, since there is *nothing* I don't say a word about), she was worried too. She stuck close to me; she didn't want to spend time at her friends' houses.

As it happened, it wasn't anything to worry about. And thirty days after this first "episode of bleeding" – thirty days which brought me to yesterday – I began to bleed again. *Thirty days!* I said when I called the doctor, and the nurse practitioner, a different one this time, said it sounded like I was menstruating.

Yes, I said, it did.

So it emerges that my next birthday, my forty-eighth, will not be my first postmenopausal one, since even if these last two months turn out to be an anomaly, I am supposed to start counting all over again, starting today. This time I'll try to keep track (the nurse practitioner said, "Please do").

If I don't bleed again for the next twelve months, I will be "through menopause." In the meantime, I am neither here nor there, neither this nor that. I was irritated for several hours yesterday, which was how long it took for me to understand what was making me so irritable. It wasn't that I figured it out, either – it was more of a eureka when Grace blew up at me because I urged her to go with the flow of the day, the not-knowing if the friend she wanted to see was coming over or not, which depended on circumstances out of the friend's control (i.e., parents). "I just want to *know*, one way or the other, so I can get on with it!" she finally shouted at me.

Well, we were both hot and tired, too. We're having a hot June this year – as hot as the June the year Grace was born. I remember lying on a blanket in the backyard for hours, days, just waiting, wanting her to be born already, sick of that final stage of pregnancy, sick of dreaming of my baby but not yet being able to see her, sick of thinking all the time about being a mother but not being one yet, and resenting for the thousandth time that I had somehow landed in Ohio – in the middle of nowhere, as I think of it even after fourteen years – so far from the ocean where I spent every hot day of my youth. Where I profoundly – sorely – wished my daughter would be able to spend every hot day of her youth.

This is no place to be pregnant, no place to raise a child, I kept thinking in those final days, landlocked, sweating, swollen, ready.

But it's worked out just fine. I miss New York City every day of my life here, and on summer days, I miss Brighton Beach and Rockaway. But we go to the pool every summer day, after I've finished the day's writing, and Grace – unlike me at her age – is a good swimmer. I didn't learn till I was thirty-five, despite all those summers in the ocean, riding waves, gliding back to shore on them. Grace taught herself to swim at our old pool when she was five, watched over and applauded by Blanche and Erika and their mothers. At the new pool, she takes lessons from a patient, gentle, and good-humored young man named J. R. She dives, she invents stylish jumps that involve last-minute turns and arms and legs theatrically posed, and I watch her with as much pleasure as I have ever watched anyone do anything. Just the other day, as I stood in neck-deep water, I watched her go off the high dive for the first time. She didn't know I was watching; she hadn't told me she was going to try it. I had been sitting on the grass near the shallow end with one of my students, talking about her impending move to New York – Shari was about to take her own leap into thin air, carrying a suitcaseful of her smart, witty short stories – and we got too hot to stay put, so we slipped into the pool, still talking, and walked together toward the deeper water, and I happened to look up and to the left, toward the diving well, and saw Grace just as she made her way out to the edge of a board so high off the ground I would never in a million years consider climbing up to it, and take a flying leap into twelve feet of water.

And if she isn't in the ocean often enough to be instantly at ease in it when we do get to a beach every few years, either back in New York or down in Georgia, visiting with her father's family (whom I have begged to drive to the coast), after the first hour or so, she's all right – more than that: confident, brave – and it's something, really, to stand beside her while the waves crash around us, and to race them back to shore, then collapse together on the sand.

This hot summer, I'm missing the ocean more than ever, and even if it's an illusion, I keep thinking it would soothe me, *fix* me, if I could spend a week or two on a beach, if I could just get away from here – the middle of nowhere.

"The middle of nowhere is all in your mind," a woman I trust told me when I complained to her. "It's the not knowing one way or another where *you* are that's getting to you, not Columbus." And she smiled – she's a New Yorker too. "Or not *only* Columbus."

She was right. *Nit ahin, nit aher,* as Grandma used to say – that's what drives me crazy. The neither-here-nor-there, the this-nor-that of it. It's what drives me crazy about Columbus, too. It's not a small town, but it's not a real city either.

I have always liked things to be clear – to be one thing or another. One *way* or another. And now look at me: I don't even know if I'm still fertile (however marginally) or not.

"They call it menopause, not menostop," said the trustworthy fellow–New Yorker. Her name is Marlene Kocan, and she is someone I think of as very wise, and not only because she often stops me in my tracks with a wisecrack.

"All right," I said, "I get it." I'm afraid I might have sounded a little crabby, though.

The not-knowing – that gray area, the place I have decided I will call "natural ambiguity," my body's own ambivalence – I despise that. I despise it the way I despise Columbus, a town that has nothing to recommend it except a job I love and the fact that it's home now – that it has been home all these years, like it or not.

Why should Grace listen to me when I tell her to go with the flow? I've lived my whole life on the edge of my seat.

I look at her sometimes now and I see her as I see myself: poised for change, ready and not ready – both at once – for the next thing, trying to find a comfortable spot to balance on as we wait, uncomfortably. And we can't wait. The only time I have ever been able to just wait was during those last days of my pregnancy. And Grace, even at night, waiting for sleep, can't just wait. She can hardly bear to lie still. I'll come in to check on her and find her sitting up in the dark, listening to dulcimer music on her CD player, thinking so hard I can practically see her brain working. "You can't sleep if you don't rest," I'll tell her. "You have to lie down and close your eyes. Breathe deeply – that'll help."

"But I really hate that in-between time," she says. "Not asleep and not awake. I prefer to just – bang! – be asleep."

That's usually the way it happens for her, too. *In mitn derinnen*, as my grandmother would have said. Grace just gives out, all at once, mid-thought, still sitting up, her mouth open, the music tinkling and plunking on.

Having spent all of my life certain that things had to be one way or the other – that I was either a failure or a success, right or wrong, in love or not, happy or not, the perfect mother or the worst one – I am learning, not easily, the lesson of middle age: that everything is vaguer and less sure, less focused, less *fine*, more nuanced and complicated than that.

My progress, in my life as in my work, comes slowly, but steadily. I won't win any races – I've never believed the tortoise beat the hare – but I'll get done what I am meant to do, in my own way, in life and in work both.

As I prepare to turn forty-eight, as I make my way toward fifty, I know something I didn't know when I was younger – when I thought, *If only I could publish a book!* Because I did, after all, publish a book, and although it was a pleasure to have people hold in their hands what I'd worked so hard on for so long, a pleasure to put the book on my own shelf and know I'd entered that community – *people who have written books!* – that I'd yearned to be part of since I was old enough to read, it didn't matter in the way I had imagined it would: it didn't make everything right.

If only I could have a child! I thought – and then I did, and it was wonderful, even better than I had imagined it would be, but it didn't make everything right either. No more than being married did. No more than the second book did. No more than finding a way to earn my living doing something I loved did.

Nothing makes everything right. That's the lesson of my middle age, a lesson I can only hope I've learned at last – the lesson I would like to teach my daughter. Nothing makes everything anything. And if absolute clarity isn't to be had, then it isn't to be sought. If life is going to be a mix of girl and old, mother and daughter, good mother and bad, successes and failures, books on the shelf and laundry (clean and dirty both, folded and un-) mounting up in baskets on the floor in every room – if life is going to be a mix of memories and ideas, sickness and health, richer and poorer – I might as well proceed along the path without fanfare, without needing to look ahead. I might look *around*. I might pause from time to time. I might not even need to stay on the carpet all the while.

If I can teach my daughter this lesson – to be willing to go on without knowing, to enjoy the path itself, to trust herself – then I will have done my job as her mother.

It was only today that it came clear to me, all of a sudden, what it is that she's been feeling as she faces this next birthday, for which we spent the morning putting up streamers in six different colors, to represent the five friends, plus herself, with whom she has chosen to celebrate. It is the not knowing she can't bear, and fearing what she doesn't know. She'd prefer to hold on to what's familiar, even though she's sick of it, she's ready to move on – she wants to grow up. But what is growing up?

And what is growing old?

I am full of hope that having gleaned so early what most of us don't glimpse until adulthood – that time is at once fleeting and relentless, that we are ever hurtling forward, that every moment (day, month, year) is precious – the passage into middle age and onward will for Grace be a more peaceful and more graceful one than most of us are granted.

We're both watching for the next wave, each of our next waves. She's watching for hers in a way I couldn't, for I didn't even know it was coming. But even though she's watching, she isn't sure what she's watching for, what it will feel like when it comes. What it will do to her.

I want to tell her that it will roll over her, it will carry her high, it will turn her around, toss her this way and that – that it will frighten the wits out of her for a while – but when she's left standing afterwards, in deeper water certainly than she'd been in before, at a greater distance from the shore and perhaps yards down the beach, carried on the drifting tide, she will still be herself. This will not necessarily be obvious to others, but it will be true.

As it will be when the next wave comes, whatever and whenever that is. And the next.

She can swim out to sea if she chooses. She can cross over to the other side. She can go under – far, far under, to the darkest places. But she cannot leave herself behind.

She needn't fear that she will. I needn't fear that I will. I think of Yetta, herself to the end. And Sheila, my mother, who had to find herself before she could carry herself with her. But she did; she has.

I have to stop writing now – there is a birthday to be celebrated.

Hope against Hope

The soul knows for certain only that it is hungry. — SIMONE WEIL

I

My daughter is twelve weeks old when she tries to starve herself. Or perhaps I should say when she *begins* to try to starve herself, for her efforts will continue at full strength for another three months, and she will not give up the fight altogether until her first birthday.

It's possible it isn't her intention to starve herself. It's possible – some would say more than possible – that a three-month-old doesn't have *intentions* in the usual sense of the word. So let me be clear: I'm not suggesting that my infant daughter makes an active, conscious decision to begin a hunger strike. What I am suggesting is that the infant in question has something to say and has no way to "say" it – that there is something she is feeling (and she is *all* feelings now; there is nothing else for her yet) that demands to be expressed, as all feelings do, and that refusing the nourishment I offer is her only recourse to expression.

I should mention that I do not understand this at the time.

I do not understand this *not* because I am dog-tired and stupid (although surely this doesn't help) but because of something more basic: I don't want to. Of course, I don't know that, either. It will be six years before I know anything at all, and then it will be only because I have no choice, because I will find myself and my daughter lost – hopelessly lost, it will seem for a while – and I will have to go back over every turn I took that got us to the lonely stretch of road on which we're stranded. Not just lost, but broken down.

And it is the old-fashioned word, *breakdown*, that describes what happens when at the age of six and a half, midway through first grade, Grace falls apart and everything comes to a halt. When there is nothing to be done except to retrace the path upon which I had set out, set *us*, with the best intentions, and rethink every indicator light I'd missed along the way, so busy concentrating on the route I'd mapped out for us I hadn't noticed all the warning signs.

I knew what *not* to do, so I thought I knew everything. The opposite of wrong, I foolishly assumed – though *foolish* doesn't scratch the surface of this – would have to be right.

Wrong. It turns out, in fact – and I, much more than foolish, had no idea – that there are a lot more ways to go wrong than to go right.

. . .

It's funny that I was so simpleminded about Grace, when I am never simpleminded about anything, when my natural tendency is to consider all sides of every question, even the most trivial one – to dig until I strike rock and then to turn the shovel to one side and keep digging, *around* the rock. "Funny" is of course not the right word. The right word is "horrifying."

Around Grace, I had a blind spot. Not a blind *spot*. A blind acre.

Like someone careening at high speed along a highway without once turning her head to see for herself what the mirrors mounted here and there won't show her, I proceeded as if there were no possibility that there was anything I might not, could not see.

I asked myself no questions, so I was I sure I told myself no lies.

It seems extraordinary to me now, but I never even stopped to ask myself why I wanted to *have* a child. Extraordinary not because the desire strikes me as a strange one, nor because I imagine that most people ask this question of themselves – it seems to me unlikely that they do – but because there's nothing I don't ask myself. I have asked every other question, big and small, serious and silly, from significant to utterly inconsequential (Why prose, not poetry? Why this man, and why that one, but not *that* one? Why get married? Why poker and not bridge? Tolstoy, not Dostoevsky? The Yankees, not the Mets?). It's a habit, or a hobby – or an obsession (Why scotch and not bourbon? Ella, and not Sarah Vaughn? Zinnias, not marigolds? Pale pink. Katherine Mansfield. Cabochard). No choice is ever left unturned, not even an *old* choice, not even one that doesn't feel the least bit like a choice. My impulse, always, is to complicate, not simplify.

It wasn't even that I posed the question and concluded that it was unanswerable, or that the answer struck me as too obvious to be worth pondering, that I shrugged and chalked it up to the great biological imperative. It was, I think, that the desire when it bloomed in me seemed so natural, so deep-rooted and inevitable, that for once it did not occur to me that there was a question to be asked.

I did not assume that I would slip effortlessly into my new role – my new identity, new title, new sense of self – or that I would find my child endlessly interesting and the day-to-day tasks that involved her completely absorbing. I "knew" (and in this I turned out to be wrong) that I would find much of my new life tedious or irritating. I pictured myself trying to endure soccer and *Sesame Street* and toys scattered everywhere, noise and cartoons and a house in disorder, and I worried. I shuddered.

But I never doubted that I *wanted*. And I never doubted, either, that I could, would, do right by my child. I believed that I had much more love to give than I could possibly unload on the people who were in my life already. I had a surplus of love. It would go to waste if I did not find someplace I could put it.

I had a child, I think now, so I would have someone to love hugely, wildly, overwhelmingly, without a moment's break. So there would be someone, always, who wanted and needed that much love from me – from me above all. I wanted the company of such a person. Perhaps I didn't know this, perhaps I didn't say it to myself in so many words, but I wanted it, I wanted *her*, by the time I was thirty-eight and pregnant, more than I wanted anything else in the world.

. . .

And yet for a long time I didn't want to have a child. All through my twenties, writing short stories (trying to write short stories and mostly making a hash of it), I made a lot of noise about my *work*, solemnly quoting – and misunderstanding – the Yeats poem, "The Choice": *Perfection of the life, or of the work*, I mused, and as was already my longstanding habit, I explained, at length, my choice of work instead of life when anybody asked me about marriage, about children. "I know what matters most to me," I said, "and I know it can't be done with those sorts of distractions." I quoted Flaubert – that chestnut about how a writer must above all have an orderly life if he is to be original in his work – and I mentioned Henry James, my role model. Sometimes I said with a smile that I wanted to *be* Henry James. I laughed; I said I was still hoping for those dinner invitations (the trouble was, everyone I knew in those days was as poor and lived in quarters as cramped as I). I wrote all day long, first in a one-room apartment on Christopher Street (my desk shoved up against the foot of the twin bed), later in a minuscule three-room tenement on the Upper (way) East Side, my desk in the kitchen (the only room big enough to fit a desk), next to the stove and just across from the bathtub. I did my freelance work at night while watching the Yankees play on my little black-and-white TV.

I knew this wasn't how Henry James had lived, but it was as near an approximation as I could get. I wrote all day, every day – that was the main thing. That, and my knowing that it was the work, only the work, that mattered.

This lasted till I was thirty. Then – suddenly – I began to think I might want to have a child after all. That there might be a bit more to life than The Work. That I was entitled, maybe, to life *and* work. That Henry James might not be the ideal role model for a young woman. I searched for other role models and couldn't find any – not among the great dead writers, anyhow. I began in my early thirties to worship George Eliot, but my efforts to assemble a mental list of great women writers and artists who had managed to have children (and do right by them – for I didn't feel comfortable including famous suicides on such a list) failed. Undaunted, I decided that times had changed. They *had*. There was Cynthia Ozick, Alice Munro, Alison Lurie, Lore Segal – just for starters! Women only a generation ahead of me, women whose books I loved, who had done it. Why couldn't I? I could! I had been a fool, I thought.

But what now? There were no likely candidates for fathering the child I suddenly wanted so badly. And I wanted only one! Was that so much to ask? I wondered. Was that so outrageous? For a while I had a boyfriend who was eager to have children – so eager, he declared he wanted *six* – and as much as I wanted a baby before it was "too late," at thirty-four I broke up with him (it wasn't just the number that we disagreed on; he wanted his six kids raised Catholic, too).

Then for the next few years the question of whether I would have a child was an abstract one, for although I fell in love twice, I could not imagine having a child with either of those men.

I did think (or tried to think) about having a baby "on my own" – to the extent possible – but it made me sad even to consider it. Sad for the child, not for myself. I was sure I could *manage* on my own. Once I was enthusiastic about something, I knew I could be counted on to have enough energy for two. And then there was the matter of my capacity for devotion. I knew myself; I knew that if I had a child, he or she would not want for love. Besides, for the first time in my life I had a "real job," with an income I could count on, year after year – at least until I came up for tenure – and health benefits. It was even a job I enjoyed, which seemed miraculous to me after so many years of eking out a living doing freelance work I disliked and by which I was so deeply bored I sometimes fell asleep while doing it, my head dropping to the manuscript with its blue pencil markings. I'd had no idea there was something I could do to earn a living that would give me as much pleasure as teaching does, something that would seem to me *worth* doing, that actually made a difference in other people's lives. I was happier than I had ever been, thanks to this teaching job – which also, as luck would have it, provided the flexibility for me to rearrange my schedule so that I could take some time to stay home with a baby.

But I couldn't quite bring myself to seriously consider single motherhood. I told myself that while starting out hopeful and then failing was nothing to be ashamed of, *planning* fatherlessness was an act of bad faith, especially for someone whose own father had been so important to her.

And then – another miracle, following on the heels of the teaching job I took such pleasure in, and the house I bought (with the help of my parents, who had never lived in a house themselves, who were still paying rent on an apartment in Manhattan) – Glen turned up: a gentle, brilliant, serious, *good* man, with whom it was easy to imagine having a child.

And then I didn't have to imagine it any longer.

2

Pregnant, I was the happiest person alive. I loved being pregnant as no other woman I have ever met – or read or even heard about – ever has.

I loved my body, pregnant. I would stand in front of my cheval glass, naked, and turn from side to side, admiring myself. I remember how pleased I was when I began to "show" – how I would turn sideways by the English Department mailboxes and pull my shirt taut over the small rise, demonstrating my progress to anyone who paused to ask how I was doing. I didn't even mind morning sickness. I kept a supply of saltines on hand at all times (driving, teaching, writing, shopping, sleeping) once I found they stemmed the tide of nausea, but with every wave I countered with a handful of dry crackers, I was reminded – as if I could forget! – that I was pregnant, and it gladdened my heart.

In general, people seemed to think I was out of my mind. Thus I learned to keep such thoughts to myself except with my best friend, Z——, who thought I was out of my mind too but almost always kept quiet about it as a token of her affection for me.

She went with me when I bought my first maternity clothes – nice ones, *good* ones, more expensive clothes than I had ever bought before: *celebratory* clothes, I thought – as soon as I began to show a little. I strapped on the "five-month pillow" and twirled and curtseyed for her in the dressing room. She smiled indulgently at me, fingered the material – silk, linen – and looked at the price tags, laughing, and pronounced me gorgeous.

I *was* gorgeous, as far as I was concerned. I stared at myself in the mirror every day. I had Glen take photographs of me and when he wasn't around and the mood struck I set up my camera on the tripod and took pictures of myself. I took baths, not just for the comfort of the warmth and the near weightlessness – toward the end this was a blessing – but to contemplate my belly, so huge in the final months that it obscured my vision of the faucets and spout, which somehow made me laugh, and to watch my baby move under my skin. *Just* under my skin, I marveled, watching. *Inside me,* I whispered to myself. I felt sorry for everybody – male and female bodies both – who didn't have a baby living and growing inside. Poor souls, all alone in their own skin. I felt sorriest for men, all men, because they had never had the chance to share their skin this way and never would.

None of this, which sounds New Age or Goddessy, *flaky*, is typical of me. Not only am I definitely an Old Age type – I don't even read my horoscope in the newspaper – but I have never before (or since) admired my own body. It's a peasant's body, inherited from the *shtetl* Jews in Russia and Poland from whom I am descended – working women whose men studied, daydreamed, spoke softly, and kept to themselves (not unlike my Southern Baptist husband, himself descended from Georgia farmers, North Carolina preachers, and, he's almost sure, Cherokees in his paternal line). I have broad childbearing hips, sturdy legs, and big soft breasts my daughter pointed out at age three "look nothing like Barbie's" (which persuaded her, bless her good mind, that Barbies weren't realistic and weren't meant to be. "Like unicorns," she said, "or Santa. They're just for fun, right?" – so that later on, eavesdropping as she played with her friend Amira, who wasn't allowed to play with Barbies because, she told Grace, her mother didn't want her "to get the wrong idea about women," I heard my daughter say, "You mean *your* mother thinks you can't tell the difference between a real live *actual* woman and a doll?" and I was both proud and mortified; later we had our first talk about superciliousness and tact and passing judgment).

I'm short, just over five foot two – though people often think I'm taller, because I'm so robust-looking, not slight or delicate, and I have so much untamed hair (that's my theory, at any rate). In the last five or six years, I have taken to wearing high heels, too – "Barbie shoes!" Grace says of my tall silver-mirrored sandals, or my strappy pale pink suedes, or my favorites, the transparent mules with the row of pastel fabric flowers on the plastic instep strap – which bring me to five-six. But even during the years when I wore Converse All Stars or went barefoot, people would express surprise to find out how tall I "really" was, and a grad school friend insisted that this was the result of my "tall aura," by which I think she meant only that I am a New Yorker (and she had come to Iowa from Los Angeles, a world away from both the Midwest and New York), that I am argumentative and stubborn, passionate, and noisily opinionated about everything, whether I know much about it or not.

About motherhood I felt I knew a great deal, even before I had a chance to put what I knew into practice. I was a mother waiting to happen, a neighbor said soon after Grace was born. Which surprised me, not because it wasn't true, but because the woman hardly knew me. For four years we'd been waving, calling Hi to each other as we worked in our gardens. Once, when my cat died, she brought me a peach pie she'd made. And I chatted sometimes with her daughter, Emily. But that summer, she greeted me one morning as I sat in my porch swing with Grace in my arms, and said what she said, and it took me aback.

It would be another five months before my neighbor's second daughter, Anna, was born, and four years before Grace and Anna noticed each other and became playmates, so that my neighbor and I would have reason to talk regularly (though the talk consists mainly of her saying, "Send Anna home, would you?" and my saying, "Just as soon as they clean up the mess they've made"). Still, she got it – got me – right.

I remember thinking that the only thing Emily and Anna's mother had gotten wrong was the indefinite article.

I wasn't a mother waiting to happen. I was the mother waiting to happen.

. . .

I am the mother to end all mothers. I am the mother any child would wish for if she knew enough to wish before it was too late.

I say this to myself as I lie in the porch swing for hours with the baby across my chest, a giant thermal cup of ice water by my side. I say it to myself without a trace of irony.

I lie in the porch swing, on the chintz-covered living room couch, on a blanket in the yard, in the La-Z-Boy recliner in my study. I move from room to room, from indoors to outdoors, from porch to garden, the baby always in my arms, or over my shoulder, or in my lap, or on my chest. I am as content as I have ever been. (What am I talking about? I have never been content before!) The brand-new mother of a newborn, I am struck by how simple, how straightforward, how obvious the recipe for perfection – the roadmap to perfection – is. It is so obvious I cannot imagine why everyone doesn't follow it. It is only this: *meet every need.*

While pregnant, I had thought quite consciously about how wonderful it was to be able to take care of someone so completely without having to *do* anything. Just think, I marveled: all my daughter's needs were being met as I went about my ordinary business of breathing and eating and walking and sleeping and writing and reading. If only it were going to be so easy in real life! I remember thinking.

I remember that I used those words: *real life.* I meant: *it will never again be so easy to take care of her, to protect her and feed her and comfort her and keep her safe, once she is outside of me.*

But then it was. At least at first, it was.

My child was hungry: I had milk for her. She was tired: she could close her eyes and sleep for ten or fifteen minutes right where she was – lap, chest, or shoulder. I stroked her sparse, copper-colored hair; I changed her diapers; I sang her lullabies and standards and folk songs I'd last sung as a teenager, "Careless Love" and "All My Trials," and songs made famous by Patsy Cline about how crazy I was for feeling lonely, or going walking in the moonlight, or not being able to forget the past, and also songs I made up on the spot (*Welcome to your life, Grace Jane | We've been waiting for you since before we both were born*), nursed her again, and rocked her back to sleep; I watched her sleep; I bathed her (with a washcloth for the first two weeks, and then in my lap as I took my own bath each night after that); I dressed her in the tiny undershirts on which I had embroidered her four-letter monogram or rows of flowers during my last months of pregnancy – the first embroidery I'd done since high school, when I used to cover my Seafarers with bouquets of French knot flowers – or which I had tie-dyed or just dyed black, because in Columbus one could not find hipster clothes for babies (later, friends in New York sent me black T-shirts and leggings, gauzy turquoise and lime green peasant blouses, Indian print skirts, and a little black dress that gave the phrase "little black dress" new meaning).

I "wore" my baby in a sling so she could catnap or nurse while I took walks or shopped or dropped into my office to collect my mail. I never used a hand-held plastic "baby carrier" – I didn't even buy one – and I had to restrain myself from asking other women why they didn't have their babies wrapped in fabric and pressed close to them while they pushed their shopping carts through the Big Bear. I'd shiver as I heard, watched, other mothers' babies crying in molded plastic baskets swinging from their mothers' hands, or set into the shopping cart along with all the cans and jars.

Besides the sling, in which she could recline, I had a Snugli, so that she could hang upright, face to my chest for comfort. And I had a front-facing pack, too, which allowed her to be upright and look out at the world when she was of a mind to. That was the way I carried her to the state fair in late summer – seven weeks old, strapped upright against my chest, facing out, in a floppy sunhat and sunglasses, bare feet dangling. My best friend, Z——, and Glen were with us, and we just walked and walked and looked at sheep and pigs and horses, massaged our feet (Z—— and I did; Glen was disdainful) on the Footsie Wootsie machines, ate corn dogs and ice cream and funnel cakes and soberly contemplated the cow made out of sculptured butter and cheered for eleven-year-old girls riding their horses in the Western pleasure competition. I browsed through the DC love comics and Glen examined every piece of glassware in the Antiques Pavilion. Z—— and I considered all of the Amazing Products in the Multipurpose Building, and I bought one (a lifetime nail file), as I have every year since 1988.

In the many photos Glen and Z—— took of the baby and me on that day, posed in front of one or another gaudy midway ride or rigged game with its display of giant stuffed animal prizes, the Ferris wheel towering far behind us, Grace looks content; I look blissed out and done in, both.

. . .

Meet every need. It is my mantra, a formula that covers any situation that arises, slamming the lid down on the anxious self-doubt that new mothers experience, the questions that plague them all day, every day. Do I let the child cry herself back to sleep when she wakes in the night, as the books suggest, or do I go to her room and take her from her crib, nurse and rock and sing her back to sleep, no matter how recently she last cried? Using my formula, there's no crisis. She needs me; I go to her.

The formula expands to what I come to think of as the commandments, fewer than ten, of motherly perfection. *Be available. Be attentive. Watch and listen. Keep your child from hunger, want, grief, loneliness, frustration.* Who could argue with this? Or, I ask myself, this (the logical exponentiation of my formula)? *Do this from the instant the child enters the world; cease only when she lets you know she doesn't require it anymore.* And I am certain there will come a time when she won't require it – require me – anymore, not in the way she does now. I am certain, as it happens, without a sense of what I mean by certainty, for the time that I expect to come is so indistinct and distant I cannot even imagine it. What I do imagine is that when this time comes, my daughter will be carrying inside her the deposit I have made – of my unceasing attention, devotion, company – because she will have absorbed it fully in every cell of her being. She will have absorbed it the way some of us absorbed our early days – months, years – of needs unmet, of loneliness and longing. She will never be lonely, I believe, because she experienced an absolute lack of loneliness early on that she will take with her out into her life, out into the world, that will protect her from all the grief the world may offer.

I explain this to Z——, talking on the phone one day as Grace naps in my lap. "It's quite the experiment," Z—— says carefully. I agree, uncarefully. "I'm 'experimenting,' sure," I say, allowing just a little bit of sarcasm to color the word. "There's no *proof* that steady devotion is what a child needs. But what's the worst that can happen? She'll be loved too much? Poor thing!" I look down at the baby asleep across my lap, exactly where she wants to be. As soon as she wakes, she'll see me – she won't even have to cry out for me.

I am always there.

3

Grace was not an *easy* baby, what people call "a good baby" – a phrase I hated and which I kept hearing in those early weeks of motherhood. (I complained about this once, to a woman, a colleague, whom I assumed would be sympathetic: "As if there could be such a thing as a *bad* baby," I said *sotto voce*, moments after someone at a department party patted Grace's head and asked if she was *a good baby*. "Actually," my colleague – also a mother – said, "there is. Which is not to say that bad babies don't grow up to be wonderful children – " But by then I'd stopped listening; I'd written her off as a bad mother, which I knew there *was* such a thing as.)

Grace didn't sleep, or not much – fifteen minutes here and there during the day and never all the way through the night. She would be fourteen months old before she slept through the night, a straight six hours in one shot. And for the first twelve weeks of her life (the fourth trimester, the writer Anne Lamott calls this, when the baby is still not quite in the world yet, is still adjusting to being on the outside after the months of dark and warmth and muted sounds), she cried for three hours nightly, from seven to ten p.m., and nothing Glen or I did had much of an effect, although we never gave up trying. Dancing her around the living room to loud music – rock and roll or R&B or Texas swing cranked up practically as high as the stereo would go – helped for a few minutes at a time, as just plain holding her did not, or nursing her or taking her outdoors (which the books recommended) or setting her atop the clothes dryer while it ran (the books again) or taking her out for a drive, which everybody I knew *and* the books suggested (but Grace hated being in the car, strapped into her rear-facing car seat; to this day, she's never once fallen asleep while being driven anywhere). So Glen and I would take turn holding her tight and dancing wildly, leaping around the room to Aretha or the Stones or Bob Wills and His Texas Playboys – the only time in all these years that I have ever seen my husband dance.

She was a high-maintenance baby. She required plenty of attention, all day long and every few hours all *night* long. A wakeful, complicated, high-strung, and *particular* baby (there was lots of music she *didn't* like during those crying/dancing months: James Brown, for instance, which disappointed me, and Hendrix, which disappointed Glen). She made her likes and dislikes known right from the start – a baby of decided preferences and opinions.

That she wanted to be held all the time was fine with me. I *wanted* to hold her all the time. I remember once, spending a day with another mother/baby daughter pair, that first summer of the girls' lives, that when the other baby cried as soon as her mother set her down, the mother burst out crying herself and said, in despair, "But sweetie, Mommy *can't* hold you all day long!" and I felt for her – she looked wrecked; she had blue shadows under her eyes and her cheeks were sunken, her eyes brimming even before the outburst – but I also thought, with real curiosity, "Why not?"

I not only loved holding Grace, I hated having anybody else hold her. An old friend who had cheerfully surrendered her own baby daughter to anyone who had so much as *looked* interested in holding her pointed out that my possessiveness was crazy, and I said I knew it, but what was I supposed to do? It made me miserable, it filled me with anxiety, to see my baby in someone else's arms. I struggled to explain it. "Look," I said, "how would you feel if someone asked if she could snuggle for a little while with your husband? Wouldn't it seem outrageous to you if some woman said, 'Oh, my arms just ache to hold him! He's so cute! You won't mind, will you? Just for a few minutes?'"

C—— clucked impatiently at me over the phone line, long distance from Petaluma. "If my *husband* expected me to hold him every minute of the day, I'd just be grateful to have someone take him off my hands for half an hour."

I knew there were babies who didn't love being held – who arched their backs away when their mothers tried to curl them toward their chests. What if I'd had that sort of baby? I wondered. I was lucky. Grace and I both were lucky. She was a baby who wanted to be cuddled and I was a mother who couldn't cuddle her enough. I had been storing up not only love but simple physical affection all my life, just waiting for someone to lavish it on.

My daughter was the baby I would have picked out for myself if I'd been given a choice. We were made for each other – that's what I said, dreamily, jubilantly, proudly, to anyone who listened.

That's why I had a child – so that at last there would be someone who was made for me. And for whom I had been made.

• • •

I wasn't going to give up my work, of course. I knew that having a child would mean there would be less time for me to write, but that didn't seem so awful now. What good had my anxiety about The Work, my insistence that it "came first," ever done me? I was thirty-eight and I had published exactly one book – a book I was proud of, yes, but I could hardly have produced less if I hadn't insisted that writing was the only thing that counted. It was time to try an entirely different approach.

The women in my family tend to live a long time, I reminded myself. Think of Grandma. Think of Dad's Aunt Lillian, who'll be a hundred in November and still goes out dancing. On both sides of my family, the women hang on (Aunt Betty died in 1997, at a hundred and four; my father's paternal grandmother, Chia, died at ninety-seven after falling down a flight of stairs, thanks to her failing eyesight – she was otherwise healthy – and my mother's great-grandmother, Ruchel, according to my grandmother, lived to a hundred and thirteen). I was only thirty-eight, for godsakes. I had the rest of my life to write books. At worst, I would slow down for a while. Then I'd pick up again where I'd left off.

But really I didn't believe I'd have to slow down all that much. My work would simply have to move over, to make room for a child. I'd have to *move* it over. Who was in charge around here, after all?

While I was pregnant, I imagined myself working in my study as the baby slept in a wicker basket by my side. This didn't seem so unlikely. An older friend, a writer whose children were grown and gone, assured me that at the beginning "all babies do is sleep. They sleep all the time – sleep, nurse, poop. That's about it." For the first few months, at least, she swore, I'd have lots of time for writing.

No one told me that I would find it impossible to put my baby in a basket, that even while she slept I would be reluctant to put her down, to stop looking at her, touching her, marveling over her. No one told me that this would go on for months, that I would lose all interest in the fictional mother and child with whom I'd been so preoccupied until then. That when Grace slept, all I'd want to do was watch her sleep.

Not that she slept to speak of, anyway. Another thing no one told me was that some babies *don't* sleep all the time, that there are babies who don't sleep more than eight hours out of any given twenty-four, even the twenty-four hours following their births, when you'd think they'd be plenty tired. Or that "eight hours" doesn't mean eight hours *in a row*, that a baby might get her eight hours by sleeping between one and four a.m. and then again from five till seven, plus three half-hour and six scattered fifteen-minute catnaps every day.

I do remember that one woman I knew – a former student who'd managed to have two babies *and* finish her first novel in the short time since she'd graduated – mentioned that nursing a new baby was pretty much an all-day occupation. But she didn't tell me why, and I didn't take her seriously. She was a fiction writer; I was sure she was exaggerating. I know that no one sat me down and explained that the "two to two-and-a-half hours between feedings" I had read about, as I studied up for motherhood as if it were the Big Test, meant two to two-and-a-half hours from the *start* of the last feeding, not from the end, so that if you had the sort of baby who liked to take her time, who took frequent breaks to rest or look around at the world (popeyed with amazement, delight, perplexity, and shock) before she finished any single feeding, nursing might take forty minutes or more – and thus the periods between feedings could be as short as an hour and a quarter: just enough time to burp the baby, change the baby (change her diaper, yes, but possibly her clothes too, since diapers sometimes leak, and the baby herself is always leaking – dribbling, or spitting up milk), change your own shirt (because these days you are leaking too – everything you own is milky now – and/or the baby spit up just beyond the border of the cloth diaper you'd put over your shoulder before burping her), then maybe eat something, because you're famished yourself (every calorie you take in seems to go straight to the baby), not to mention incredibly thirsty, and finally close your eyes for a few minutes while the baby catnaps – logging in one of the quarter-hours toward the eight hours that seem to be all she needs – until she's hungry again.

If anyone had told me that the mother of such a baby might well be too tired and dazed (and probably too dehydrated) to do anything but contemplate her baby, I wouldn't have believed it anyway. Maybe that was why nobody bothered to say it – because what was the point?

• • •

But maybe the reason nobody told me was that nobody knew.

Motherhood – like so many things – turns out to be a little bit different for everyone who tackles it. It also turns out to be a lot of different things all at once for any *one* person.

Books about motherhood, I've noticed, mostly tend to fall into one of two camps, and both propagate the same insidious lie: that motherhood is one thing or another: either glorious, delightful, and fulfilling – pure bliss – or else (a confession made not without pride by the mother-authors) boring, painful, lonely, and endlessly frustrating. That, unlike life itself, motherhood isn't everything mixed up together. Sometimes everything mixed up together at the same time.

The lie seems to know no genre boundaries. The two sides have set up camp in books both popular and literary, in accounts both serious and comic, in the coolly journalistic and the autobiographical. It's a trend, I've told myself. It will pass, as all trends pass. It's just the latest fashion in motherhood lit.

But maybe not. Maybe the trend is toward simplification overall: toward trying to make the complex uncomplex. The way the culture looks at motherhood, I'm beginning to think, is just one piece of it – one piece of the greater simplemindedness of our time and place. So that, in the interests of simplicity, there is a spate of books by women reveling in motherhood's glories, reminding us – Career Women at the turn of the millennium – that the joy of bearing and raising our children should not be overlooked in this post-feminist era. Then a backlash spate follows, saying, essentially, *that's a load of shit* – and, by *the way, that is exactly what motherhood boils down to: loads and loads of shit.*

But motherhood "boils down" to nothing. Or rather, it boils down to everything: it cannot be *boiled down.* It's bliss and painful, thrilling and boring, gloriously fulfilling and excruciating, rich with desperation, dangerous, scary, and soothing. But this is only a partial list. Today alone I have already been amused, delighted, irritated, alarmed, impatient, tense, heartbroken, and full of joy. And as I write this, it is only noon, a Sunday. By day's end, who knows what else will have transpired, or what feelings dredged up from the bottomless motherwell.

Motherhood, I discovered early on – though not so early as some – is *difficult.* Marvelously difficult, if you like that sort of thing (hard crossword puzzles, the genome project, *Ulysses*) but much harder, I think, than anything else that's hard, because unlike other hard things

– unlike doing subatomic particle physics or writing a magnificent villanelle – it doesn't *seem* difficult much of the time: it's easy to imagine, sometimes for fairly long stretches, that what you're doing is simple, that you could do it blindfolded, one hand tied behind your back.

This is an illusion.

And the difficulty seems to come as a surprise to everyone. Even to women who know it's going to be hard. They don't know which part will be hard for them, and so they're caught up short when they come smack up against whatever that turns out to be. The mothers I've known who were worn out and frustrated by their babies' need to be held "all the time" came up against their first difficulty almost immediately – but I'm not sure it made much difference overall. That is, when the next hard part came, they were still caught off guard. It's not something you can train for, or practice. Even if you're the mother of two (or four, or eight – or so I have been told), each child brings a "special challenge." This is a nice way of saying: you never know what variety of hell is going to break loose.

Even if you know yourself damn well – which I believed I did – and know what to look out for, what "special challenges" are going to be built in, thanks to your own personality, chances are you'll hit a wall or two. Even with the best intentions. Even if you start out brilliantly.

4

Grace is twelve weeks old, and we are at war.

In the beginning it isn't war, or I don't know it is. In the beginning it is only a series of discrete skirmishes. The first day, she turns away after nursing for three or four minutes – nowhere near long enough, I know – and even as I try and fail to persuade her to nurse a little longer, I tell myself she's "just not very hungry today." I am anxious but I don't yet panic.

I panic the next day, when instead of merely turning, she *wrenches* herself away, pulling back as forcefully as she can after nursing for no more than a minute, and then begins to cry – to howl – and refuses to return to my breast although I know she must be very hungry.

One more day, and the war has begun in earnest.

She will not nurse. I will not let her starve. All day long I try to nurse her, and all day long she refuses to nurse. She refuses loudly, furiously, red-faced. I try to take advantage of the open mouth she's howling with, but as soon as I do, she clamps it shut again, then tries to bury her face *under* my breast. She will do anything to get away from me, and I don't know how to fight her.

The pediatrician is no help at all. I take Grace to see her – I'm crying, Grace is crying – and, just as I'd feared, my daughter isn't gaining weight: she's stalled at eleven pounds. "She may have lost a few ounces in the last few days," the pediatrician says. "In any case, she certainly isn't growing the way we like to see. Fourteen ounces overall since I last saw her? That was" – she frowns at Grace's chart – "six weeks ago. That's terrible." *Terrible.* The word is a knife. There is nothing I have ever heard that is more terrible than this word *terrible.* I ask her what to do. "Just give her a bottle of formula, for goodness sakes," she says, and adds, "I hope you're not one of those breastfeeding fanatics."

But I have already tried – it was the first thing I tried, when it became clear that she wouldn't nurse – to give Grace a bottle. Not of formula, but of my own painfully, tediously, at-long-length hand-expressed milk, because apparently (having read so much – as I prepped for the Big Test – about the benefits of breast milk versus substitutes available in cans) I *am* one of those "breastfeeding fanatics."

Grace had refused the bottle, as I'd expected she would. I tell this to the pediatrician. Miserably, I say, "And it's my own fault, too," because I had never offered her a bottle before and had thus missed "the window for introducing the bottle" discussed in every one of those books I'd read. I had intentionally missed the window. I wasn't planning on using bottles. I thought it was ridiculous for me to pump and fill bottles with my milk when I would be available myself, when I had no intention of being farther than arm's length from her until she was six months old, when I would return to teaching. I had arranged the whole year's schedule around that plan. And when I did return to teaching, I had my classes set up so that I would never be away from her for more than three hours at a stretch, and by that time, I had read, her nursing sessions would be at least four hours apart. Besides, she'd be eating solid food by then. She wouldn't starve while waiting for me to get back from campus.

The best-laid plans. I tell this story at the local La Leche League chapter meeting I force myself to attend even though I have never liked clubs or groups of any kind – I am not a joiner – and I hate the structure and artificial social setting of meetings. But this is an emergency, and I am frightened enough to take my place in the circle of women sitting on metal folding chairs in our neighborhood branch library's meeting room. Most of the women gathered have babies on their laps or crawling on the carpet, and there are half a dozen toddlers playing in the corners and periodically waddling up to their mothers and pulling up on their untucked shirts to nurse. *Jesus*, I think, and tell myself something else that I will end up being wrong about: *I'll never let my daughter do that. A year of breastfeeding – that's it, and I quit.*

That is, if I ever get to start again.

Grace is asleep – asleep and starving – in my lap. When it's my turn to speak, I introduce myself; I introduce Grace. Everyone smiles. I speak calmly about missing the "window of opportunity" to "intro-duce the bottle" and everyone nods empathetically. This is heartening: no one here thinks I'm out of my mind. I explain about the flexibility built into my job, but every other woman in the room – it's ten a.m. on a Wednesday morning, after all – is at home full-time with her child; they're not that impressed. One of them mentions how lucky she feels not to "have to work." Another says, "It's hard on a baby, you know, to lose her mother at six months." I say, doing my best to keep my cool, "She's not *losing* anything. I'm going to be teaching, not dying," and I take a deep breath and tell the part of the story I came here to tell, and ask if anyone has any ideas that might help me. As soon as I ask this question, I start to cry, and the woman sitting next to me puts her arms around me (as well as she can; she is seven months pregnant) and then suddenly she's crying too, in sympathy. The mixture of sympathy and antipathy from a group of other mothers is something I will get used to, later on. But it's new to me that day, and what with my anxiety about Grace, and my exhaustion, I can't cope with the conflicting emotions – theirs or mine – and I don't stop crying for a long time. The woman crying with me won't stop until I do, and for most of what's left of the meeting, she rubs and pats my back, the two of us weeping into each other's hair.

• • •

I will never know if Grace would have been willing to take a bottle during this period if she had been accustomed to one from the beginning. The lactation consultant to whom the La Leche group leader sends me wastes no time in conjecture. She tells me briskly that there are mysteries about our babies that we'll never solve, that we're not supposed to solve. "We just have to deal with them, that's all." She arranges for me to rent an electric breast pump so that my milk production won't stop while I continue to try to get Grace to nurse, and she rattles off a list of suggestions to help me do that. I take notes, and try everything she mentions. Most of it doesn't work, but she prepared me for this. "Keep trying things. Try something different every day," she said, and I thought of the poem, a favorite of mine, by Elizabeth Bishop, "One Art" – the line, *Lose something every day*.

I discover that changing position – surprising Grace into nursing because she doesn't see it coming – helps. But after two days she learns to recognize that my looming over her on all fours ("That's it, all the mystery is gone," says Glen sadly the first time he sees me on my hands and knees on the bed, the baby beneath me) means that food is coming. As soon as she makes the connection, she stops nursing this way, too.

Then I find, even more usefully, that she will nurse *in her sleep*. I bring her back into our bed, between Glen and me, where she had been during her first month. Now, even though she continues to refuse to nurse all day long, I can get her to nurse at night, some nights virtually *all* night. She nurses, asleep, for hours at a time – less effectively, no doubt, than she would if she were awake, but effectively enough, it seems: she begins to gain weight again. At sixteen and a half weeks, she weighs eleven pounds, thirteen ounces; at eighteen weeks, twelve pounds, three ounces; at twenty weeks, twelve pounds, nine ounces. It could be better, the new pediatrician admits, but at least the baby isn't *losing* any more ground. "You're getting there," Dr. Sheets says. "Just keep doing what you're doing." She pats my arm. "You're doing great."

But I am not doing great. For one thing, I am getting almost no sleep. I nap, on and off, all night long, but mostly what I do is anxiously watch Grace nurse, stroke her head, and occasionally shift my weight so that she can nurse on the other side. I have learned to nurse while lying on my side; I have learned to offer both breasts from *one* side.

Grace wakes up calm and happy each morning. I have outsmarted her. She seems to have no memory of what's happened in the night, and I feel guilty about tricking her this way. I remind myself that I am tricking her for her own sake. Still, it's the kind of thing I'd sworn I'd never do.

I am more tired than I have ever been – even during Grace's first weeks, for at least then I'd sometimes sleep for two hours between nighttime feedings – and I am more anxious, tense, and tearful than I ever imagined I *could* be. I am still trying to get her to nurse in daylight, to persuade her to behave as she did on days one through eighty-four of her life (or perhaps not *exactly* as she did then, since one thing has changed for the better: the nightly three-hour crying bouts have stopped).

With the help of the lactation consultant – a profession I would have mocked at any previous time in my life – and her bottomless store of tips for getting reluctant babies to nurse, I learn that Grace will nurse during the day if I follow a complicated, rigid, grueling routine: I must be alone with her, in a room that is completely dark – lights off, windows curtained – and silent (even a passing car, or a bird chittering on the windowsill outside, will stop her). I can't nurse her sitting up, as I did for the first three months; I must be lying down. I must take my shirt off, too, and not merely lift it.

This means, obviously, that I can't go anywhere – or that I can go places only from which I can quickly return home no more than three hours from the start of the last closed-door, shuttered, silent nursing session. (I do try, several times, to nurse her this way in other people's bedrooms, but it is very awkward – removing half my clothes in someone else's house, shuttering someone else's windows, lying on an unfamiliar bed – and because I find it more stressful than the rush home, I give up.)

Months pass. I am a recluse. I store the milk I've pumped (I'm still pumping several times a day, because Grace's nursing isn't regular or forceful enough to keep up my milk supply) in baby food jars in the freezer, and every day I try to give her some defrosted breast milk in a "sippy cup" that she mostly pours over her head. She is still too young to manage a cup, but I am assured by the lactation consultant that if I keep trying, she will learn, sooner than promised by the books.

We are concentrating now on getting my milk into her any way we can. When she is old enough to digest solid food, but still young enough so that her main source of nutrition continues to be breast milk, I will mix defrosted breast milk into cereal, into rice, into pastina, into everything I *can* mix it into. Muffin batter. Scrambled eggs. Meat loaf. If she eats even a few bites, I am ecstatic. I make breast milk popsicles – my sister-in-law Donna's suggestion – and these are a big hit: Grace sucks on them rapturously, sitting in her high chair; in between sucks, she raps them on the tray and laughs uproariously.

She is six months old, then eight months old. She becomes interested in avocadoes, in skinned whole plums, in quartered grapes, in certain sour fruits she discovers she loves – fat, barely ripe blackberries; star fruit; even lemon halves, which she merrily licks and sucks on. She drinks her breast milk, ice cold, from a cup.

And so she doesn't starve, after all. And finally she is a year old, and breast milk is no longer an essential part of her diet. We celebrate her birthday with a huge party, at which I serve all the foods she likes best now – London broil, and pasta salad with chick peas and lots of garlic and fresh cilantro, and all the sour fruits she's so fond of – and her very first cake, an orange cake with orange icing, decorated with kiwi and lemon slices, and vanilla ice cream, another first. I call Allison Hazelbaker, the lactation consultant, one more time, to thank her. "It's over," I tell her. "Thank God."

And so the crisis ends. Or so I think.

In fact it just goes underground.

5

Saul Bellow once described the perfect circumstances for his writing as *solitude with someone waiting on the other side of the door.* I am not quoting, only paraphrasing – I'm sure he said it much more elegantly – because I can't look up the quote. I read it years ago in a magazine while standing in line at the Big Bear with a cart full of groceries, well before the days of Grace strapped to my chest, during the first year or two after I'd moved to Ohio for my teaching job. The article was a compilation of well-known writers' answers to this question and several related ones, such as, "What would you be today if you weren't a writer?" but Bellow's answer to this one is the only bit that has stayed with me, both because he's one of my favorite writers and because of my reaction to what he said.

I remember that when I read it I thought it sounded good but didn't seem feasible. Not in my life, anyway. The person on the other side of the door would be preoccupied with other things, wouldn't be waiting for me. And in the unlikely event that someone would be waiting for me, the way I supposed Bellow's wives, one after another, waited patiently for him, then knowing that someone was waiting would make me feel pressured, guilty, rushed. Annoyed. And selfish, for barricading myself behind that closed door to begin with.

What I'd have to have, I remember thinking, was someone waiting for me in suspended animation. Not doing anything, not even waiting, but just there, silent and unneedful. Frozen. When I came out, this frozen companion would spring to life – glad to see me, interested in conversation, ready and willing to keep me company.

I knew this wasn't realistic. Not only because I knew that human beings can't be put into suspended animation, but because who would want to live with someone who existed only when she was present, even if it were possible? Actually, it was a creepy thought. I had freaked myself out a little just by thinking it. But there was something else that bothered me about this – and not just about my daydream variation of Bellow's prescription, but about the prescription itself. Because in fact the only time I ever *wasn't* lonely was while I was writing. The second I quit working and opened the door, the loneliness rushed in again. And frankly I wasn't sure that having someone waiting for me, even if I wanted someone to be waiting for me, would make any difference. I was already around people practically every minute that I wasn't writing. I had dinner out all the time (at last, in my mid-thirties, in Columbus, Ohio, I had attained that much Jamesianness in my life). I had a best friend. I had lots of other friends. I had students, colleagues, friendly neighbors. And I always had a boyfriend, or an ex-boyfriend I was still seeing on the sly even though he was involved with someone else. Practically a cast of thousands. None of this so far had made even a dent in the loneliness.

No, that was not entirely true. Some of it had made a *dent* – the way your own hand will leave a crease across your cheek or forehead if you happen to fall asleep with your head in your hands. I'd had glimpses of non-loneliness – the early days or weeks of being in love with someone, long talks on the phone with women I've considered my best friends, soul-searching conversations over dinner or in bed with one boyfriend or another, long afternoons of shoe-shopping with Z——. Always, though, I knew that even if I wasn't feeling lonely then, that very second, I would be lonely once more soon enough. He would turn his attention to his work, or to someone else who required it, or to a basketball game on TV. She would hang up the phone, or go home to her own life, and I would be left alone with mine.

The only time in my whole life, except while writing, that I have *not* been lonely or felt the presentiment of loneliness, was when I was pregnant and during the first three months of Grace's life.

Pregnant, I remember thinking, *I'll never be lonely again* – and I knew enough to make fun of myself, to think, *Oh, sure. Now there's a romantic idea* – but then my daughter was born and I still wasn't lonely. I had secretly been afraid that I would miss being pregnant; I had worried out loud, during my third trimester, that I was enjoying it too much, that I would miss having another life inside me. The woman I said this to – one of the women who worked in the kitchen at MacDowell, the artists' colony where I spent my seventh and some of my eighth month – laughed and said, "If you like pregnancy that much, you'll love what comes next even more – that little bundle of living company."

By the last few days of my pregnancy, I saw that she would be right. I was so anxious to see my daughter by then that those final days, after my due date had passed, were the only hard ones of the pregnancy. I couldn't wait anymore, I kept saying; I couldn't wait another *hour* to meet her.

The love of my life, I called her the day she was born, and Glen and Z—— (who had been in the hospital with us all night, in the labor room with us counting down the seconds during each contraction until five a.m., and then sitting on the floor outside the delivery room for two hours, white-knuckled) exchanged glances. I saw the look that passed between them.

Jealous, I thought. Both of them. Poor things.

· · ·

Having a baby *was* better than being pregnant. My infant daughter turned out to be splendid company. It didn't matter that she couldn't talk: she was alive and in the world with me. Just looking at her filled me with pleasure, and I talked to her all day long. I narrated her life to her down to every mundane detail: diaper changes, trips to the Big Bear, opening the day's mail. She was clearly as enthralled by the sound of my voice as I was by everything about her. We were riveted on each other; we were the perfect couple. It was love at first sight *and* love that expanded every day. Every hour.

Even then, it wasn't all rapture and gaiety, though. These were the days when she was nursing like any other baby, round the clock, day and night, every couple of hours, and I had trouble falling back to sleep after I nursed her. And then there was the strain of those nightly three-hour sob sessions. Plus, as I've already noted, I had turned stupid, which came as a shock to me – the girl who'd been smart all her life. I couldn't hold up my end of a conversation, or write, or read anything but books on baby care, baby behavior, baby psychology. I was grateful, I remember, that I'd gotten so much writing done at MacDowell, and that I'd read so gluttonously all through pregnancy (a book a day at least, craving novels, particularly nineteenth-century novels, just as I craved watermelon, liver and onions, and vanilla malteds) now that I couldn't read anyone but Penelope Leach and T. Berry Brazelton.

I don't know why I bothered reading "the experts." I knew exactly what I meant to do. I'd worked it out years before, not consciously but constantly, and during my pregnancy it had floated to consciousness. By the time Grace was born I'd written a map in my mind – merely taking notes, I'd thought, on what I already knew. I was like Kekulé and the benzene ring: it was as if I'd dreamed the truth while sleeping – while living, the first thirty-eight years of my life – and now I just had to copy out what I had seen, which I was sure was the truth, dancing in my head like those carbon atoms Kekulé saw clinging to one another, making a circle.

I spent the earliest part of my daughter's infancy as I had spent my pregnancy, in a swoony, dazed, amazingly (and utterly amazed) unlonely state, still under the influence of that dream – the dream of perfection.

. . .

Pregnant, a new mother, I walked around (and sat around, and lay around) feeling as if I were encircled by something like the swirling glow around Glenda the Good Witch each time she materializes – the glow of good intentions. For months I had the sensation that sparkling, glittery white light surrounded me – the light of blissful certainty, or certain bliss; of change all for the good, and of goodness itself.

I had never felt anything remotely like this – magical, aglimmer, *graced* – and it was for this, the feeling I had from the moment I knew I was pregnant, that my daughter was named. If the baby had been a boy, Glen and I were prepared to name him for the two grandfathers we'd lost – my mother's father, Sam, and Glen's father's father, Tullie – men we'd loved as much as each of us had ever loved anyone, men we still missed terribly. It grieved us both that our grandfathers would never know our child. And so it was our own good fortune that was responsible for our naming our baby after a feeling, not a person – because all the women we loved were still alive then, and I am an Ashkenazi Jew who is enough of a believer in tradition to refuse to consider naming a child for a living relative.

Glen gave Grace her middle name – Jane, after no one and nothing. A name that was all her own. A name to keep her grounded. This was a good idea, I thought. A child named for a state of mind and heart (especially for such a fate-tempting state of mind and heart!) needed a good solid name, a *basic* name, for ballast.

Grace Jane, ecstasy brought down to earth – that was how I saw it.

But when I told Glen this, he shook his head. He just liked the sound of it, he said, those two single syllables and the way the $\backslash g \backslash$ and $\backslash j \backslash$ sounds worked against each other. I didn't believe him –

no more than I have ever believed him when he's told me straight-faced that his still lifes are all "about" their composition, and rolled his eyes when Grace or I interpreted them out loud. (When she was little, Grace would identify the three of us in Glen's paintings – and it *was* curious that after she was born so many of them featured three objects. When there were three apples or three pears, it was easy, she said: they were named for their sizes, like the Three Bears. But when there were three different objects – a peach, a cherry, and an olive, say; or a thimble, a shotglass, and a marble – she would explain solemnly how she'd assigned each one its character, and as much as I enjoyed these narratives, Glen hated them.)

Both Grace and I have by now quit talking about her father's paintings as if they were stories. We don't want to torture him. But really I don't think he minds that we *see* stories, metaphors, and themes in them. He just doesn't necessarily want to hear about it.

And I don't think he minds the way I think about our daughter's name. He just prefers to keep things simple, or at least to keep them simple on the surface. The trouble is, in Grace's case, even on the *surface* nothing ever has been simple.

6

Grace is just over a year old when she begins to nurse again willingly. Now that she doesn't have to; now that she has to ask me for it. She will nurse, as it turns out, until she is four years old. One of the legacies of my La Leche League days, and the whole new group of books I read then, is a decision to let her wean *herself* when she is ready – a natural extension, it seems to me, of my determination to meet her needs rather than doing things "for my own convenience," as I am wont to put it.

She nurses less and less frequently with each passing year, and for shorter and shorter periods. In the end, except for when she's ill (when nursing is a blessing, since breast milk is a "clear fluid," and no matter how awful she feels – even when she has the stomach flu and a fever of 104° – she will lie beside me and nurse on and off, so I don't have to worry about dehydration), she's down to once a week or so for no more than a minute or two – a quick hit; keeping her hand in, I figure. Sometimes she forgets for as long as ten days, and

I feel obliged to tell her that my milk supply is dwindling, that it's a supply-and-demand system, so that one day she will try to nurse and there won't be any milk, that she should be prepared for this. And then one day it happens. She says, "That's it, Mama. Nothing, not a drop," and adds, "I guess you'll have to find another way to comfort me now, huh?"

. . .

She is such a cheerful, articulate, smart, sensible child. How can there be anything wrong?

But there is something wrong. Well before the "breakdown" there is something wrong, only I don't see it until later. In kindergarten, she refused to throw away what was left of a piece of construction paper after she had cut shapes out of it. Neither her teacher nor I found this worrisome ("Kids," Mrs. Brant said, and shrugged. I didn't think to ask if other children in the class were secreting away their paper scraps; perhaps they were). By the end of the school year she had begun to keep and hide any piece of paper she had written or drawn on, even "mistakes": if there was even one mark on a sheet of paper, she would save it. This didn't seem so odd to me. In fact I was impressed that she so honored her own efforts. I thought it was the word or two that she had written, the half-finished drawing, the "rough draft" of a poem that she wanted to save. It didn't occur to me that what she was saving was anything she had touched – that she couldn't bear to part with anything once she'd come into contact with it, however briefly.

Not even when she moved on to candy wrappers, empty juice boxes, the packaging her toys came in. The price tags snipped off her new clothes. Discarded wrapping paper, no matter how crumpled and torn, at other children's birthday parties (so that she left her friends' houses with a goody bag of candy and cheap plastic toys and a shopping bag of wadded up giftwrap; the mothers didn't mind, though some of they gave me strange looks). Sometimes she picked things up in the street and begged, weeping, to keep them. Just seeing something was enough to make her feel sentimentally attached to it. She even explained that to me. "It's too hard to let it go, it makes me too sad."

But she was unlike other children her age in all kinds of ways, and I chalked up this latest eccentricity – that's what I called it – to her sensitivity and her intelligence and her depth, which were considerable. Everybody said so. That she could articulate so precisely what she was doing – well, I was both vain and blind enough to be proud of that.

She was, I further reasoned, the only child of older parents who were themselves vastly different from the parents of the other children she knew. Naturally she would be a bit of an oddball. And didn't Glen and I have a basement full of stuff *we* couldn't throw away?

I was right about all of this – that is, all these things were true: that Grace was sensitive and smart and "deep," that she was an only child of older and somewhat eccentric parents (artists, "not from here," in a conservative Midwestern town in which people seemed to pride themselves above all on fitting in), that unlike all our neighbors we have never held a garage sale – but that didn't mean there weren't other factors to consider. It didn't mean there wasn't something wrong.

There was something wrong even before this, when she was three and a half, when my friend Vicki was first diagnosed with cancer. I knew this would be terrifying, terrible, to any child. But I misunderstood how frightening it was to Grace, and why. I didn't see the gap – huge and growing huger daily – between what Grace, smart as a whip, *knew*, and what she could understand. I didn't see that for her, as close to me at three, at four, as she had been as a newborn – so close we might as well have been one person – the thought of a mother vanishing forever was the thought of *herself* vanishing forever.

We were five hundred and fifty miles away from where Vicki was sick, so we didn't see her very often. And each time we did, I prepared Grace as well as I could. She knew Vicki would be bald, that she would have no eyebrows. She knew that Vicki might have to throw up sometimes, and that this, like the baldness, wasn't because of the cancer but because of the "strong medicine" we hoped would cure the cancer.

When we visited, she knew that she and Silas, Vicki's son, would have to play quietly, and probably indoors, and that Vicki would be resting while they played. Sometimes I'd look up, while we were there, and see Grace in the doorway of the playroom in the Brooklyn Heights apartment, watching Vicki and me as we sat on her couch, holding hands and talking.

When my second book came out, just before Grace and Silas turned five, Vicki and her family came to the reading I gave at the Jefferson Market Library, my old branch library in the Village. She brought me flowers and took photos and introduced herself to everyone as the "for Vicki" to whom the book was dedicated. But by the next evening, she was too sick to join us at the book party uptown. Grace asked a lot of questions – more questions than anyone else asked – about *how* sick Vicki was that day: in exactly what way, and did she have a fever, and was she in pain, and was it the cancer making her so sick this time or the medicine she was taking for it?

Back in Columbus, I called Vicki every day, and Grace would watch me, waiting for the moment when I made the call. She watched me take the phone out of earshot, out of her view. Even after I hung up, I'd have to stay out of sight for a few minutes while I composed myself. When Vicki had first called with the news that cancer was suspected – that there was "something" on an X-ray that was suspect enough to require immediate exploratory surgery – Grace had been beside me, at the kitchen table, and she had watched me fall apart. I was sure that was part of the trouble – that she had seen me so frightened. She had never seen me that way before.

She never said *she* was frightened. But from the beginning, the first months after that phone call, she became preoccupied with what she called "scary thoughts." She tried to fall asleep at night and couldn't: her mind was flooded with pictures that frightened her so badly she would scream, and I'd come running. "Mama, take a fork and pluck those pictures out of my brain!" she would shriek, and smack her forehead, grab her own hair and tug on it, trying to pull the thoughts out of her head.

Some of these images were concocted out of the air, and some had to do with Vicki, or with Silas. Others were from books. One that appeared again and again was from Dr. Seuss's *Hop on Pop*, which by then we hadn't even looked at in months; she had dismissed it as a "baby book." It was the picture, Grace explained when she could catch her breath and speak, that was captioned, *Jim is after him*, the one that showed Jim biting on the tail of a sharp-toothed creature that had just been trying to bite Jim.

I understood that the "scary thoughts" had to do with death – with Vicki's, with the possibility of mine. She mocked herself for the assurances she'd asked for when she was two, that I wouldn't die until I was "very, very old" ("I'll do my best," I'd always said). "I was so stupid then, I didn't know anything," she told me. She sounded very bitter.

She wasn't even four years old. I tried to meet her on her own ground intellectually. What else could I do? I admitted that sometimes people do die earlier than they should, that the strong medicine Vicki was taking might not work, that this was a worse sickness than any normal sickness, that Vicki might die. But I told her that no one in my family, on either side, had ever had cancer, and that "scientists believe that this is part of the story" ("Did anyone in Vicki's family?" Grace demanded, and I told her yes, both of Vicki's parents died of cancer. "I hate cancer," she declared, a four-year-old again). I told her about Ruchel, "your great-great-great-grandmother," and my father's Aunt Betty, "your great-great-aunt," and reminded her that my own grandmother was close to a hundred when she died, that the odds were in our favor.

But I wasn't dealing with anything but the surface – the complicated surface. I didn't know what was below the surface because I was below it *with* her. Neither one of us could see a thing.

7

It's possible that there has never been a mother with better intentions. But it didn't matter how good my *intentions* were. I failed my daughter. There is simply no other way to look at it. Or – a more precise way for me to say this, and the way that pains me most – it was *because* of my intentions that I failed her. If Grace and I ended up stalled, lost, under a pitiless sky in a place I'd never meant for us to go, I can blame no one but myself. I paved the road myself – using a map I'd drawn myself – with my excellent intentions. The proverbial road; the road to hell.

The first tiny flames, I now believe, began to lick at Grace's feet, so that I had to jump back, still holding her in my arms, while she was still an infant – before she knew anything; only *felt*. I was all feelings, too. The difference was that I thought I knew things, and I had words for everything I knew. I had plans and ideas. A baby has nothing – no ideas, no plans, no words, no thoughts, no understanding.

And yet. And yet.

I believe now that even then the baby knew something I didn't.

When she suddenly stopped crying for three hours every night and her hunger strike began, I didn't wonder at the synchronism. I was just relieved I didn't have to deal with both at once. But what I wonder now is whether the end of the "the fourth trimester" – her little brain clicking into place, her whole self shifting from part-of-me to a separate being, still mine but her own too – allowed her a more sophisticated way, a more *specific* way, to register a protest. Against me. Against my good intentions.

Get out of my face, Mama.

That's what I think she was saying. But I couldn't hear it.

. . .

I could not have heard it. It wasn't possible for me to hear it – not that, of all things.

And even if I had heard it, it would have made no sense to me.

Purposefully, consciously, in *good* conscience, I never left her alone for a second. I was sure that if I did, she would suffer; she would grieve. It was all or nothing for her. For me.

I met every need without ever stopping to think whose needs they might be. It was *obvious*, I thought.

I didn't *think*.

I felt what I felt and called it knowledge.

I could not be more ashamed. I could not be more sorry.

. . .

My own mother's serious depression during my infancy and child-hood, I have always imagined, had to do with me. No one in my family has ever endorsed this explanation, but then the only person in my family who has ever been willing to talk at all about what things were like in the years just after my birth was my grandmother, who favored "explanations" that either blamed my father or relied on an image of my mother as "too good to live" – that is, as the embodiment of perfection itself, unfit by definition to cope with an imperfect, ugly world. If I had pointed out that the birth of a baby, the care of a baby (particularly such a baby as I'd been, according to my grandmother herself: a sleepless, crying, extra-needful baby – *so unlike your brother, when he came along! He was such a quiet baby, such a sleepy, easy baby!*) must have been a part, at least, of what came as so great a shock to the "too-good," protected, untried girl my grandmother described, she would have said, "Narishkeyt, mamaleh!" Foolishness! She would have said, "A thought like this should not even be inside your head." The fact was, she would no more have allowed me to hold myself responsible than she could take any of the blame herself.

I know very little of substance about how my mother was raised, but it seems plain enough that at twenty-two, when she became a mother, she barely knew how to look after herself. She had been simultaneously over- and under-tended all her life: cosseted and fussed at, kept clear of ordinary everyday activities (so that she never learned to cook, for example, and didn't know how to use a broom or mop; she knew nothing about money and was afraid to talk to store clerks), and suppressed – forbidden to be angry, or to show any other unseemly emotions, to express her own personality (and perhaps she had no idea what that might be) – and yet certainly she never felt unabashedly loved, supported, treasured by her mother, who had her own difficulties. My grandmother was busy tending to three older (and by all accounts rowdy, sometimes unmanageable) boys in a tiny apartment; her husband, my grandfather, left early every morning for work in the hat factory and returned home late – sometimes stopping to play cards, or to go to the opera, where he'd get a standing room ticket. He had a life of his own, which aggrieved her – and he left her to take care of everything difficult, which made her angry and must have also (though she never admitted this) frightened her.

My mother had been treated by her mother as if she were a doll not meant to be played with – the kind made of bisque, beautifully painted and dressed, with unglazed china fingers that could easily be broken off. One took good care of such a doll, kept her on a high shelf, and didn't handle her too much. My grandmother fussed at my mother. But she had no tenderness for her.

Was my mother already depressed when she married my father? No one says; perhaps no one – not even she – knew. My father was seventeen and "tough" (at least he looked it) when they met; my mother was fourteen, shy, pretty, an A student. He'd been watching her for some time before he gathered up the nerve to speak to her in the neighborhood candy store in Brighton Beach.

He must have been both an antidote to her childhood – he was loud, brash, nervy, confident, and restless, sometimes even explosive, ever *present* – and a familiar sort of harbor: he was as willing (eager, even) to treasure and protect her as her mother had been. And his bluster must have been familiar too to a girl who had much older, rougher brothers. He was nothing like her father – whom she adored and longed for; she'd spent her whole childhood hungry for that never-enough present sweetness that came and went with him.

In the wedding pictures, neither of my grandparents looks happy. My grandmother looks grim, resigned; my grandfather looks anxious and suspicious.

My mother – smart and a beauty, both – married my father at nineteen. He had no prospects then (just out of the army, twenty-two years old, a high school dropout working in his father's hardware store) but he had *ideas*. He talked big. His personality was as overpowering as my grandmother's, and although in those years he and my grandmother were enemies, they were in cahoots where my mother was concerned. Between the two of them, they kept her on the shelf, out of harm's way.

She had started at Brooklyn College after she graduated from Lincoln High – the same high school my father had given up on three years earlier – but she quit "to get married," she explained when I was a child, and it was presented as something unassailable, though I remember wondering (but thinking I could not ask) why she couldn't have been married *and* a college student. After she left school, she had an office job for a short time; she quit that, too. Briefly, she gave piano lessons. But then I was born.

I imagine that being faced with the job of taking care of me – the first serious, demanding task of her life, and one from which there was no rest – must have been overwhelming. It's easy to imagine that the responsibility for a baby might be enough to send a fragile person over the edge. Over one edge or another.

So I suppose it's not unreasonable to believe that this – that I, in need of constant care, constant attention – was responsible for her tumbling into the dark place that swallowed up my life as well as hers for years. I know that there were periods in my childhood when the darkness lifted for a while – that we would count the days, then weeks, and sometimes months, that Mommy was feeling all right – before it descended again. When it did, it was like a heavy curtain falling, signaled by the morning that she wouldn't rise to get me ready for school. Nobody talked about it. My father and I only exchanged glances, mine sorrowful and scared, his angry and grim.

My brother claims to have no memory of any of this. Perhaps by the time he was old enough to start to gather up memories – and his begin much later than mine, even taking into account the almost four-year difference in our ages – my mother *was* well; it was all over. My mother herself has protested my memory of her as "depressed all the time," but she will not talk about it beyond that – or perhaps she would, if I were to insist, which I cannot bring myself to do, since it makes her so uneasy and unhappy. When I was in my early twenties, I did press her once to talk about it – I had just moved out of my parents' apartment and was living on my own, trying to make sense of who I was and how I had become myself – and she began to cry. And her crying reminded me too much of the way she'd cried all those years ago. It alarmed and upset me, and it also made me angry – and that alarmed me, that my mother's sobs could make me so angry – and so I said, "Never mind, it's all right, forget it." Since then, I have not asked her to go over that old ground. I allude to my childhood only passingly, in a way that doesn't ask for comment or corroboration.

My father doesn't speak of it at all. It's too long ago, another life – that's how he treats it. Only my grandmother would talk about it, but she is gone now – and even when she was still here, and her mind was still clear enough for her to look back through it, she never spoke to me entirely truthfully about those years. That is to say, while she spoke the truth as she understood it – which was more than anyone else in my family would do – and she remembered things that no one else seemed to, she described my mother's "sickness" in a way I knew wasn't quite right. In her account of what had happened, she herself had been a bystander, innocent, doing what she could to help. And if I pressed her, she would say what she always said when anyone brought up anything upsetting: "Let's talk about good things." I would sigh – sometimes I'd groan – but I would do as she asked. How could I fault her for preferring happiness?

I will never know "the truth," only what I can remember. And what I remember is feeling all alone, neglected, yearning – wishing, hope against hope, for the company and conversation, the attention, the *recognition* of the person lying down behind a closed door, in the dark.

I was marked for life by this, just as we are all marked by our early troubles – troubles of one kind of another, many of them much worse, more crippling, than mine. Still we are all *marked*, in ways we can see and ways we can't.

. . .

We start out such soft, small, urgent selves, and from the first we're etched, scraped, engraved, impressed upon. It isn't very long before there's almost nowhere left to *make* a mark, a scattering of tiny almost-hidden bare spots here and there, for the last bits to be written on – the addenda, all the later troubles, the ones that are sharp enough to find and penetrate the few still unmarked places.

By three, my daughter, like anyone, was *marked for life*. I think of her now, newborn and delivered into my arms unsealed, unstamped – that soft bundle of living company, the essence of Grace – impressed daily (hourly, minutely) with my presence, my attention, my interest, my devotion. She didn't know what it felt like to be ignored. She didn't know what lonely felt like, what without-me felt like. She didn't know what *in need* felt like.

And why should she? I would have said if anyone had spoken of it. Perhaps someone did. Glen's grandmother, his father's mother, bluntly said once as she watched Grace nursing, during one of our visits down South, "What will happen to her if you ever get sick, end up in the hospital? It will be the end of the world for that child." I was appalled; I wanted to say, "What do you suggest? That I let her practice for my illness, my death, just in case?" but what I did say – cheerfully and at top volume, the way I say everything to Grandma

Holland (who can't hear a word my soft-spoken husband says) – was, "Oh, I'd rather not concentrate on possibilities of that kind. I figure I'm lucky to be so available to her. Don't you think I'm lucky, and that she is too?" Grandma Holland clicked her tongue. "Oh, lucky," she said, as if talking about some foolish luxury – a too-big house, or jewelry. A meal in a restaurant.

I'm thinking we both missed the point – Grandma Holland in her way, which is too chilly to suit me, and me in mine, too damp and overheated for her taste. I know what kind of mother she was: I've seen the evidence, lived with the long-range results. It's the middle ground of motherhood I've had so much trouble locating. It's the middle ground that almost everyone seems to have trouble locating.

My presence in my small daughter's life was so extravagant that even when we were apart, it was as if I were still there. That was what I'd had in mind, of course – that she would "internalize" my presence, that I would be so much in the life of her mind, she would have a sense of my comforting presence even when I was far away. Not that I was ever far away.

It didn't occur to me that maybe she shouldn't have a sense of my comforting presence all the time – that perhaps she did need to know what lonely, what in-need, what without-me felt like. That even an internalization of another person might be too much company, year round, round-the-clock.

I try to imagine now what the forever hovering in Silas's future – the forever without his mother; the forever for a child without a mother – could have meant to my daughter at four, at five, when she didn't even know the meaning of a minute without me. It must have been more terrifying – can such a thing be possible? – than it would have been for another child, one who had the slightest sense that he could manage on his own, that he existed on his own, apart and separate from his mother.

8

Grace is six. It is the summer before first grade, and we have made a toy boat together, out of a four-by-ten-inch rectangle of styrofoam and a couple of popsicle sticks, aluminum foil, and a sheet of green construction paper. It isn't very seaworthy (our forte is art, not engineering) and after we've floated it in the tub once and the construction paper sail is soaked through, it's pretty much a goner. Still, we keep it around for a while – the way we keep everything around – and it gets stepped on and kicked aside and eventually mangled, because "around" means on the floor in a corner of the playroom, mixed in with all kinds of other unclassifiable toys that aren't in bins, and toys not in bins always get stepped on and kicked aside.

Finally, when there is nothing much left of it – the popsicle sticks have come loose from the styrofoam base, which is chipped at all its corners and broken almost all the way through in the middle, the paper sail has crumpled, and the foil is hanging halfway off – I throw it away. I don't often throw things away: we're a save-it-just-in-case kind of family, with a basement full of broken and defunct machines and furniture and miscellaneous items – Glen's motorcycle helmet from when he had a motorcycle, five years before we met; two sets, his and mine, of rusting darkroom equipment; the bathroom sink I replaced when I bought the house; two IBM Selectrics; Grace's crib and changing table, her stroller and high chair, her tricycle, her plastic potty – to testify to that. And I know that our daughter has inherited or learned, or inherited *and* learned, Glen's and my packrat tendencies, so something has to be truly useless, finished, of no possible worth to anyone at any time in the future, before I discard it.

The boat goes. And then, not too many days later, Grace asks for it and I have to tell her it's gone, and she cries. "I loved that boat," she says. She *wails*. "We *made* that boat. How could you have put it in the trash?"

Naturally I feel awful – she is weeping as if she's lost a loved one – but I know this is excessive (her weeping, and my feeling awful, both) and I point out that it wasn't even a boat anymore, that it wasn't good for anything. I tell her we can make another boat. "A better boat," I say. "One that doesn't tip over as soon as you put it in the water. One that's properly balanced. Maybe Daddy can help us this time. Someone who knows what he's doing." I try to make her smile but she's still crying. "And we could put a sail on it that makes more sense. A sail made out of fabric, maybe."

But she doesn't want another boat, she wants this boat. Children say this sort of thing all the time. Every parent knows this – this is what I tell myself, trying to keep from feeling like the worst mother in the world. I know I didn't do anything awful, throwing the remains of a poorly homemade boat in the trash. But she sobs, I try to soothe her, and we are both miserable. We both feel terrible.

But I have no idea how terrible she feels. Or that the episode of the boat will be what pushes her over the edge. I didn't know she was on the edge. I didn't even know there was an edge for her to be on.

• • •

She begins to have nightmares about the boat. She wakes up screaming, and when I run into her room she's sitting up in bed weeping, thinking of the boat we'd made that's now buried in the city dump. In daylight, she asks me questions about what happens to trash, how and when it decomposes; she wants to know what the dump is like. She wants to know if I'll take her to visit the dump, and when I say no, she cries. She wants to find her boat, she says. She can't stop thinking about the boat, something she made with her own hands – she says this again and again – alone and rotting in a heap of other trash.

She is unable now to throw any trash away. This has crept up on us, because at first it hadn't seemed that different from what she'd been doing since kindergarten. And I begin to understand that it isn't any different – but now it's clear that there is something wrong, that her behavior can't be written off as eccentricity or sensitivity, that it can't be written off at all. There's trash hidden all around the playroom and her bedroom, bags of crumpled paper everywhere because I'm still equivocating, "compromising," letting her keep paper trash – but nothing dirty, I insist – "just for a while," I say vaguely, because it is so painful for her to let it go. And I get the metaphor (how could I not?), and she and I talk about it, just as we have talk-talk-talked (so Grace says) about everything, all her life – we talk about how hard it is to part from things, about loss and letting go – but (as Grace points out) the talk-talk-talk isn't doing any good: she still feels bad. Very bad. And at the same time something else has started, something she calls "catching up." She mentions to me, with studied casualness, that if she bumps one foot – "like this," she says, and shows me – she has to follow up by bumping the other foot in the same way.

"What happens if you don't?" I ask her.

She gets a bad feeling, she tells me.

"Would it help if I gave you a name for the bad feeling?" I ask her, and she says she doesn't know, maybe it would. So we talk about anxiety. But for once – maybe for more than once – names don't help, and now she'll see me watching her when she half-trips on a hitch in the playroom rug, and goes back over it to make herself stumble again, and she says, "I can't help it. The anxiety made me do it."

I talk over her behavior with people who know about such things and I'm told that yes, it's worrisome – "It's a little obsessive-compulsive, sure" – but that what I need to watch for is whether it interferes with her daily activities. Whether it's screwing up her life. It doesn't seem to be, I say. She seems to have incorporated these things into her activities. "So see how it goes. It might be a passing thing, a way to handle anxiety, 'the bad feeling,' for the time being."

But then something truly bad happens, something that screws up everything. Something unspeakable. Glen's mother is beaten nearly to death in a robbery in the tiny Georgia town where my in-laws live.

Grace and I are sitting on the floor playing Monopoly for the first time when the phone call from Glen's father comes, and everything screeches to a halt the way it does when the unspeakable occurs. Within hours, Glen and Grace and I are on a plane to Macon, Georgia – three-quarters of an hour from where my in-laws live, but the nearest town with a hospital – and for the next few weeks we are holed up in a hotel room half-a-mile's walk from the hospital where my mother-in-law is in intensive care.

Glen is with his mother all night long, every night. In the daytime, when his sister and his father are with her, he tries to sleep a little, but he can't, really, so he returns to the hospital. Grace and I play board games in the hotel room – we take a cab to Wal-Mart one morning to buy some games, since we'd left home too quickly to bring much of anything with us, just whatever we thought to grab on the way out the door – and once a day, so that she has something to look forward to, we go up to the hotel's tiny rooftop pool. There is never anyone else there.

We visit Glen's mother every day, too, but we never stay long; it's too frightening to Grace. She and I talk – we have to talk – about the badness in the world, a subject I've been keeping in deep background, and which has never come up "naturally" in the bad-guys/good-guys way it seems to for children who watch television or go to the movies. Grace has never seen a movie that divides the world in this way; in fact, she's never heard of anything like this before. Now she wants to know what would make someone do such a thing, and I can't say "because some people are just evil." I have to try to find a way to talk about this with her, but it's much too complex; I am at a loss. What she can "get" intellectually, I realize, she can't possibly feel her way through.

I do my best. I talk about how people who are treated badly never learn to treat others any better than they have been treated. About how some people may be so hurt and angry they don't care *what* they do: they forget that other people have feelings, too – or they don't forget; it has simply never occurred to them.

This feels hopeless to me – it feels ludicrously reductive – but she listens intently to every word I say. We talk for hours, for days.

And we wait, in the damned hotel room. Or beside the hotel's rooftop pool. Or in the hotel's restaurant, Grace eating plate after plate of bacon from the breakfast buffet. The whole time we're in Georgia, all she eats is bacon, something she's never had any interest in eating before. She murmurs, "Bacon in Macon," again and again over the course of the day. There's nothing else to eat, nowhere else to go, nowhere we can get to without calling a cab, and we don't know where to tell a cab to take us.

And all the while, Grace is sad and solemn, but not hysterical, not overwhelmed by grief or anxiety. She actually seems *less* anxious than she was at home, all summer before this happened, and it crosses my mind – but oh so briefly, *too* briefly – that she seems "better" because she and I are spending so much time together, alone in each other's company. We haven't spent this much time together since she was a baby. We are even sleeping together, night after night. There are two queen-sized beds in the hotel room, but Glen is at the hospital every night at bedtime, and I'm back in the habit of lying beside her until she falls asleep, something we'd just recently stopped doing. Most nights I fall asleep right along with her, and I just stay put, not even bothering to roll out and get into the other bed if I wake up in the middle of the night.

Does it cross my mind that this intense bout of togetherness will make things worse when we get home, when she goes back to school, when life resumes "normally"? I don't think so; I think I'm only thinking now about Gerry, my mother-in-law, bruised almost beyond recognition, in and out of consciousness, parts of her brain deadened, lost, the neurologist's warning that she'll never be "the same," and my husband sitting patiently beside her hour after hour, keeping her company in the silent, undemanding, reassuring way that only he, of anyone in his family – of anyone I've ever known – is capable of doing.

Arguments rise up out of the tension in the family. Glen and his sister Donna. Glen's father and me. Glen and his father. Two of Glen's sisters, with each other. Arguments flutter around us and then die out. Grace keeps her cool, playing quietly with the few Barbies that she's brought from home, playing Junior Monopoly (she shuddered in Wal-Mart when I picked up the regular Monopoly game, and so I bought the junior version, which is boring and soothing to her, "just what I need," she tells me earnestly) with me or with her cousins if they stop by the hotel.

Weeks pass. And then one night – in the middle of the night, as Glen sits by her – Gerry opens her eyes and speaks lucidly for the first time, asking him about Grace. He welcomes his mother back to the world, tells her calmly that he'll only be a minute, and races to our hotel room to wake us, to take us in Donna's van, which he has swiped, to see his mother – to make sure that before she closes her eyes again, she can see Grace for herself. And so that Grace can see her, awake and herself. We know this moment may not last.

Grace is in her pajamas and in her father's arms for the entire visit – it doesn't last long – and she is remarkably composed. "Hi, Nana," she says. "It's good to see you."

And thus Gerry's recovery begins – a virtually complete recovery, eventually, which none of the doctors had predicted. Today, exactly three years later, Gerry writes, reads, sews, drives, sails the Internet, and keeps the books for her husband's business. (She was even the one to file the mountain of paperwork that would reduce the hospital bills, since she and James are uninsured; she was the one who wrote the letters arguing for the county's responsibility for what had happened, for it turns out that the feebleminded young man she had hired to haul away some trash from behind the shop, and who had beaten her with a brick and left her to die when he snatched the business checkbook, had been recently, mistakenly, released from jail.) Today, her vision is slightly impaired and she will sometimes have to cast about for a moment to find the word she has in mind to describe something. And she has switched – permanently, it seems – from left-handedness to right-handedness. These are the remnants of what she calls "the accident."

Glen stays on in Macon to be with her after Grace and I have to leave. Back in Columbus, school is starting. We arrive the night before the first day. Thus Grace starts first grade in a flurry of confusion – we haven't yet bought school supplies; we haven't gone school clothes shopping (a ritual I remember with mixed feelings from my childhood, but which I feel awful about skipping) – but she seems okay; she's *coping*, I think. Whatever was troubling her earlier in the summer, it's not in action now.

But of course it isn't *gone*. It's only dormant. The six months that follow are hard ones, with plenty to distract us. Meanwhile, inside Grace, what she herself will later call her "problems" are nourishing themselves underground, like the tulip bulbs that she and I plant every fall, which will break through the ground in spring.

At the end of six months her grandmother will be out of the hospital, in rehab, relearning to walk and write and bring a fork to her own mouth and handle the simple, daily chores of maintenance, washing herself and her clothes, brushing her own hair, and doing puzzles and crocheting bookmarks to practice her small motor skills. Grace's school, to which Glen and I have been deeply committed (and so regular a presence in the classroom, where we each volunteer one day a week, that some of the boys in Grace's class who have no fathers at home, have begun to call him "Daddy"), will have disintegrated. The undoing – the ruination – of this school, which we love, has been faster and more devastating than we could have guessed when the school's maverick, dedicated principal was removed at the end of Grace's kindergarten year (an act of pure politics we couldn't find a way to explain to her) and a new principal, one who had no business at an "arts impact" school, was installed. By February, I will have spent five months lobbying downtown on the school's behalf, showing up at school board meetings, taking my turn at the microphone along with all the crazy people who stand up each week to rant about one thing or another (as often as not only marginally related to education), and sitting in the office of the assistant superintendent – the superintendent herself refuses to meet with me – who makes empty promises and repeatedly praises my "level of interest" in the school, in my daughter's education, and in "the children of the city of Columbus."

The new principal is bringing the school down single-handedly, with the full support (or utter lack of concern – I can't tell which) of both the school board and the superintendent of schools. I plead for a replacement who might be better suited to our school's arts-through-the-curriculum program, someone who will at the very least be smart enough, and self-confident enough, to take advantage of the experience and advice of the teachers, many of whom have been at the school since its inception under the old principal, fourteen years before. I am told I must give the new principal a chance.

By midyear, the school's arts program has been denuded to the point of meaninglessness, a frill. Even those of us who never had to be convinced that art is important to a child's education are stunned by how rapid the school's deterioration is once music and dance and visual arts and theater, which last year had been threaded through the children's day, have been reduced to the vanishing point. Even the teachers who had been there longest hadn't understood the extent to which improvisational theater and dancing to Saint-Saëns and Stravinsky and painting self-portraits and banging on drums and plucking dulcimer strings had been keeping large numbers of children in the school functioning – interested and engaged, attentive, *learning* – or how quickly such children would collapse under the weight of the constant drilling and test preparation that have been instituted in their place.

Grace's first grade classroom teacher, Mr. Trent, had already suggested I consider removing her from the school, but instead I'd been begging the assistant superintendent to send us classroom aides – a

wexner bookshop hours:
mon-fri 10am-6pm
saturday 12noon-6pm
for holiday and extended hours call:
614.292.1807

TASCHEN

TITLES FROM TASCHEN
AVAILABLE **ONLY** AT THE WEXNER CENTER BOOKSHOP

SAMPLE TITLES FROM THE ICONS SERIES– $9⁹⁹

CASE STUDY HOUSES, SOME LIKE IT HOT– $150⁰⁰
LIMITED EDITION MONOGRAPHS
(IMAGES ON REVERSE)

BOOKSHOP

last-ditch effort. I don't want to remove Grace from Mr. Trent's class-room; he's too good a teacher. And Glen and I are so involved with so many of these kids now, and with the school itself, that we're hoping we can win, that we can take the school back from the philistines before it's too late.

But it's already too late. I have stuck it out too long, and I am harrowed, stupefied with guilt, when finally I do have to take Grace out of the school – in the middle of the year, in the middle of a week, mid-February.

By then, she is a nervous wreck. She has begun to insist each night that the towers of stuffed animals that have long "slept with" her in her bed have to be arranged just *so*; if one falls, she sits up and restacks all of them. The three pillows have to be step-staired behind her head precisely, two inches of pillow showing between each, and the three blankets she uses in winter smoothed out so that their ends match up, so that everything is even.

I tell myself that it was school that was the problem – the chaos there. But when she's been in her new school for weeks and she is still checking and rechecking the lineup of her blankets, restacking her stuffed animals, measuring the distance between pillows, I conclude that the shock of the transition is the problem. And that the new school, in its new way – peaceful, quiet, orderly as it is – is itself a problem. There is not one girl in her new class whom Grace can call a friend.

The equalizing of bumps and trips, the "catching up," has become by now so much a part of her day, of her life, that it *is* interfering with her play, her sleep, her daytime concentration. She tells me she can mostly keep it under control at school, and if she can't, she does what she has to do secretly. But the stress of restraining the impulse to "catch up" at school takes its toll, and when she gets home she is a bundle of tics for hours. At school she's so tightly wound it seems to me a miracle she's learning anything.

The trash-saving has gotten worse, too, bad enough so that her new first grade teacher calls me to talk about it, asks me if I can do something about it – and she doesn't even know that Grace is picking things up off the street now (broken bits of plastic, string, empty packages) and begging to take them home with her. The first grade teacher at the new school is young and inexperienced and tense; she's been thrown a curve and she likes things just *so* (you'd think she'd sympathize with Grace's troubles). She doesn't take to Grace, and this is a first for my daughter: a grownup who is not charmed by her precocity – who actually seems unnerved by it; a teacher who isn't grateful to have her in her classroom. Grace comes home in tears, wondering what she's done wrong, why the teacher is so stern with her. "She scolds me for not knowing what I'm supposed to be doing when nobody has even told me what to do. I have no idea what's supposed to happen when or where or how in this place."

One afternoon she sucks her thumb in class and the teacher stops what she is doing – reading to the children as they sit on the carpet around her – and stares hard at Grace until she takes her thumb out of her mouth. "I would've done it sooner," Grace tells me when she gets home, "but it took a long time before I figured out *why* she was looking at me and what she wanted." When I phone the teacher and ask her, as nicely as I can manage, to cut Grace a little slack ("This is a rough time for her, as I'm sure you understand," I say, and I think I hide my despair and rage), she says, primly, "I'm afraid I can't do that. I can't allow thumb-sucking in my classroom. The other children might copy her – as you know, children are so impressionable at that age! – and then where would I be? I'd have a whole classful of parents complaining."

The teacher is the problem. And the new school. And the old school. Everything. There are so many problems, and all of them are *the* problem. But there's more to it than this, and it goes deeper. As problems always do.

9

We are on the way to Cincinnati, a two-hour drive, to see a psychiatrist I have been assured will not automatically pronounce Grace obsessive-compulsive and offer a prescription to drug her symptoms into submission. Who will take the time to determine what the underlying dynamics of these symptoms are and help us deal with what's causing them.

I've already spent countless hours on the phone trying to find a psychiatrist in Columbus who specializes in the treatment of children and is analytically trained, someone who won't jump to the most obvious conclusion and provide a quick fix – the easy, the cheap, the *standard practice* route – and so I am unfazed by a roundtrip of four hours for a two-hour consultation. I'm still angry, as we set out, which is all right: it keeps me going, keeps me focused and strong despite how much I have always disliked driving and how phobic I am about highway-driving in particular. Besides, the hostility is mutual. The general consensus in the Columbus psychiatric community about me seems to be that I'm nuts, maybe in need of a good psychotropic drug myself.

This is why we are going all the way to Cincinnati to see Dr. Knox. It is a trip we will make numerous times over the next few weeks, so that she can talk to Grace – so that Grace can talk to her – and a thorough diagnosis can be made. If Dr. Knox determines that the trouble *is* a neurobiological disorder that has to be biochemically treated, so be it; but if, as I suspect, Grace's symptoms are trying to tell us something, I want to know what they're saying, and not just shut them up.

Another symptom has been added to the mix in the days leading up to this trip, and it's even scarier to me than the others. Grace now feels – pressingly, consumingly, irresistibly – that she must tell me everything that's on her mind, every passing stray thought, no matter how trivial. At the same time, the other symptoms, especially the "catching up," have worsened, and the combination of the new symptom and the catch-ups is especially disturbing, since much of what's on Grace's mind *is* catching up.

The night before we leave for Cincinnati, before she finally passes out from sheer exhaustion, she sits up in bed talking nonstop to me for hours – a frantic rapid-fire monologue her own mouth can hardly keep pace with, as she simultaneously describes what happened at school that day and what she thinks about it now and oh, *right this second I just thought about Tenara and I wondered what her day was like at the old school and I'm thinking about Mr. White and when he taught us about "organic shapes" last year, remember? and that shadow – look, Mama, it's an organic shape, what's it a shadow of?* but doesn't wait for me to answer, says, *Wait, wait, I know, look – it's just my shoes and leggings all mixed up together in a heap and the way the nightlight makes a shadow too of the stuffed animals piled in a basket on the floor beside it and remember when you gave me this nightlight?* and how her tongue just touched the roof of her mouth when she said that, and so now she has to touch her tongue to the roof of her mouth again and *just when I did that, I had to swallow, see? Like this* – she swallows audibly – *so now I have to swallow the same way again, like this, like this,* she says, *see?* and she swallows again, and it's so hard for her to get everything out before it disappears forever that she starts to cry – *It's gone, Mama, I didn't get to tell you and now I've forgotten what it was.* She's sobbing while she's talking, and she's talking so fast I'm afraid she's going to hyperventilate, and I interrupt, I take her hands in mine and say, *Breathe, just breathe, ten times, slowly,* but it's torture to her to stop talking even long enough to take a few deep breaths.

This has been going on for days. If she doesn't tell me that she just saw a shadow cross the wall, or that she heard a car honking outside, or that her tongue just clicked against her teeth or that she just thought for a second about a girl in her class who spoke cruelly to her – or the one who almost made her cry by saying something nice – then that thought, that experience, will disappear, she says, I'll never know she had it and it won't be real, it will be lost forever – *and?* I say, and she says then *she* won't be real, *she* will be lost forever.

She is still holding herself together, just barely, at school, but the instant she is out for the day, the instant she sees me waiting to pick her up, she rushes into my arms and starts talking, talking, talking. Her monologues betray the lie of literary, artful, organized stream-of-consciousness. It's just what I have always told my students: if we really were to put things down exactly as they pass through our minds, it would be unintelligible. Even the most exhaustive-seeming literary stream of consciousness is about choice, about making choices. But Grace has stopped making choices; she cannot make any choices. If she doesn't speak of every single thing that flies through her mind, if she tries at my urging to keep just one thought to herself for a few seconds, to see how that feels, she is consumed by anxiety. "I *know* how it feels," she says, "and I hate how it feels. I can't."

Just as she can't keep from making things, everything, come out even. I beg her to sit with the impulse for a minute, half a minute, see for herself that "the bad feeling" that fills her when she bumps her left knee and doesn't bump her right one right away won't drown her, won't eat her up – won't do whatever she fears it will do. But she can't "sit with it." She has lost the ability to simply be.

And so we are on our way to Dr. Knox.

Grace is in the backseat talking a mile a minute and clicking and ticcing away, pausing periodically for no more than half a minute, at my insistence, to take the deep breaths that do help, at least a tiny bit, although after each deep breath she tries to fill in what I missed – what she missed saying – while she paused to take it. Then we are halfway there, and I say, "I need to talk now for a minute, all right? Take a few deep breaths," and she does, gamely, tearfully, and I say, "Do you understand why we're going to see Dr. Knox? Who she is, what kind of doctor?"

"Yes," Grace says, and, "wait," and clicks her tongue against her teeth, explaining, "I had to click my tongue just then again because a second ago it clicked against my teeth on accident – and now I have to put my tongue on the inside of my right cheek because – "

"Take a deep breath," I tell her. "Take ten deep breaths. Slowly. Don't talk. Just breathe. Get some oxygen. Oxygen will help to calm you."

She does, and then she says, politely, "Thanks, Mama, that helped a little," and, "Yes, I know who Dr. Knox is. She's Charlotte."

I had truly thought I was well past being surprised, but what can this mean? I wonder. Cautiously, I ask her, "Can you tell me why?"

"Of course I can," she says – a break to click, to tap elbow to knee, finger to seatbelt buckle, wrist to the side of her booster seat, tongue to teeth again, and then her oral report on all of these activities – "because Charlotte saved Wilbur, remember?"

Ah. "In *Charlotte's Web*, you mean."

"That's right, in *Charlotte's Web*. And Dr. Knox is going to save me."

I look at her in the rearview mirror. She's been drawn and pale for weeks. She's exhausted, and who wouldn't be, going through what she's been going through? But for the moment she looks radiant. And humble.

• • •

It is Dr. Knox who disabuses me of the notion that I am doing everything right. She is all I have been promised and more – both brilliant and wise, as well as sensible, patient, calm, thorough, gentle with Grace, and tough on me. Grace talks freely with her, usually while they sit playing on the floor. In the waiting room, I can sometimes hear them laughing; once, Grace comes out to show me a mechanical creature she has made – it's battery-powered and can walk, forward and back – with googly eyes and long wiggling springy arms.

Under questioning, Grace tells Dr. Knox everything she can think of about our life at home, about school, about what she can remember from when she was younger, about what happened to my mother-in-law last summer, and about what she calls her "problems." On her first visit, Dr. Knox later tells Glen and me, Grace sat down on the couch, crossed her legs, and in answer to the opening question, "Do you know why you're here?" said, "Yes, I have three big problems. Here's what they are: I save trash, I have to say everything I think, and I do this thing called catching-up" – and she stood to demonstrate the technique, running across the Persian rug, purposely tripping before she reaches the other side of it, then going back and re-tripping. "See?" She sat down again, folded her hands. "Oh, and there's a fourth sort of problem, too, I guess. I need to make sure everything around me is in perfect order. I have to check again and again to make sure. This is called a checking compulsion" – and, in case Dr. Knox thought she'd made that up – "my Mama told me that."

Then she waited for Dr. Knox to spin the words in her web that would save her.

The words are all for us, though. After several sessions with Grace, Dr. Knox arranges for an hour with Glen and me. Z—— makes the drive to Cincinnati with us to keep Grace company in the waiting room. I don't hesitate to ask this favor of her, even though it's been six years since she was last a part of my day-to-day life, and even though I know the trip will be inconvenient for her – and she doesn't hesitate before she says yes. Z—— is someone who can be turned to in a crisis. Like my husband, she is at her best in a crisis.

I seem to have made it my business to have such people in my life: those I know I can count on at the eleventh hour, if not always at hours one through ten.

While Z—— builds geometric Polydron creations with Grace on the waiting room floor, Glen and I sit side by side on Dr. Knox's couch and listen to what she has to say, which is plenty. She tells us, first, that she does not believe that Grace is suffering from a biochemical disorder that requires pharmacological treatment, and I am so relieved I begin to cry. But she goes on at once to say that this doesn't mean that the situation isn't serious, extremely serious, that we must understand – her tone is so stern by now that I find myself shrinking in a way I haven't since my own childhood – we have *a very sick child on our hands.*

This phrase is etched on my heart. Even thinking of it now, a little more than two weeks before Grace starts fourth grade, on a Monday morning half an hour before she's due at her friend Tenara's house to spend the day – at least till three, when Glen will take her out to Hilliard for their double horseback riding lesson, when she will mount Saint, an Appaloosa, and trot and canter in a circle for an hour while Ernest, their very laid back teacher, murmurs directions – and in the meantime she's downstairs by herself practicing the Beatles' "Thank You, Girl" on her guitar, for *that* lesson on Thursday (and I'm about to call down to remind her that before we leave the house she has to change the bedding in her guinea pig's cage and the water in her fish's tank), I am lightheaded with fear.

But in Dr. Knox's office, I sit very straight. I don't speak. I just listen. She is purposely frightening us into action – I will understand this later – since it will be what we do, and especially what I do, that will be the most important part of Grace's "treatment," and she has to be sure we *get* this, she has to put things in the starkest, most frightening terms possible. And Grace *is*, at this moment, very sick. I don't know why it hurts so much to have someone say that, to hear what I already know, but as the psychiatrist in whom I have placed all my trust tells me that things will have to change at home, and right away, that there's no time to waste – that indeed it was probably the first small changes that had recently been made, changes Grace has talked about with Dr. Knox during her diagnostic sessions, some inevitable and some purposeful (Glen has started taking over for me at bedtime once a week; neither he nor I are lying down with her at night to help her fall asleep), that lit the fuse, "which needed to be lit. This is a good thing, not a bad thing," Dr. Knox adds. "This *needed* to explode" – and that Grace is likely to fight tooth and nail at every stage of what's ahead (and I remember as she says this the way Grace wailed, gasped, shrieked No! as if she had been told that someone she loved had just died when I let her know that I would not be lying down with her at bedtime anymore, that she would have to fall asleep on her own from then on), I am so overcome with anxiety and dread I have to remind *myself* to take deep breaths.

. . .

The key will be helping Grace to get caught up – "a different kind of 'catching up,'" Grace volunteers when I explain, in the simplest terms I can, what we will be doing, and why – to where she is supposed to be. Her symptoms are the expression of a severe developmental delay around "issues of separation/individuation" – this is the gist of what Dr. Knox tells us, and what we will continue to talk about with the therapist, a clinical psychologist named Dr. Meltzer, whom Grace will begin to see weekly in Columbus as Glen and I concentrate on making the changes at home that will help her to "catch up." Dr. Meltzer will point out, gently, that there will probably always be a lag between Grace's actual age and her intellectual age, at least until she is an adult, and that this gap makes the developmental gap even more pronounced and painful: the distance between her emotional and mental ages is vast. What we are to work on – what we *can* work on – is bringing her up to where a normal six-year-old should be in terms of feeling differentiated from her mother. Drs. Meltzer and Knox are in agreement that if we can help Grace do that, the symptoms will subside and eventually vanish.

And they're right. In retrospect, and written down, it sounds too simplistic and too obvious to be true – and it also sounds easier, much easier, than it actually was. Grace does fight, as if her life depends on it, every one of the initial changes we make. They are in the main what feel like stupid, programmatic, forced (and most often, to me, cruel) steps toward "normalcy." Each time Glen and I meet with Dr. Meltzer to plan the next step, I cry. I cry because everything we have to do goes against my "instincts" and because I dread telling my daughter what the next step will be, because I can't tell the difference between cold/uncaring/mean and "appropriate." It seems I have become stupid again. *Stupid* is how I feel (I am paying someone to tell me that my daughter can no longer take a long bath in a tub full of bath toys while I sit on the bathroom floor and play with her! I must be stupid – incompetent; a failure). I cry too because Dr. Meltzer understands exactly how I feel, because her empathy and gentleness open up a little place for me in which I can fall apart and it's all right, while at home, with Grace, I have to be cool and matter-of-fact.

I have to be cool and matter-of-fact even as every single thing I do is counterintuitive.

Glen and I begin to switch off nights, so that Grace has equal time with each of us during her most vulnerable, anxious hours of the day. For the first time, she has play dates at other children's houses without my being present; she is dropped off at birthday parties. Even if she begs me to stay, I leave. She can no longer sleep with towers of stuffed animals arranged around her. Or a pile of blankets at the foot of the bed (I begin to see that what she has done is create a sort of crib around her). When she wakes in the night, she must try to help herself get back to sleep before calling me into her room. She must throw away all the bags of accumulated trash and she is forbidden to save any more of it, no matter how sad it makes her.

Even after she stops protesting each of these changes with shrieks and sobs, plunging into grief for hours – even after it becomes clear that she welcomes the changes, that she's been needing them (because she protests only *for* those hours, then calmly, even cheerfully, adjusts to each; because after she shrieks and sobs over my announcement, for example, that she must not wake me in the middle of the night before trying on her own to go to sleep again, she sits down with a piece of paper and a gold gel pen and makes a list of things she'll try before she calls me – a long list – and tapes it up on the wall above her bed) – I am grief-stricken. That's how I begin to understand what I have done.

• • •

We're very lucky that the crisis has exploded now, both Dr. Knox and Dr. Meltzer tell us, more than once. They have both seen the same kind of delay surface in adolescents, when it's much more difficult to treat, when the damage has taken root so forcefully that it can't be unearthed. Grace has time on her side. We are warned that we are likely to see tantrums beyond the specific protests to the changes we are making. Tantrums "about nothing" – irrational, apparently random attacks of anger and frustration. All the tantrums she never had at two.

"There are reasons two-year-olds have tantrums," I am told, and my shame – which I had not thought could reach any deeper inside me – scoops down to the core of my being, for I have not forgotten how much I had prided myself on having the only two-year-old anyone had ever heard of who *didn't* throw tantrums. Proud of her, proud of myself for being such a good mother – was I anything less than perfect? Evidently not – for here, sitting serenely in her stroller beside Silas's empty one as he flung himself to the ground and bawled *I won't go home I won't I won't* as Vicki and I packed up to leave the Aquarium in Coney Island, was my sweet, smart, charming daughter. "But Silas," Grace would say when he was throwing himself around, turning red-faced, kicking, telling Vicki he hated her, "it's time to go home now. Don't you want to go home? We can play with my toys there – can't we, Mama? And we'll have a snack. We've been here all day. We can't *live* here" – trying to crack a joke, and sometimes it worked; sometimes she could calm her friend Silas down when his mother couldn't. But later she would confess that his "fits" scared her. "Why does he get so angry? And over nothing?"

When people complimented me on my daughter's extraordinary "maturity" and pleasantness, and asked if she didn't ever "lose it" when I said no to her, I would blush – embarrassed: *can I help it if I live with perfection?* – and shrug and say, "Well, the thing is, there's never really any reason to say no to her. She never asks for anything unreasonable." And this was true; I can't recall a time she ever did.

"A tantrum is a protest," I remember telling Dr. Knox, that day when she met with Glen and me for the first time, to talk about her findings over the several sessions she'd had with Grace by then, "and there was nothing for her to protest. She was . . ." I stopped; I didn't have the words for what she was. Or rather, I had the words, but I couldn't say them, because I knew they must not be the right words after all. *She was perfectly happy. She had everything she needed. She was perfect. I was perfect.*

"Completely fulfilled," Dr. Knox said.

"That's right," I said.

Dr. Knox contemplated me. And even then, even with everything that had happened, was happening, I felt proud: I had managed to completely fulfill my daughter.

"But that's not what she needed," Dr. Knox said. She said it gently. It was the first gentleness she had shown toward me. "It wasn't your job to 'completely fulfill' her. How do you suppose a human being learns to handle frustration, sorrow, strife, any sort of difficulty? These are skills that need to be developed."

"You're telling me she needed to be sad or frustrated? That I should have – what? Neglected her?"

Dr. Knox cocked her head. "Does anything less than 'complete fulfillment' constitute neglect?"

"I don't know how to make those calibrations."

"Yes, well, that's a problem."

But it wasn't Grace's problem – or, that is, it wouldn't have been Grace's problem if I hadn't been her mother.

Meet every need. I didn't know that sometimes it might not be so clear whose needs were whose. That the instinct to meet a need might be an instinct to meet the need of someone other than the one you're taking such good care of. The one you think you're taking such good care of.

That sometimes – maybe even more often than sometimes – mothers and their children's deepest needs will be at odds with each other in ways that aren't in the least apparent. And that even the smartest mother might not know that; that even the smartest and most conscious and purposeful mother has an unconscious.

You'd think I would have known that.

I would have thought I'd known that.

The funny thing is, I thought I did know that. I thought I knew, and had it licked: I thought I could beat the system by sheer intelligence, determination, concentration.

But I couldn't concentrate enough to figure out that my own instincts weren't instincts in the sense of pure, true mother-feeling – as I swore they were – but miswired impulses that were disguised as instincts. Who knew that impulses could be so cloak-and-dagger? That one's own old griefs could be so clever about hiding and emerging in full costume?

Grace wasn't the one who dreaded being all alone.

Or she didn't start out that way.

Who knew that there were worse things than loneliness? That never having the chance to be lonely, and figure out how to live with being lonely, might be worse by far in the long run for a child? A child: a child who isn't you but has been entrusted to your keeping – some other bundle of genetic material and experiences, one *not your own*, her *own* package of self – her own personal genome project.

Who knew that not learning how to let things go just might be worse than never having them at all?

10

Babies and children have developmental stages, passages. These vary from child to child, but there's a normal range for everything: seven to twelve months for the first, simplest words – *mama, dada*; twelve to fifteen months for *bird, ball, dog*; twelve to fifteen months for first steps (but there are always asterisks: *****note that some children will begin to walk sooner, and some will not take their first steps until they're twenty-one months old*). I knew all this. I knew it all (I'd read it all).

Large-muscle control proceeds from head to toe. First infants learn to control their heads, then they crawl on their bellies, dragging their legs by pulling with their arms, and finally they control their legs and feet in walking. Fine-muscle control begins with flexion and proceeds to extension.

I noted each of Grace's physical and intellectual landmarks – literally noted them, writing them down. It was only the second time in my life that I'd kept a journal. And this one was for Grace (my plan was to turn it over to her when *she* was a new mother), so I kept it up religiously. I wrote everything in second person, addressing it to her, and I annotated every entry.

First time rolling over: ten weeks (I set you down on the fluffy rug by the tub while I took a quick shower. I put you on your back as usual, so you could look around, and when I opened the shower curtain there you were on your belly!).

First steps: ten months (we're on the beach at Tybee Island after a visit with your paternal grandparents in Cochran, Georgia. You're walking like a drunk. You can't walk a straight line, and you're laughing the whole time. And when you spot a seagull rooting around in the sand you chase it, yelling "Doggie, doggie!").

First complete sentences: fourteen months (sort of complete, that is; you're still missing all your articles and prepositions and some verbs: "Mama, read book right now," "Grace Jane hungry oatmeal").

First time all colors correctly identified: sixteen months (and I do mean all. Between your father's color wheel and your mother's shoe collection, you can point, when asked, to "yellow ochre" as well as "magenta" and "turquoise." This is your daddy's doing).

First pun: twenty-three and a half months (you stripped off your diaper and sat on Sanchez the bear and called out, "Look, Mama, bear bottom!").

I devoted pages and pages to language development – jokes cracked (7/5/95: *"I love a mama sheep. A mama sheep is a* EWE. *I love a* EWE, *Mama! Get it?"*), stories told (9/20/95: *"One day a little girl went walking in the woods. She picked up a pebble. 'Don't throw me!' said the pebble"*), metaphors made (9/27/95: *"That steam looks like hair"*) – but the journal was long finished, every space on every page filled in, and tucked away in a manila envelope in the closet in my study, where it remained for years, before I understood that I had failed to take note of my daughter's psychological passage (or rather the absence of it) into autonomy. Relative autonomy, the normal stages toward autonomy.

Of course, it's harder to define, harder to write about the way I wrote about her first steps, her first jokes. Even the books I read – all those books I read! – didn't address emotional stages in the programmatic, clearly defined ways they did "fine motor skills" or "teething" or "speech development." Because it's too hard; because the signs are too subtle, too tricky. Because the whole business is much more complicated.

I wouldn't have taken seriously a chart that listed psychological stages to be checked off. I would have mocked it as ham-handed, simpleminded. I've devoted myself – devoted my life, my work – to complications, to the subtle, to the psychological. To the *inner life*. I knew better than to think this could be boiled down to a list.

But I didn't know enough to know that my own daughter was stalling – that I was stalling her – because I was stalled myself.

My psychological development had come to a standstill in her infancy.

No one talks about the developmental stages of mothers, but we have them. Why wouldn't we? We start out new, from scratch – newborn mothers. I didn't think of this until Grace did, until on her fourth birthday she had a revelation she was delighted to share with me: "Before this day in 1993, you were just plain old Michelle. But on this day, Mama was born. So" – she beamed – "happy birthday, Mama!"

Why wouldn't it stand to reason that a mother born the day her child was born needed to grow and develop emotionally, that at every stage of the child's development, she would have to stretch to accommodate the change?

(Which means, I suppose, *every day*, one way or another.)

But I didn't stretch; I didn't accommodate. I'd found bliss – how could I "accommodate"?

I had already said goodbye to lifelong loneliness while pregnant. When I took that child in my arms for the first time, I experienced, beyond the absence of loneliness, the perfect connection with another human being.

And I damn well wasn't going to give it up.

That's how I got stuck – stuck in my mother-infancy. I've spent the last two and a half years trying to catch *myself* up.

. . .

If I'd been paying attention, I would have seen that there were clues, a series of clues, that my bliss had come to an end anyway, a matter of months after Grace's birth – that I was trying to hold on to something that couldn't be held on to.

For although I started out ecstatic, aswirl in that golden glow – and, after all, I had become a mother so suddenly, after close to forty years of being just myself, it's not surprising that the transition was accompanied by the sort of twinkling that spins Lesley Ann Warren as the Rodgers and Hammerstein Cinderella into her ball gown and slippers, her kerchief falling away as her hair is swept up into a tidy bun, crowned by a tiara, the smudge of ash on her cheek wiped clean – and although I spent weeks, months in a state of giddy, hazy joy, it didn't last.

When Grace was six months old, and it was time for me to start teaching again, I fell into a deep funk. I chose not to call it a depression. *Depressed* was what my mother had been. I was blue. Very blue. I was under the deep blue sea.

And that was how it felt. I was underwater – doing everything in slow motion, crying all the time. Seawater. I was so blue I couldn't sleep; I couldn't eat. I drove to and from campus in tears, taught my classes brusquely, poorly. Talked to no one about how I felt; made small talk, instead, for the first and last time in my life (and this alone should have alarmed me, for I never suffer silently; I never keep my troubles to myself. I was drowning, and everyone around me must have thought that I was waving).

I did my best to analyze the trouble. I thought I *did* analyze it. I was sure I did, in fact. I thought I understood what I was up against, thought that I could see, through my veil of tears, two separate layers of trouble. On the first, the surface level, was my grief about being away from my baby daughter for the first time (a little obvious for my taste, but still true enough). Just below that, however, was a vast store of guilt – guilt because a part of me did want, did need, to get back to my "own" life. I felt guilty, I thought, because it had turned out I *did* have a few needs of my own I could not erase, as hard as I had tried to. Never mind getting back to teaching (about which I had no choice, since it was the only steady income we had, not to mention the source of our health insurance – plus, I reminded myself glumly, I *liked* teaching, or I once had: there were students, I vaguely remembered, to whom I was committed, who had been waiting for me to come back for many months); more to the point, I was beginning to feel hungry to get back to writing. I had never in my life, not since I was in second grade, gone so long without writing. Of course I missed it, I said to myself – it was only right, inevitable; what did I expect? – and yet I felt awful about missing it. I was putting it – my work, *myself* – before my daughter. Something I had sworn I'd never do.

That was my analysis, and sunk in gloom as I was, I was also a bit smug: I'd figured myself out. That it didn't help – that I still felt so bad it was hard to get out of bed in the morning – angered me. I had placed my faith in analysis, in insight, and it was letting me down.

During this bleak period, I remembered something I had done my best to forget, something that had happened months before, when Grace was no more than two months old and possibly even younger.

Something I hadn't written about in the journal I was so scrupulously keeping.

I had decided one evening that I would watch a movie on TV – which doesn't sound earth-shattering, but for me, at that point, it was. I wasn't even reading then; I wasn't doing anything but taking care of Grace. Still, that evening it occurred to me that I could use a diversion. Nothing too demanding, nothing that required real concentration. Just some entertainment; just for a little while.

I don't remember what the movie was. It wasn't important, I know that. It wasn't that there was a movie on that I wanted to see; it was only that I wanted to see *something*. And Grace was quiet. She had just finished nursing – this was in the days before the nursing strike – and she was in my arms, content and drowsy.

I turned on the TV. I arranged myself on the futon couch across from it, reclining, comfortable, little pillows all around me and behind me, the baby settled on my chest. I watched the opening shot. The title sequence.

And then I realized that my heart was racing. Slamming in my chest, like a fist pounding a door. I felt the fist – *wham, wham, wham* – underneath the baby, against *her* chest.

I was ignoring her. Those were the words – *ignoring her* – that came to me. *You are ignoring your baby. What kind of mother are you, after all?*

I looked down at her. Whatever was happening in the movie, I was missing it. Five minutes in, ten minutes in, and already I was lost. I couldn't pay attention to the movie. It was the baby I was supposed to be paying attention to – paying *all* my attention to. There was something wrong with me.

There was something wrong with me – I remember that I felt this; I remember precisely what it felt like – because I wasn't content to devote all of my attention to my daughter. Because I wanted *diversion*. Because I wanted to be taken away for a couple of hours, *wanted* to be distracted – even as I remained in the same room with the baby. Even as I continued to hold her. There was something wrong with me because I wanted something else. Not only her.

Finally she began to cry, which I took as a sign that she was as distraught as I was, that she objected to my looking at a movie and not her – and that was the end of my movie-watching.

Months later, when I began to itch to get back to my own work, when I saw in despair that I couldn't spend every minute of every day with my eyes on her – that I wasn't up to the task, as I saw it – it was no wonder I took to my bed.

And then of course I *was* drowning; I was drowning in guilt. I was doing exactly what my mother had done. I made an effort to smile for my daughter, to play with her – I would not turn my face from her, I would not return her animated looks with a closed, remote one of my own; I never once shut myself away in my room, away from her – but still I was in a panic. Every time I wept, I panicked. I would want to close my eyes, and the desire to rest, to give in to my exhaustion – and we must not forget that at six months Grace was still battling with me over nursing (*we must not forget*, I say, but at the time I found that "no excuse" was justified, that no task should be too much for a devoted mother, a serious mother, a *real mother*) – the desire to rest filled me with shame. Shame and fury.

Selfish mother. Failed mother. The worst mother who ever lived, because unlike my own mother, I knew better. I had no excuse.

I redoubled my efforts. I put my nose to the grindstone – the re-doubtable grindstone of motherhood.

And I ground my baby daughter down.

. . .

The worst mother who ever lived – this is what I think of myself, again and again, the year that Grace is six.

Not because of the damage I've done – although I excoriate myself often enough on that account, too – but as a result of my efforts to *undo* the damage.

Every change I have to make that year involves a battle with myself, one so painful and protracted that I wonder, each time, how I will get through it, if I will get through it.

You are a cold, cruel, dreadful mother – the worst mother who has ever lived. This is what I hiss at myself as I lie in bed in the dark, listening to Grace, suddenly awake at three in the morning, down the hall in her own room. I wake up because I hear her wake up. Even after six years (even after nine years!), a change in her breathing is enough to wake me. I have never slept well, not even in my own childhood – when I was famously not only an insomniac but also a sleepwalker – but since becoming a mother, it takes nothing to wake me. The quiet creak of my daughter's mattress springs as she sits up in bed, the sound of her taking a drink from the water bottle on her nightstand, her footfalls as she walks across her room to try "Getting Back to Sleep Tip Number One" – turning on her CD of dulcimer music – any of this will rouse me from my light, always restless sleep, and not just rouse me but jolt me wide awake and staring in the dark.

She is fine – I know she's fine, or she'd call out to me – but I don't feel as if she's fine. What I feel is: *It's the middle of the night and she's alone, I've told her not to "bother" me, I've left her to fend for herself. What kind of mother am I?*

I know what kind of mother. The worst mother who has ever lived.

11

It is far too soon for me to know if Grace will be able to forgive me for the damage I did. Right now she adores me. I am everything to her, or almost everything. She gets angry with me in a way she wasn't able to when she was younger, and mixed in with my grief each time she screams at me (because I have told her to clean her room, or said *No, Hannah can't come over, you have homework*), telling me I'm mean, I'm ruining her life, is joyous relief: she feels free to feel this way. When she "talks back" – which drives her father mad (*Where did she learn to talk this way?*), it pleases me; it thrills me. I approve of sass, I approve of feistiness and independence, I hate the *yes, ma'ams* and the lowered eyes and voice of Glen's sister's children when they speak to their parents – but most of all I'm grateful that my daughter is herself, a separate person, that she got out from under after all.

For a while I wasn't sure she could, and even now sometimes she regresses to a desperate *we-are-one* state of mind. It's hard to say exactly what brings it on (transitions, always – from school to summer and back, bad arguments between Glen and me, my infrequent non-serious illnesses or, this past summer, the worry that I might be truly ill) and it's fleeting, but it's still terrifying when it happens. "Don't leave me, Mama," she cried on the first day of Kabuki theater camp last month, and when I pointed out that I had to leave, that I had things to do, she said she didn't care: she couldn't bear for me to leave. By then she had her arms around my waist. I reminded her that she wouldn't, didn't, want me around all the time, and promised I'd be back at three to pick her up. But she was sobbing, begging me not to go.

"What are you afraid of?" I asked, and she said what I imagine babies feel but have no way to say.

She said, *"I won't exist if you're not here."*

My child who has words for everything, reaching inside herself for the small hidden part that's still stuck, stalled – where I stalled her.

Just a couple of nights ago, she had a dream about that day camp. She dreamt, she said, that she and everyone else at camp had to stand "on cliffs, right at the edge." They were all screaming. And it didn't matter that she knew – "even in the dream I knew" – that it was "just pretend," that like everything else they did in camp that week, it was only acting, not life. She was still scared to death. She woke up crying, and she called me into her room for the first time in years. She was so shaken she asked me to stay with her until she could get back to sleep, and I hesitated. But I remembered the test Dr. Meltzer suggested I give myself when something happens that I feel I can't trust myself to handle by instinct: I asked myself if staying was for her sake or mine – if she really needed me to stay, or if I needed to stay.

Whose need this time? I wondered, as I held her – she was still trembling, although she had stopped crying – and even though I fear I'll never know for sure what the real answer is when I ask myself this question, I took a chance that this time it was hers, and I lay down beside her and stroked her hair and told her everything would be all right.

I fell asleep myself, there in the bed with her, as I used to every night when she was small. But when she was small, I would start out every night with her, too, staying till she fell asleep. More often than not, I'd fall asleep and wake up an hour (sometimes two or three hours) later, and stumble to the bathroom and then to my own bed. Most nights I'd have to return to her midway till morning – and some nights more than once before morning finally came.

After her Kabuki dream, I slept till morning with her. She'd woken at a little after three; we were both asleep again by four. I woke at six-thirty, her legs wrapped around me – one across my neck, one across my waist. Her left hand was on my cheek. It was the first time in a long, long time – in more than two years – that I'd woken in her bed. I didn't even realize I was crying until I looked in the bathroom mirror.

Mostly nowadays she's strong, independent, involved in her own life, happy, whole, more interested in friends and dogs and horses and books and the Beatles than in me. When she woke up, an hour after I did, the morning after her bad dream, she was in good spirits, full of plans for the day, eager to call Kristin and get things started. And even last month, after that dire moment of separation at camp, when I phoned her half an hour later as I'd promised I would, she was fine – it had really *been* just that moment ("Can't talk, Mama, sorry, we've got rehearsal, see you later").

Sometimes she talks nostalgically about her "problems." "Remember 'catching up'?" she'll ask sometimes, and want to talk about it, what it was like, how it "went away." She is fascinated by her symptoms and by the way they were "solved" so mysteriously. That they don't frighten her as they do me – I still can't think about that winter and spring without my heart constricting – is a good sign, a strong and healthy sign. I am always on the lookout for such signs.

Someday, I imagine, she will want the whole story. Someday she will be able to understand the whole story. But what will she feel, then? Will she be grateful that we were able to rechart our course, make the necessary corrections and begin again? Or will she be bitter because I didn't do right by her from the start? And how will the way she feels toward me – forgiving, understanding, bitter, grateful, angry – creep into how she feels toward her own daughter someday if she is lucky enough to have one?

. . .

Perhaps Grace will be the mother, at last, who *doesn't* do harm.

It surprises, *shocks* me, still, how narrow the channel of rightness is, how easy it is to make mistakes, even devastating ones. My own mother did the best she could with me. She wasn't thinking about what her own sorrow, her illness, was doing to her baby daughter, her four-year-old daughter, her six-year-old daughter. She *couldn't* think about it. She had neither the strength nor the resources; she barely had the strength to open her eyes each morning. And *her* mother was a child when she married my grandfather. Fifteen years old, she had no idea how to live, no idea what it meant to be a mother. Then in short order there were three boys to look after, boys who were "always wrestling, hitting, always in some kind of trouble, and making so much noise!" she told me, and even though, by the time she spoke of this to me, "the boys" – Aaron, Isaac, and David – were in their fifties and sixties, she still sounded bewildered, worried, fretful.

Her husband, my beloved grandfather, stayed out of the way as she tended those terrible boys, shopped, plucked chickens, pummeled bread dough, sewed, stewed, peeled and chopped and baked and steamed, relentlessly cleaned the tiny apartment they were all crammed into. And then came my mother – the baby. What was my grandmother to do with a quiet little girl who stuttered, who needed attention? A delicate little girl, a piano-playing little girl, a little sister who screamed, "Ma, they're killing each other!" of the older brothers she adored?

My mother's mother didn't have a clue what to do with her. She hushed her. She hushed her for so long, so hard, my mother thought *hushed* was the only way to be. Quiet, contained, restrained, *good* – always good.

Good, and good for nothing. Equipped for nothing, able to do nothing. My grandmother's legacy to her. Unpurposeful, unintended, unconscious – yes. But still. But *still*. Bequeathed.

• • •

What sins will Grace visit on her own child? Surely she will be as conscious, as purposeful a mother as I. But conscious of what, and purposeful in the service *of* what? And what will she fail to see?

Is it possible that she will be able to see it all? To miss nothing? Already there are times when she shows more insight than I, when she's a good quick step or two ahead of me. So I have high hopes. But even with my high hopes, I wonder: is it possible not to fail to see *something*, is it possible to do everything right?

To actually be as good a mother as I hoped to be?

I thought I knew what I was doing. I was sure I knew what I was doing. I would be, for Grace, what I wished for myself: the person waiting in suspended animation on the other side of the door.

12

That I was a lonely child, left mostly to my own devices, was certainly not purposeful. But like everything that happens in a child's life, it served a purpose. It helped me become a writer, which is something like saying: *it helped me to become myself.* I began to write – poems and plays and finally stories and the novel I typed out on my father's hand-me-down Smith-Corona when I was eleven – to keep myself company and to entertain myself, and to find a use for all the thoughts that I was storing up. I found it suited my theatrical bent, too, and turned my excellent memory into a tool, when already it had sometimes seemed a burden (because no one else's memories matched mine, because I'd remind A—— of something she had said a month ago and she refused to believe me, told me I was making it all up).

Because my first efforts at writing were praised and rewarded, and because it was a pleasure to have stumbled upon something I was good at, and – perhaps most of all – because when I wrote, I wasn't lonely, I kept at it. It seemed to me a miracle that I could escape my loneliness by writing.

It is a paradox, I know now, four decades after I began, of the writer's life: even though we work in silence and in isolation, we don't ever feel altogether alone. I'm talking to you now, telling you the story of my life as a daughter, as a mother – and whoever you are, there is at least a possibility (the potential that tantalizes me!) that you will understand me perfectly.

Back then, all I knew was that it was absorbing as nothing else was, and that I was in control of it, as I could not be in control of anything else. As much as I loved – worshiped – my father and my grandmother, they were in charge of anything that passed between us. In my writing, I was in charge of everything. And in my writing, there was no price to pay, as there always was with the people I loved, who needed my attention and devotion as much as I needed theirs.

If I became a writer even in part because of my troubled childhood, then I must be grateful for the trouble. Every unhappiness has some happiness buried inside it; every wrong has some rightness. And so I tell myself: if I failed my daughter by being too much present for her, giving her too much of myself – so much that it became difficult for her to be herself, alone, to know what "herself" might be – I also managed to do some things right. I loved her so completely she will never wonder what it feels like to be loved; she will always know, down to every cell in her body. She will never feel insignificant, or all alone in the world, or unable to be understood by any living soul – she will always carry with her a sense of her significance, a sense of my company, a knowledge of my understanding. I held her back, it's true – but I didn't *only* hold her back.

This is what I tell myself when I am at my lowest. This, and that in the end – before the end, before it was too late – I did learn how to let her go.

13

Motherhood is like riding the flying trapeze – swinging through the air and grabbing hold of the next bar as it swings by.

A balancing act. A tightrope walk.

It's like being shot out of a cannon.

Like knife-throwing.

As thrilling, as terrifying, as gorgeous, as ridiculous as that.

As ridiculous as the sad clown, the clown with the broom, the little car jam-packed with clowns.

Motherhood as a three-ring circus – that's how I see it now.

. . .

When I say *balancing act*, I don't mean the balance today's have-it-all "mom" (I hate that word – its jauntiness, its single-syllable all-American friendliness, its lack of *weight*) is supposed to attain between career and children and husband and house and "time for herself" (including regular exercise and a beauty regimen). That's a part of it – I don't mean to say it's not – but it's the part that's too much talked about, as if this struggle were all there were to *the* struggle: the three-ring circus, the road trip of motherhood.

I am not the first woman to say what I am about to say: that the notion that one can "have it all" without collapsing under the strain of competing forces – the brilliant career, the thriving marriage, the fit and youthful body whipped into shape by Pilates or Nautilus plus daily five-mile runs, the happy, healthy children tucked into the corners of everything else – is *shit*. You try to have it all, to *do* it all, and the career takes a hit, the marriage takes a hit, the body takes a hit. Your children take a hit. There's no point kidding yourself about it. Some kind of hit, from one direction or another.

Never mind their fathers. I'm not suggesting that they're not important. I'm just saying flat-out that fathers aren't mothers, and that there's no child alive who doesn't crave his or her mother.

The mother of all parents – that's what mothers are.

My generation, the post–*Feminine Mystique* generation – those of us who were in elementary school in 1963, when contemporary feminism was born – was spoon-fed a primitive version of the career/family conflict. Or if not spoon-fed it (some of us would smack away a full spoon aimed at us), then at least handed to us on a silver platter. The conflict had been uncovered *for* us. Perhaps that was the trouble; I have sometimes thought so, thought that this was why it's been so oversimplified. But even though what's on the platter has been made more complicated (and more interesting, and more palatable) for the two decades' worth of women who have followed us, who have understood from birth, it seems, that they have the option of ordering *some of both, please,* or *first one, and then the other, thank you,* we still haven't acknowledged that what's on that platter is just one part of the meal, not all of it.

(Another metaphor: motherhood as feast.)

And if it's reductive to think that "solving" this problem will make the whole thing – motherhood itself – a snap, what about the insistence on the part of some that they *have* solved it – that (A) it's *obvious* that children benefit by the example of mothers who are thoroughly engaged in the world, who are *forces* in the world, who are *taking care of themselves* (just think of the example we're setting for our daughters! No child would be happy, raised by a mother who is unfulfilled, resentful, bored, or angry – and who could argue with that?); *or* (B) it's absurd to imagine or pretend that our children don't need their mothers front and center in their lives, not just for a few hours in the evening and on weekends packed with chores and errands (and cell-phone calls and e-mail from the office, paperwork to finish, charts to read, numbers to crunch), and what's the point of having children if you're going to pay someone else to raise them? – *plus,* argues this camp, today's full-time "stay-at-home mom" cannot be compared to the forties and fifties pre-feminist mothers who raised us, since today's mom makes a conscious choice, unlike Betty F's respondents, who did what was expected of them (and became depressed): today's homemaker-mom demonstrates to her children not only the principle of choice, important in itself, but also that she's chosen them, forsaking a career or else a good chunk of one, making it clear to the kids just how important they are and how much they mean to her – and who could argue with how much our children mean to us, or say that we shouldn't let them know that?

When Grace was a baby, I would sit tensely in a roomful or a playgroundful of other women and their children, listening to the low rumble of debate, the judgments passed, the disapproval masquerading as a question or even as admiration (*How many hours did you say you leave him at the sitter's house? I wish I could bear to do that! And You must have inner resources I don't! I'd go stir crazy at home all day alone with her. And You're so brave to be able to leave him at the day care center when he's still so young*), and the uneasiness and fear and even panic I could hear just underneath what everybody said (*Am I doing the right thing? Am I screwing up completely?*), every mother implicitly criticizing whatever anybody else was doing if it were even the least bit different from what she was doing – since doing things differently was an implicit criticism of *her* way.

It was exhausting. I would come home and lie down, still clutching my baby, and sometimes I'd cry.

What never crossed my (weary, anxious, sorrowful) mind then was that focusing on this – the mother's work, the mother's time at home, the hours in day care or with sitters – obscured the larger, messier, more complex and unwieldy problem. That once the basic needs for food and shelter have been met, the problem of motherhood becomes an intricate one, inextricable from the problem – the *problems* – of humanhood: the experience of being alive and joyful, or suffering, or in doubt or in a cloud of gloom or worry, or living through a moment of quiet, perfect pleasure, or any other tone along the spectrum of emotion, an infinite variety of shades of feeling. Not to mention thinking – thinking hard, making decisions all day long, year after year.

Contemporary feminism, I believe, has done a terrible disservice to motherhood by trying to frame as simple and manageable a problem that cannot be simplified. Has taken the three-ring circus with orchestra and lights and elephants and lions and elaborate costumes and the stink of dung, the clamor, the crowds, Madison Square Garden *and* the subway that gets you there – and put it on TV, one camera aimed into the center ring, the music muted. What the hell, let's make it black and white too while we're at it. It's small, it's manageable, it's no big deal, see? If you just look at it this way.

But even when it looks like no big deal, it is. There's nothing black and white and small about it. Even when it looks effortless, it's hard. Even when it *looks* hard, it's way harder than it looks, and in different ways than it seems to be. And sometimes even when you know it's hard, you still do it badly – very, very badly. Even when you've made every effort. Even with the best intentions, *Mom.*

The complicated, noisy, circus truth of it is that nearly every minute is hard. Nearly every minute requires some kind of decision that will affect much more than the single decisive moment. Most of all, the question of whose needs count, or have to count more, at any given moment, and the question hidden inside that one, the question I have had such trouble with – *whose need is this, anyway?* – are never far from the center ring.

And underneath those questions are the questions one has to ask just to live, mother or not, if you're trying to live the fullest possible life, a life that won't feel wasted: Who am I? What is my purpose? What must I do to *do right?*

Being responsible for launching another human being – who will ask the same questions, again and again, over the course of her life – just doubles the questions, crisscrosses them.

If you mean to do right by your child and be true to yourself, too – and you understand that it is not always clear what being true to yourself is, that what seems true to your *self* is complicated by what you do or don't understand about your self – and you understand that the question of making yourself "happy" is not necessarily related to what will constitute doing right by your child – then you are in for years, decades, of trying to figure out something at least as hard as working out the repeating lines of a poem in which the first five stanzas are triplets and the last stanza is a quatrain, and the first line is also the last line in the second stanza and the third line is the last line in the third stanza. Or as hard as investigating the properties of Fermions, half-integral spin particles that obey the Pauli principle, and Bosons, integral spin particles that don't, or the anomalous magnetic moments of leptons, or the quark structure of matter.

. . .

Motherhood as subatomic particle physics. Motherhood as poetry.

As a circus act – as all the circus acts at once.

As a cross-country trip, interstate driving with unreadable signage, lane changes at high speeds, traffic, trucks bearing down, the weather treacherously changeable.

As an elaborate meal, one course after another, cookbooks open everywhere, pots boiling over, the kitchen a mess.

Motherhood as mixed metaphor.

Motherhood: the mother of mixed metaphors.

. . .

Grace learned the phrase "the mother of" just this past year, in third grade. Two of the boys in her class – the two who are "always" getting into trouble, she reported (the only two in an otherwise extremely tractable group) – had a fight in the classroom. A quick, contained fight – a nothing fight by the standards of her old school. A slap, a punch, someone knocked down. Nobody hurt. But in the heat of the moment, one of them – she wasn't sure which one – yelled, "Fuck!"

Both boys got "yellow boards" (Grace says she doesn't know what this means, but she is certain it will involve their parents), and while the teacher was busy issuing the mysterious yellow boards, one of the girls took it upon herself to whisper to Grace, "You know, don't you, that that's the mother of all bad words?"

Grace nodded. Sure she did, she said. But when she got home, she asked me what Katy had meant. First she wanted to know about "fuck." She'd heard the word before, but only at poetry readings. She had never asked what it meant, and I had always figured she'd assumed it was a "poetry word," like erstwhile or o'er.

Grace knows all about "bad words" even though the category doesn't exist at our house. Her friend Hannah, who lives across the street from us – two houses down from Anna – has read her chapter and verse on the subject. Indeed, it's thanks to Hannah that Grace has learned most of the "bad words" other families forbid. We've talked about how every family has its rules, and how some of them are bound to seem eccentric to the rest of us. Hannah is not allowed to go on sleepovers, or to wear sunglasses, or to say "damn" or "hell"; Anna is forbidden to play with the Ouija board (the work of the devil) or to listen to certain of 'N Sync's songs; Amira for years wasn't permitted to wear nail polish or temporary tattoos or to chew gum (but now that she's twelve, we've noticed that the ban on polish seems to have been lifted). Grace's street friends consider me peculiar because I won't let her dash back and forth across the busy street between our house and theirs, something Anna and Hannah have been allowed to do since they were very small. Of course, that's only a small part of why they think I'm peculiar.

I told Grace what "fuck" meant – what it was slang for – and she gasped. "No wonder you're not supposed to say it in public! That's a very private thing!"

She didn't want my help with the "mother of" part. She worked it out for herself. I watched her think it through, and then she said, "Oh! I've got it. The one that counts most, right? The best or the worst – it could be either, I bet."

"That's right," I told her. "Excellent."

"So you know what you are, Mama?" She said this slyly.

"No," I said. "Tell me. What am I?"

"You're the mother of all mothers."

I laughed. "Only to you," I told her.

She raised her eyebrows. She looked all around her, pointedly.

"There's nobody else here."